Managing Your Band

Artist Management: The Ultimate Responsibility

3rd Edition

ISBN 0-9651250-3-3

Cover Design: David Kerzner
www.gogaia.com

For information:

HiMarks Publishing Co.
P. O. Box 2083
Wayne, NJ 07474-2083
Fax: 973.720.2217
marcones@wpunj.edu

Managing Your Band

Artist Management:
The Ultimate Responsibility

3rd Edition

- Touring
- Publicity
- Contracts
- Marketing
- Trademarks
- Copyrighting
- Merchandising
- Record Companies
- Enhancing Creativity

1. Scope of agreement

Musician hereby employs Agent booking agent, manager and represe vices, appearances and endeavors as a musi the undersigned musician and to musicians leads or conducts and whom Mu "A.F.M." refers to the A Musi

2. Duties of agent

(a) Musicia

For every musician who, against unbelievable odds,
was given the chance to play in the major leagues and blew it!

Contents

Acknowledgments ix

Introduction x

CHAPTER ONE
    PERSONAL MANAGEMENT 1
        Do I need a manager? 1
        What is it? 2
        An art or craft 2
        Who should try it? 3
        Patience 3
        Recognizing the true artist 4
        Choosing a manager 5
        Choosing a team 5
        The daily ritual 6
            The contract 7
        Project management 10
        So what's the secret? 15
        Summary 16
        Projects 16

CHAPTER TWO
    THE CONTRACT 19
        Why is it needed? 20
        The basic parts to any contract 20
        The agreement 21
        Summary 26
        Projects 26

CHAPTER THREE
    LEGAL ASPECTS 29
        Selecting a name 29
        Completing a search 31
        Registering a trademark and servicemark 31
        Starting your own business 33
            Proprietorship 33
        Partnership 34
        Corporation 35
        Limited Liability Company 36
        Bookkeeping 36
        Group breakups 37
        Summary 38
        Projects 38

v

CHAPTER FOUR

MARKETING THE ARTIST 41
    The marketplace..41
    Scope of today's market...42
    The role of the artist 44
    Creating the image 45
    Managing the image..45
    "Delabeling" the star...45
    The media tools 46
    Media mix 47
    The campaign 47
    The image makers..51
    Direct to consumer marketing 52
    Summary...53
    Projects 54

CHAPTER FIVE

THE TRANSNATIONALS...57
    Integration & concentration 58
    The big five 58
    Summary...63
    Projects 63

CHAPTER SIX

THE RECORDING COMPANY..65
    Its role in the industry..66
    Advances...67
    Types..68
    The Structure 70
    Product flow 71
    Where the money goes..88
    The company's share..90
    Summary...92
    Projects 92

CHAPTER SEVEN

THE RECORDING CONTRACT...93
    The ingredients 96
    Its value 112

CHAPTER EIGHT

CARE AND FEEDING OF THE CREATIVE 155
    The creative process. 156
    The creative product 161

Media check...181
Guiding the creative talent...182
Summary..184
Projects...185

CHAPTER NINE
    TOURING..187
    Brief history..187
    Tour objectives..188
    Preparing...190
    Routing..190
    Booking...193
    Budget...198
    Travel and accommodations...198
    Choosing an opening act..198
    Concert rider...206
    Choosing material for the performance.....................................208
    Publicity..209
    Entourage..210
    Manager's responsibilities..210
    After the tour...213
    Summary..214
    Projects..215

CHAPTER TEN
    MERCHANDISING, ENDORSEMENTS, & SPONSORSHIP......217
    The history...218
    Definitions...219
    Merchandising Agreement..222
    Summary..229
    Projects..230

CHAPTER ELEVEN
    BUSINESS MANAGEMENT..233
    The role and function of a business manager............................234
    Financing a project..235
    Summary..239
    Projects..239

CHAPTER TWELVE
    LEGAL BATTLES...241

Acknowledgments

This book took a long time to write. It became more a labor of love as the years went on. I started it when my son was learning how to talk and finished it during the tail end of my divorce. Like I said, the book took a long time to write.

I started the project by hooking up with Mark Spector, then manager of 38 Special. We met for a while, but I guess that neither of us had the interest or perseverance to see it through. I put it down for several years and then got the itch not to give up on it.

A while later a former student and attorney, Jeffrey Aber, put a bug in my ear to collaborate. I must thank him for the tedious work he did on the recording contract. He was very helpful. He explained the details and put up with my ignorance. Jeff became busy and then moved to L. A. I put the book down again.

A colleague of mine, Karl Guthrie, is a practicing entertainment attorney and a great talker. During several of his weekly visits to the college to teach Law and Ethics in the Music and Entertainment industry, we would talk (sometimes, I might confess, through a good deal of the class period) about the current state of affairs in the industry. Karl enjoys my insights about current events. Karl kept asking about the book and stirred my interest to move it along. He also was very willing to share most of the agreements found in this book with me and I am thankful.

Lastly, as a [former] board member of the Music and Entertainment Industry Educators Association I am in contact with most of the industry educators throughout the country. There is an expressed need for a text that can be used in a personal management/entrepreneurship course. They too helped me find the energy to finish.

I purposely left the acknowledgements from the first edition in this edition as well. Although this edition is more comprehensive, it still deals with the basic issues of entrepreneurship and artist representation.

For this edition, I thank friends Adam Kornfeld, Dave Lory, Walter O'Brien, and George Tortarolo, for the updated contracts and advice; my students who completed my personal management course for their contributions to chapter twelve, and general insight into what is expected in a text; David Kerzner for his outstanding cover design; and lastly my wife, Angela, for her computer skills and most importantly, putting up with me during this task.

S. M.

September, 2001
Wayne, NJ

General Introduction

With barely a music graduate degree in hand, I was given the opportunity to play in the major leagues. As a band that wrote and performed its own material, we somehow generated some interest at Epic Records to give us a chance and sign us. The group was holding down a six nights a week, six sets a night summer gig at **THE** club in Lake George New York and packing the place. We rehearsed almost everyday and were probably as tight as any band could be. We sounded great and people paid to hear (and see) us. Things were happening pretty fast and it was all exciting (and foreign) to the six of us.

As we began our first tour of arenas (as an opening act) we were told on numerous occasions to concentrate on the music and let "them" worry about the business. This was the fall after the summer of Woodstock 69, and it was obvious to many that there was now big money to be made from rock 'n' roll. We had management. A friend of ours who could be trusted, a doctoral student at Syracuse University, had been booking the band and had the intestinal fortitude to put up with us. He could swim, and although we didn't know it, but not with the barracudas!

A short time later, while we were still in demand, we realized his shortcomings and decided to try another manager. We found one, or I should say, he found us, and had his attorney draw up an agreement. He came to us with experience, and we all liked him. After all, he was hipper than our friend, lived in NYC, and had gotten high with us on several occasions. What was not to like!

We received the contract that the attorney composed, read it and were shocked that this guy, our new found friend, would demand what was written on the pages. In fact, we were so appalled (and green) that instead of asking our attorney to respond with an equally outrageous counteroffer, we decided to run (not walk) back to our original manger/friend and ask his forgiveness.

Basically this is where the story ends. In fact, we committed industry mortal sin number two and went on to manage ourselves. After all, The Beatles did it (without success), so why couldn't we. Well, this is how I learned what not to do.

Only a few years later I realized that many musicians are being short changed. That, for the most part, the record business is not controlled by the players. With the right education and information, musicians could be in control of their own destinies. However, it would take time. Today the more successful musicians understand the business, make decisions, and some control their own careers, production and record companies.

This book has been written to help the cause. Personal management is still the weakest link in a business that operates by fragmenting its product. That is, an artist must give pieces of his/her product to several people that control different fragments of the business. Holding on to all of it doesn't work. **ONE HUNDRED PERCENT OF NOTHING =NOTHING**, no matter how you slice it. An artist must understand and learn to live within this concept. The trick is to give it to the right people for the shortest amount of time possible. I hope this book helps artists choose the right people to give it to, and right people learn how to do it right!

Introduction to Third Edition

As soon as I started using the second edition of this text in class, again, I noticed some gaping holes. So in this edition, along with updating the statistical material, I have tried to fill in some of those spaces. I have omitted a bit of the italic comments in the sample contracts to allow for more classroom use.

Throughout the book, the web is discussed as a tool for many of the artist's needs, however, I consciously did not include web addresses. I feel that the list would be outdated before the book is in print and most people interested in this subject are fluent web users.

In Chapter Two, I included an updated personal management contract. The agreement is shorter than the previous agreement, including the italic comments.

Chapter Five, The Transnationals, was completely rewritten. It discusses the Big Five, and most of the information was found on their respective web pages.

Chapter Seven includes an updated recording agreement with current industry language.

Chapter Nine has been expanded to take into account the many changes in concert promotion.

Chapter Ten includes a sample merchandising agreement with comments in italics.

In Chapter Twelve several legal battles have been added.

I have tried to include a more inclusive index.

The Instructor's Companion has also been updated accordingly.

The subject of how to remain fair to both genders was never an issue to me.
Throughout the book I tried to use s/he and his/her when either applied.
My intention was (and is) to emphasize equality.

CHAPTER ONE
Personal Management

"Good personal managers have become an endangered species in the music business today."
Bob Donnelly. Billboard Magazine. *February 20, 1999.*

By the end of this chapter you should be able to:
1. Discuss the role of a personal manager
2. List eight characteristics of a good manager
3. Discuss the three characteristics of a potentially successful artist
4. Discuss how an artist should choose a manager
5. List the artist's "team" and discuss their individual roles and how they are chosen
6. Discuss two key points found in an artist-personal manager agreement
7. Manage a project in an organized manner
8. Define talent and success as it relates to the industry.

Do I need a Manager?

At one time or another, most artists/musicians ask the $64 question….. "Do I need a manager?" The answer isn't always as obvious as one might expect. In fact, it may be more complicated than first imagined because there are several types of managers, and a big difference between two types most often employed in the entertainment industry: a personal manager and a business manager.

The second question that is asked is……. "When do I need management?" Is the role of the manager most important when: an artist is looking for a record deal; a new artist has reached the status of Celine Dion or Puff Daddy; an artist has become a veteran performer (ie: Mick Jagger); or an artist has reached the residual stage of Jimi Hendrix?

The answer to all of the above is that at each stage the artist may not recognize that s/he needs a manager, but it is clear that s/he needs management. And unless the artist is committed to giving the 24/7 to the business side of the career, someone must take the responsibility.

What Is It?

The role of the personal manager in the music and entertainment business can be compared to the role of a football coach. Short-range strategy plays an important part of every possession in every quarter of the game. Long range strategy plays a role in determining a successful season. Each play is determined by the team's strengths versus the opponent's weaknesses. During a losing game, it must be extremely frustrating to watch from the sidelines and not be playing.

The personal manager coaches the artist and his or her team. Every musical set of every gig is important in winning over an audience. Each gig has an effect on the long-range game plan. How much can the team do to insure the success of the next performance? During a weak concert, it must be extremely frustrating to watch from the wings and not be playing.

Most managers will confess that when they got their first client, they thought they knew a great deal more about managing then they really did. Most managers will also confess that they learned management by "doing it." Furthermore, managers that have survived in this business will confess that the most crucial aspect to surviving was ADMITTING that they neither knew the CORRECT answer to certain questions, nor did they know WHAT the correct information was that they SHOULD HAVE known. Some managers will even admit that they STILL don't know everything they should know.

So What Is It?

Personal management means being responsible for every part of the artist's career . . . twenty-four hours a day, seven days a week. It involves making decisions you and your artist can live with and developing a trusting relationship with an artist. It's a relationship that matures over time and grows out of mutual respect. This respect may be gained in two ways: by maintaining a record of not "screwing up", and by truly considering the artist's opinion about his or her career. A personal manager should never let the artist feel that his or her opinion is worthless. In fact, the artist's opinion can be and <u>should</u> be an integral part of the decision making process. Empowerment is a strong motivator.

An Art or a Craft?

Well it's both! The mechanics of the job can be learned, so the craft isn't very mysterious. Learning the fundamentals and routines is easy. The creative or artistic side of the job is more complex.

A successful manager has the ability to motivate people, and generate excitement about a project. A successful manager senses other people's needs, not only the artist's, but the needs of the other people who are part of the "army" that works for and with the artist. This part of the creative aspect is seldom learned. A person either does it or doesn't. Personalities play a major role in the business, and at times, personal relationships are even more important than talent.

Who Should Try It?

The short answer is anyone who wants to. However, Figure 1.1 lists eight characteristics that contribute to success. A discussion of some of the points follows.

A good personal manager is

1. a self-starter

2. patient

3. organized

4. able to make decisions and take responsibility

5. able to recognize creativity and talent

6. able to recognize uniqueness

7. able to recognize the potential value of an artist in the marketplace

8. knowledgeable about the music business

Figure 1.1

Patience

A successful manager is a patient one. The creative process takes time. Composing songs or developing a concept for an album should not be rushed. Deadlines and timetables constantly need readjustment. Truly creative people cannot turn on creativity precisely at a designated time. The manager must feel comfortable with the unpredictability - - with changing schedules and unanticipated cost overruns.

A manager must also wait for information to be collected. Being "ultra" busy in this business seems to be a status symbol. It takes days and repeated phone calls before decisions are finalized. Many record executives (decision makers) divide their time between NYC, LA, and the rest of the world, and even some very successful and prominent managers have trouble pinning them down.

Artists' careers evolve through many levels. However, they don't always appear to be moving in the right direction (or any direction). Stars must "pay their dues," and a manager must wait for each level of success to be reached before another level can be attained.

In this business, success does not provide instant gratification. An audience may go wild during a concert or a critic may write a positive review of a recording, however, success is measured **quantitatively**. How many tickets were sold? How much airplay did the record receive? How high up the charts did the record go? It takes time for impact of these measurements to be felt. And it takes patience by the record company to allow time for success to happen. "Patience is a virtue" . . . a necessary virtue for success.

Ability to Recognize Creativity and Talent

How does one develop the ability to recognize creativity, talent, or uniqueness? Does one either have a feel for it or not? Can it be developed? Can it be taught?

Everyday, successful personal managers receive many demo tapes from new artists. (One manager said that his office receives up to 200 tapes each week!) It's hard to explain how a manager reaches the conclusion that someone has a unique talent. Record company a&r people use their personal judgment when deciding who will be permitted to record. They say it's a feeling that one instinctively gets when they hear or see it. The late John Hammond, indisputably Columbia Records' greatest talent scout, had the ability. (Hammond brought, among others, Benny Goodman, Bob Dylan, and Bruce Springsteen to the label.) If someone has potential to recognize talent, it can probably be developed with practice, but it can't really be taught. A personal manager must possess the ability to recognize the talent in undiscovered artists. Related experience in the industry may help, but the confidence must come from within. No one is infallible. Every successful manager has "passed" on at least one successful artist.

Recognizing the True Artist

Every successful performer has true artistry, or some combination of artistry and craftsmanship with market value. However, given this ingredient, what other characteristics are essential when choosing an artist with success potential? Consider the following.

1. Desire, determination, and patience

   Serious determination is essential in order to survive in this business. Many stars have ALMOST quit more than once. Since success is seldom instant, an artist must have the maturity to wait for the industry and the audience to react.

2. Credibility

   On stage or off, an artist must have a clearly focused image in order to succeed. (Creating an Image is discussed in a later chapter.)

3. Potential to withstand changes in the marketplace

A manager should ask him/herself if this person has the potential to make recordings that will last a generation. Also, will the artist's personality mature with his or her craft? Every artist should strive to become a classic.

It's also true that many "artists" make a great deal of money for only a short time. When managing such an artist, one correct strategy is to find a reason why the public would want to buy the act on a short term basis rather than looking to that artist for the lasting potential. Although big money has been made with both kinds of artists, most managers would choose to handle the "classic" artist.

When asked why he chose to work with a particular artist, one manager summed up her qualities by saying, "her personality is clearly defined . . . she articulates a sense of self . . . with the proper guidance, she has the potential to sellout arenas."

Choosing a Manager

Most artists would like to be managed by a person with strong industry contacts and a proven track record. These elements improve the chance of success. Credibility is as important for a manager as it is for an artist. However, given these qualities, what should an artist look for when choosing a manager?

A management agreement is essentially a legal contract to enter into a relationship. **Mutual trust** is crucial to a successful working relationship. The artist and manager should have **compatible personalities**. When describing their managers, most artists will list the positive qualities and conclude by saying "and I like him or her."

Choosing a "Team"

Typically, an artist's team is composed of a manager, an attorney, an agent, a publicist, and an accountant or a business manager. The artist must feel comfortable with the team members that are directly involved with the financial aspects of the career; namely, the manager, attorney, and accountant. However, the manager must be able to work with all of the team members. A good manager will offer the artist suggestions as to who should play certain roles, and will specifically chose who will play others. The following are guidelines that maybe helpful when choosing the team.

Attorney

Attorneys play a major role in the music business. Sometimes it seems as if there is a contract for every aspect of a career. Therefore, the manager should offer an artist at least thee names of three attorneys with whom the artist would feel comfortable doing business with. Three who have exhibited sound judgment and distinguished experience . . . and leave the responsibility of choosing one with the artist. The artist should interview them and actually choose the attorney him/herself. The legal documents have the final word in business, so why should the manager take full responsibility in an area that could sour and lead to mistrust?

Booking Agent

A manager must maintain a close relationship with the artist's booking agent. They will converse on the phone several times on any given day. This relationship is far more important than the booking agent's relationship with the artist. As always, the artist should be given the chance to offer input into this decision, but the manager should make the final choice.

When choosing an agent, and before signing an exclusive agreement, the manager should evaluate the degree of enthusiasm for the artist that exists **throughout the entire agency**. Large agencies usually divide the country (or world) into territories, and assign an agent to each territory. Agents will also be assigned to specific categories of the business, such as state fairs, amphitheaters, or southern colleges. Therefore, overwhelming support by one agent and no interest displayed by other agents, could present booking problems at a later date. Broad support by the agency is more beneficial in the long run.

Publicist

The proper creation of publicity and handling of an image are crucial to a successful career. Most often publicists are hired to manage specific campaigns, projects, events, or tours. It is the manager's responsibility to hire the right person or agency for the job.

Business Manager (accountant)

The business manager holds the fiscal responsibilities, and controls all collections and disbursements. This allows the manager to concentrate on the more creative endeavors. When choosing a business manager, again, several names should be suggested, and the artist makes the final choice.

The Daily Routine

In this business, each day brings a new offer or a new crisis. Some days the mail is opened in the morning and some days it sits until late afternoon. Some days the phones light up before the office is opened, and on some days things unravel in an orderly fashion. There are though certain constants. Each day the manager should ask these questions: "Am I making as much money for my artist as I possibly can? Are as many records, concert tickets, T-shirts; etc. being sold as they're possibly can? What could I be doing to make more money for my artist?"

Asking these questions on a daily basis ensures that certain "career maintenance" routines are completed. The manager talks to the record company everyday. If his/her artist is touring, he or she will converse with the agent several times during the day; contact will be made with every individual that pertains to the amount of money being made.

Even though it seems like business can be maintained by fax, cell phone, e-mail, the net, etc., managers who are not located in one of the centers of the industry (NYC, LA, Nashville, or London) are at a distinct disadvantage. Personal contacts are of great importance. In this business, absence does NOT make the heart grow fonder. In fact, "out of sight - out of mind" fits this business more closely. Daily contact is the key.

Everyone must work towards clearly defined short and long range career goals. Musicians are conditioned to live from job to job (gig to gig). Most worry if the phone will ring again. Most don't approach their lives in a career-oriented manner. Artists talk about what's happening today, where as every day the manager must adjust the career plan to focus on the long-range objectives.

Recently, this author asked a former student working in management, George Tortarolo, what his responsibilities are. His response follows:

> *My responsibilities are eclectic to say the least. As one of four managers in a firm of eight people my time is currently spent on projects that relate to Melissa Etheridge, Dave Koz, and Jeremy Toback. All three have albums that were released in the past month. The year leading up to the album releases was spent developing marketing plans, working with their labels to create artwork, staying on top of the press and PR departments to see that they arrange for TV, radio, and print spots. My law background allows me to review, consult on and negotiate the various contracts that come to the artists. Such agreements are recording, publishing, produce/engineer, management, tour riders, movie and TV licensing and songwriter. I monitor regional album sales through the use of Soundscan and airplay by BDS. In conjunction with an artist's business manager, I keep ledgers of any income and spending as well as oversee the payment of invoices. I arrange for rehearsal time and space, I assist in the hiring of session players, and I arrange for sponsorships with manufacturers such as string and amp companies. I have produced one website (www.socalrecords.com). I respond to email from fan websites. Recently a lot of time has been spent relating to the tours of Melissa and Jeremy. I assist in routing (calculating which markets the four should to play, and in what order so that a logistical path is followed.) With the help of a travel agency that caters to the needs of the music industry, I arrange for tour flights, hotels, and ground transportation. I also spend time looking for a job that pays a better salary!*

The Contract

(A full discussion of the contract appears in Chapter Two.)

Several industry sourcebooks listed in the bibliography include artist-personal management agreements with appropriate comments (see the latest edition of

Shemel & Kravilovsky, or Passman,). When it all boils down, these are key points that are important to both parties.

1. Term

Both parties must agree on the length of the contract, option periods, which party has the right to extend the agreement. Contingencies concerning extending the agreement must also be agreed upon, as some contracts include a minimum gross income the artist must make for the manager to continue.

2. Compensation

How much should the manager be paid? Is the commission based on gross earnings, net earnings, or some formula that represents a mixture of both?

Most or the remainder of the agreement contains fairly standard clauses that are negotiated in a routine manner. However, an attorney MUST represent the artist throughout the negotiations.

Stages of an American Career

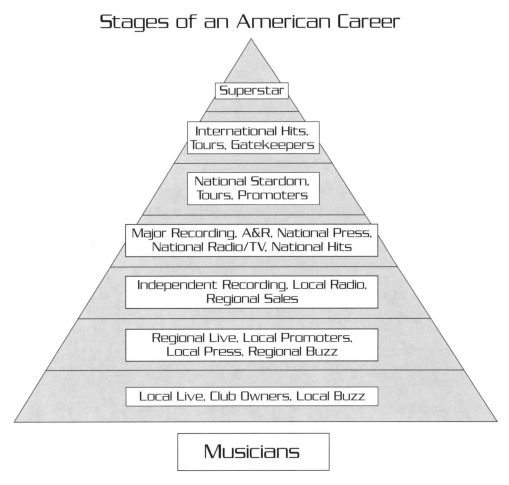

Figure 1.2 Stages of an American Career. Frith, S.(ed.) Facing The Music. N.Y. Pantheon. 1988.2

Career Plan

Figure 1.2 illustrates the various stages of an American artist's career. While the lower levels of the hierarchy are fondly known as "paying your dues," it is the graduating up to the third level, **indie recording and regional sales**, that is considered a major goal and is more easily attained with sound project management and a career plan than not. It is the level that most driven musicians attain but unfortunately never leave. Crossing the bridge from level three to level four is what stumps even the most assertive. It is here that the well thought out career plan is essential.

The artist's career plan may be completed in several ways. It's true that long range and short range goals are important, however, only the more successful managers follow some form of a set procedure. Setting goals is simple. Attaining them is difficult.

A successful career includes talent, organization, and planning. Given that the artist has a certain amount of talent (or at least appeal), it's the manager's responsibility to oversee the organization and plan. Invariably the "plan" is the weakest link.

A successful plan includes:

a) preparation,

b) securing the proper information,

c) having the proper attitude, and

d) establishing goals.

The goals should motivate both the artist and the manager. The strategy for reaching them should be flexible. A timetable should be set and tactics developed. This type of planning is helpful in successfully completing any project. Projects are developed to solve specific problems or complete specific tasks, and once they are completed, they end. Figure 1.3 lists eight ingredients that are important to a successfully managed project. The following is an explanation of each point.

Project Managmement

1. Problem Statement

2. Background Statement

3. Objectives

4. Procedures

5. Plan

6. Schedule

7. Budget

8. Success Indicator

Figure 1.3

1. Problem Statement

The problem statement is an explanation of what is perceived to be needed, therefore creating a problem. For example, if the artist wants to change record companies, an investigation into why this is perceived to be a need should be made. Exactly what is the problem that the artist believes a new record company will solve? The solution may really be another producer or songwriter. A manager must be certain that if there is a real problem, it's clearly stated, and the perceived solution (project) is the correct one.

2. Background Statement

Information about the background and significance of the problem is very useful in determining the value of a project. For example, if the artist wishes to record with a specific producer, the producer's track record may include significant information pertinent to attaining a hit record.

3. Project Objectives

Are there many objectives or only one? If there are many, a prioritized list is essential. One method of writing objectives is to put each objective in a behavioral form. For example, instead of listing an objective as "learn" three new songs, in behavioral form it might read "perform" or "arrange" or "memorize" three new songs. This form makes it more obvious when an objective is completed.

4. Project Procedures

What steps must be completed to meet the objectives? Each step should be listed in chronological order (the project's critical path). Both **creative** and **organizational** tasks should be listed. For example, if the stated project is to complete another recording, all the creative and organizational tasks that need to be completed before arriving at the studio, during the recording process, and after its completion must be listed. Obviously, some tasks occur simultaneously, but a chronological list is still useful.

5. Project Plan

Who will complete which tasks? Who will make certain each task is completed? What strategy will be used to complete each task? For example, who will write the new songs? Who will search for an outside writer? Who will hire the producer? Specific tasks must be assigned to specific people. This is what makes a plan work.

6. Schedule

Realistic timetables work. Set realistic deadlines and don't require tasks to be completed long before they are needed. Schedules with a natural flow help to complete the project.

7. Budget

What is the money needed for, when is it needed, and where will it come from? These three questions need to be answered. Also, remember to include a 10-15% miscellaneous expense category for unforeseen expenses.

8. Success Indicator

How will the success of the project be determined. Realistic goals should be set. If an artist's second recording sells 2 million copies, 3 million short of the first's sales, is it not successful?

Career planning is one of the most important functions a personal manager performs. Being organized is also important. Preparing a well-organized plan greatly improves the artist's chances of success.

What follows is an example of a class project. It has been included here with the permission of future industry leaders David Allu and John Landieri.

YOU WERE SPIRALING

by

David Allu and John Landieri

I. Problem Statement:

A. The perceived problem:

The manager of *You Were Spiraling*, Michael Kahn, believes that more exposure is needed. He would like us to obtain more exposure for the band. The way he would like us to do so this is by getting airplay for the band at college radio stations throughout the northern New Jersey, New York City, and eastern Pennsylvania area.

1. Why is this perceived to be needed?

The band and Kahn want more people to be aware of the band. There are some other ways of getting the name and sound of the band heard: performing, print, TV, and the web, to name a few. Our group chose to focus on airplay to meet the need of getting exposure for a number of reasons. **Firstly**, print media is being covered by the other group in the class. **Secondly**, the band can not perform this month. All of their time and energy is going toward the recording of a new demo. When the recording process is completed they will resume performing. **Thirdly**, obtaining airplay on college radio stations will reach the most people. The only TV programs that the band might be able to perform on are public access TV programs. We think a college radio station will reach more consumers than a public access program.

II. Background Statement:

Why would a band want to have their music played on a radio station? Radio has been and still is a crucial form of promotion for a recording artist. Throughout the history of rock 'n' roll, and even years before rock emerged, the radio has played an integral role in promotion. Other means of publicity such as MTV, VH-1, Letterman and The Tonight Show have also been important. However, at the level that *You Were Spiraling* is performing, music videos and national TV exposure are not possible. As a form of promotion, radio is number one. So, at our level, radio remains the medium that has the greatest exposure. Furthermore, radio play is free (discounting the cost of the promo CD, the paper the bio is printed on and postage). Many other forms of marketing tools and advertisements require money that the band does not have.

Why did we choose college radio? The perceived market for *You Were Spiraling* is the college age group. Many college radio stations are central to the campus' music scene. Colleges have traditionally been a place to "brake" new music and artists. We will persuade college radio stations to play the CD to increase the awareness of the group on each campus.

III. Project Objectives:

Have as many college radio stations as possible in the area put a *You Were Spiraling* song in rotation

IV. Project Procedures:

1. Choose ten college radio stations in the north Jersey, New York City and PA. Area.
2. Make telephone contact with the program director at each station informing him/her of *You Were Spiraling*. Ask his/her permission to send a CD and Bio.
3. Send a CD and Bio (make note of the date sent) to each station that we have spoken with and have granted us permission. Compose a letter to enclose in the package. The letter should thank the individual for his/her time and inform him/her of the songs we are pushing. These songs are "Your New Boy" and "Crisis @ 92 Credits".
4. Call the program director 4-5 working days after the package is sent. Ask if s/he has had a chance to listen to the CD. If s/he has, ask what they thought. Ask if s/he preferred either of the suggested songs. Persuade to add a song(s) to the playlist.
5. If the program director has not listened to the CD, call back in another 1-2 days (proceed with #4).
6. Have friends and band members call station and request the song.
7. Call each station every three days to get feedback.

NOTE: On occasion, the DJs of college radio station will choose which records the station will air. Many DJs have their own shows and choose the material for the show themselves. In this case, speaking with the program director may be point-less or only mildly helpful. As a result, we should substitute the DJ of the pro-gram director as the person addressed in our phone calls.

V. Project Plan:

1. Dave and John have five CDs each. Each will be responsible for his CDs.

2. Dave will contact the following five radio stations:

a. WFDU 91.3 FM	Fairleigh Dickinson College
b. WGLS 89.7 FM	Rowan College of NJ
c. WFMU 91.1 FM	formerly Upsala College
d. WRSU 88.7 FM	Rutgers University
e. WPRB 103.3 FM	Princeton University

3. John will contact the following five radio stations:

a. WLFR 91.7 FM	Stockton State College
b. WMCX 88.9 FM	Monmouth University
c. WPSU 91.1 FM	Penn State University
d. WKDU 91.7 FM	Drexel University
e. WTSR 91.3 FM	located in Trenton

4. Each member will follow the project procedures.

5. John and Dave will inform each other and Michael of each task as it is completed and the stations that add the song(s).

VI. Schedule:

10/27/97	All materials are sent out.
10/31/97	All stations have been contacted.
11/7/97	Each team member should have airplay on at least one station.
11/21/97	Each team member should have airplay on at least three stations.

VII. Budget:

The group will be reimbursed for the following expenses incurred:
gas
postage
telephone
mileage

VIII. Success Indicator(s):

A. Airplay

In order for the project to be deemed successful Michael Kahn will be happy with airplay on five of the ten stations. As a manager for a band, he feels that any support is appreciated. So, even radio play on one station will make him more content than none. However, the challenge is to have as many spins as possible.

B. The Conditions for a Successful Project:

1. The band feels as though they benefited from the group's work.

2. The group has participated in a positive successful learning experience.

The band song(s) will be in rotation 2-3 times per day on at least one but preferably five college radio stations in the area.

So What's The Secret?

Well there really isn't a secret. How big of a star the artist becomes will be determined by many factors, the least of which is how well the manager keeps the artist a **priority** among the industry gatekeepers. If there were a secret that's what it would be.

In his book Tarnished Gold, the late R. Serge Denisoff defines the two concepts of *talent and success*. He states, "**Talent** is the *commodity* that has economic potential."[1] In other words, creating an original musical presentation that is marketable to record buying audiences. And it's the industry gatekeepers, namely, club owners, agents, radio programmers, promoters, and record company "ties" (personnel) that define the talent. They make the decision as to who gets the chance to be seen and heard.

Talent alone does not guarantee success. "**Success**," Denisoff writes, "is the artist's *ability* to persuade the industry gatekeepers to recognize the talent."[2] This persuasion not only comes in the form of music, but in stage presence and overall excitement and charisma as well. Furthermore, the artist must then choose the industry leader whose evaluation of his/her talent is correct.

So there's the formula, now go do it. Play in the major leagues. It's a tough road to stardom. Not many who try make it. Again, according to Denisoff, "only 17 new artists per year, it is believed, ever record a Top 40 hit, while in the same year 23 persons are statistically likely to be struck dead by lightning."[3] If you have what it takes, those odds shouldn't stop you!

SUMMARY

1. A key to successful artist management is obtaining the proper information.

2. The artist's opinion should be part of the decision making process.

3. Management is an art and a craft.

4. The most important characteristic a manager can have is patience.

5. Artists striving for success should have talent, desire, determination, and patience.

6. An artist must have a clearly focused image.

7. The artist's and the manager's personalities must be compatible.

8. The artist's team is composed of the personal manager, attorney, booking agent, publicist, and accountant.

9. In this business, there is no such thing as a typical day.

10. Each day, the manager should ask: "Am I making as much money for the artist as I possibly can?"

11. The artist and manager must agree on the length of the contract and manager's compensation.

12. An organized career plan is essential for success.

13. Talent is the commodity that has economic potential.

14. Success is the artist's ability to persuade the industry leaders to recognize the talent.

15. The manager must keep his/her artist a priority with the industry leaders.

PROJECTS

1. Using the outline for project management, create a fictitious project and complete a detailed plan.

2. Role-play an initial artist and manager meeting.

3. Negotiate a fair artist - manager agreement.

NOTES

1. R. Serge Denisoff. <u>Tarnished Gold</u>. Transaction Books. New Brunswick, N.J. 1986. pg. 37.

2. Ibid.

3. Robert Burnett. <u>The Global Jukebox</u>. Routledge Press. London, U.K. 1996. p. 126

4. Op. Cit. Pg. 38.

CHAPTER TWO
The Contract

*"Fellows, forget about the contract. If it's not working like a marriage,
the contract is not going to help!"* – Anonymous

By the end of this chapter you should be able to:

1. Discuss why a **written** agreement between an artist and personal manager is typically used in the industry.

2. Discuss the four basic parts of any legal contract.

3. Discuss what it means to act in a fiduciary manner.

4. Discuss all the parts of a typical artist/personal manager contract, identifying fair deals for both sides.

5. List the areas where advice and counsel should be offered by the manager that are in accordance with the American Federation of Musicians' guidelines.

6. Compose a fair artist/personal manager agreement.

On several occasions, as a member of a band, the author was involved in negotiations with prospective managers and was asked to sign artist/personal management contracts. Depending upon where we were in the negotiations, some contracts were more elaborate than others. Some contracts also favored the manager more than others. Regardless of the situation, when band members inquired about the language in different sections of the contracts, the various attorneys representing the managers invariably used the marriage analogy. They assured us, in each case, that the contracts would not bind us to managers we no longer wanted to represent us.

They also assured us that we, as artists, were truly "the bosses." "The manager works for the artist, and it's never the other way around. So if the manager isn't performing to the artist's satisfaction, he or she should be fired." My response was always the same. If this is true, why do we need to sign a written agreement? If the relationship is supposed to work like a marriage and the artist is the boss, why should any problems arise? The answer is simply that problems do arise.

It's been reported that Elvis and Colonel Parker never had a written contract. Their deal was consummated with only a handshake. Unfortunately, the estate on behalf of Elvis' daughter, Lisa Marie, has sued the Colonel for a number of misappropriations (see Chapter 12). Seldom is an issue of *Billboard Magazine* is published without an artist/manager suit reported.

The contract is there for protection. It's signed by both parties so that each is protected from each other. It's signed with the understanding that although it is a relationship, it's first a business. And the business is more important than either party individually. In this way it works like a marriage should work.

Another reason for a written contract is that a manager, as an employee of the artist, acts in a fiduciary capacity. This means that the relationship is one involving a confidence or a trust. For this reason, the manager should never have an unfair economic advantage, and reputable managers refuse to enter into agreements where the artist is employed by a company in which they have a vested interest. For example, if a manager also owns a concert promotion company, s/he would have an unfair economic advantage if that company booked the artist, and s/he also would collect a commission from the artist on the date.

Acting in a fiduciary manner implies that the artist's interest must come first, and the manager's interest second. The manager is obliged to operate in the artist's interest, and this has been the basis of many artist/manager disputes.

Most people believe that a contract must be in writing and signed by both parties to be valid. Terms of most contracts only have to be agreed upon by both parties, and if the agreement is witnessed, then it is a valid agreement. Contracts are put in writing to avoid one party denying that they agreed to something. Besides, as more time passes, people have different recollections as to what actually occurred. So even though it may take a long time to negotiate, it's easier in a long run if the contract is in writing.

There are **four basic parts** to any legal contract of this type. They are: **mutual assent**, **consideration**, **capacity**, and **legality**.

Mutual assent — This is the offer and acceptance by both parties. For example, John Jones wants to manage the "Dumbbells." The "Dumbbells" want a manager. This is the section of the contract that begins with "Whereas."

Consideration — This is the trading process. Something of worth changes hands when services are performed. For example, if Jones manages the "Dumbbells," they agree to perform and appear where they are told to.

Capacity — This means that both parties are of sound mind and body, and have the legal capacity to perform the necessary functions to carry out the terms of the contract.

Legality — The contract must be for a legal purpose. A contract for a deal to buy a car that you know has been stolen, is not legal.

The following is a typical artist/personal management contract. The term "typical" is used because there is no such thing as standard contract. Although the language may vary, the items addressed in all contracts are common. *For educational purposes, comments that address each issue in terms of its fairness to both parties have been inserted in italics, however, the comments still leave additional room for discussion.*

"THE DUMBBELLS"
EXCLUSIVE WORLDWIDE
PERSONAL MANAGEMENT AGREEMENT

In consideration of the promises and covenants set forth in this deal-memo, and for other good and valuable consideration, the sufficiency and receipt of which are hereby acknowledged, when signed by **SLICK** Management ('us" and "we"), on the one hand and **Heavyweight, Middleweight and Flyweight**, collectively p/k/a "**The Dumbbells**" (individually and collectively, "you"), on the other hand, this deal-memo shall constitute a legally binding agreement (this "Agreement") regarding your engaging our services as your exclusive personal manager throughout the worldwide entertainment industries.

The artist should make certain that the individual manager's name appears in the opening statement and not solely the name of a business or corporation so that the manager is personally responsible. The same is true for the manager. The manager should insist that each member of the performing group have personal contracts with the manager.

1.   (a)   You hereby engage us as your exclusive personal manager throughout the worldwide entertainment industries for a term (the "Term") that shall commence upon the date of the Agreement and shall last until the earlier to occur of (i) end of the second album cycle (such two (2) album cycles shall hereinafter be referred to the "First Album Cycle" and the "Second Album Cycle", respectively) and (ii) five (5) years from the date of this Agreement, provided that, in the event that such five (5)-year period expires during the Second Album Cycle, then the Term shall continue until the end of the Second Album Cycle. In the event that either the applicable album released in the First Album Cycle or the applicable album released in the Second Album Cycle or the applicable album released in the Second Album cycle sells at least five hundred thousand (500,000) units in the United States prior to the end of the Term, then we shall have the option (the "Option") to extend the Term for one (1) additional consecutive album cycle, which additional cycle shall commence as of the expiration of the Second Album Cycle. The Option shall be deemed exercised by us unless we notify you in writing to the contrary prior to the expiration of the Second Album Cycle. As used herein, an "album cycle" shall mean the period of time commencing with the initial commercial release of a long-playing studio album embodying your newly-recorded featured performances and continuing until the delivery to your exclusive record company of the next long-playing studio album embodying your newly-recorded featured performances in fulfillment of your recording commitment.

Clause 1 (a) defines the term of the agreement. The term of this agreement is based on both the recording cycles and years. It also states that management will have the exclusive right to pick up the option period, and it lists the requirements. Furthermore, it states that management can exercise their option without notifying the artist, and if they choose not to exercise the option, they must notify the artist "prior to the expiration date", which could be interpreted to mean that a notification at 11:59 PM of the cycle will fulfill their legal requirement, leaving the artist no time to secure new management.

It should also be noted that five years is a long time period for an initial term.

Notwithstanding anything to the contrary herein contained, in the event that you have not entered into or substantially negotiated the terms of a recording, production or distribution agreement with a "major label" (defined below) within twelve (12) months of the date of this Agreement, then, upon our receipt of written notice to such effect, you shall be entitled to terminate the Term of this Agreement. For the purposes hereof, "major label" shall mean (i) WEA, CEMA/EMD, SONY, UNI, or BMG, or (ii) any other record, production or distribution company whose records are distributed by one of the companies set forth in the preceding clause 1(b)(i).

Clause 1 (b) describes the contract termination requirements. If a record deal is not secured, then the artist may, in writing, terminate the agreement. There is no grace period for this notification.

Other contracts use a gross income amount as a barometer for how the relationship is working. If the artist does not make a certain dollar amount by a certain date, then the contract can be terminated. Also, some use both.

2.   We shall render all services customarily rendered by personal managers in the United States recording industry. Our services hereunder are non-exclusive and we shall at all times be free to perform the same or similar services for others, as well as to engage in any and all other business activities.

According to the American Federation of Musicians (the union), the artist's representative should offer to advise and counsel and render services in five specific areas. They are:

> 1.   *the selection of literary, artistic, and musical materials*
>
> 2.   *all matters relating to public relations*
>
> 3.   *adoption of a proper format for the best presentation of artist's talents*
>
> 4.   *selection of a booking agent*
>
> 5.   *the types of employment the artist should accept.*

Clause two also states that management is free to manage other artists. There are many advantages to employing management that manages other acts of the same genre, such as record company and booking agency contacts.

3.   (a)   During the Term, you agree to account to and pay us, promptly following your (or any of your designees") receipt thereof, a commission equal to twenty percent (20%) of all the gross earnings received by you (or any of your designees) in any and all forms and from any and all sources in the entertainment industry, subject only to the exclusions set forth in **Exhibit "A"** attached hereto incorporated herein by this reference.

This is the compensation clause. Twenty percent is within the scope of personal management commissions in the entertainment industry, however, be aware that a symbol such as this in a contract (%) is begging to be negotiated..... in this case, down to fifteen percent. It is important to read Exhibit "A" to understand what is excluded from commissions.

Commencing upon the expiration of the Term and continuing for a period equal to two (2) times the length of the Term (the "Post-Term Period"), you agree to pay to us a commission (the "Post-Term Commission") equal to the following percentages of all of the gross earnings received by you (or any of your designees) in any and all forms and from any and all courses in the entertainment industry, subject only to the exclusions set forth in Exhibit "A"; (i) fifteen percent (15%) for the first one-third (1/3) of the Post-Term Period; (ii) ten percent (10%) for the second one-third (1/3) of the Post-Term Period; and (iii) five percent (5%) for the final one-third (1/3) of the Post-Term Period. For the avoidance of doubt, with respect to gross earnings derived from master recordings, videos and musical compositions, the Post-Term commission shall only apply to the gross earnings derived from those master recordings, videos, and musical compositions that are substantially created during the Term.

This is the "golden parachute" or "sunset" clause that protects management from loosing out on commissions from income subsequent to the termination of the agreement that they believe they are entitled to receive. Usually a manager will want to continue receiving commissions on any contract that s/he negotiated, even if, for example, all of the albums under the recording contract have not yet been recorded. Note that the "Post-Term Period" is twice the length of time that the initial term represented, which could be ten years! Even though the commission rate decreases, the entire clause should be negotiable.

4.   You agree to reimburse us for any and all direct expenses incurred by us on your behalf, including, but not limited to, long-distance phone calls, FedEx or similar overnight courier charges, messenger charges and travel costs, but specifically excluding our so-called "overhead" costs. We hereby acknowledge and agree that when we travel with you or on your behalf, we shall travel in the same so-called "class" as you (including, but not limited to, with respect to air transportation, ground transportation and lodging); for the avoidance of doubt, the foregoing shall not preclude or prevent us from traveling with you or on your behalf in a superior "class", provided that any such resulting excess costs shall be our sole responsibility and obligation. We shall not, without your prior consent or request, incur any costs on your behalf in excess of (i) Five Hundred dollars ($500) for any single expenditure or (ii) One Thousand Dollars ($1000) in aggregate costs per month.

Management requires payment of expenses that go beyond normal costs. Number four also states that if the artist travels first class, then management is entitled to as well. Also, it sets a ceiling for both single and monthly expenditures.

5.   Your obligation under this agreement shall be joint and several and, for the avoidance of doubt, your obligations to pay to us commissions shall cover each of you as members of "The Dumbbells" as members or leaders of other projects and in any and all other entertainment related activities, including, but not limited to music, motion pictures and television.

The agreement requirements members of the performing group to sign and become libel individually as well as collectively.

6.   We shall have the right to assign this agreement, in whole or in part, to any entity in which SLICK Management, has a substantial ownership or control interest. You shall not have the right to assign any of your rights or obligations hereunder.

Management is stating that they have the right to assign the contract (or artist) to another subsidiary company. This entire agreement lacks a "key man" clause, which customarily states that if an individual leaves the company, the artist has the option of going with the individual or staying with the company. The artist should not sign an agreement without it. The two situations are related and should be set forth in this clause.

7.   Neither party hereto shall be deemed to be in breach of any of its respective warranties, representations, agreements or obligations hereunder unless and until the alleged breaching party shall have first received from the other party specific written notice by certified or registered mail, return receipt requested, of the nature and details of such breach and such alleged breaching party shall have failed to cure said breach within thirty (30) days after receipt of such written notice.

This is the breech and cure clause, which allows either party to respond to an alleged breech within thirty days of written notification.

8.   WE HAVE ADVISED YOU THAT WE ARE NOT PERMITTED TO SEEK OR OBTAIN EMPLOYMENT OR ENGAGEMENTS FOR YOU AND THAT WE DO NOT AGREE TO DO SO. WE HAVE MADE NO REPRESENTATIONS TO YOU, EITHER ORAL OR WRITTEN, TO THE CONTRARY. YOU ACKNOWLEDGE THAT WE DO NOT HEREBY AND HAVE NOT HERETOFORE OFFERED TO, ATTEMPTED TO OR PROMISED TO OBTAIN, SEEK OR PROCURE EMPLOYMENT OR ENGAGEMENTS FOR YOU AND THAT WE ARE NOT OBLIGATED OR EXPECTED TO DO SO.

Clause eight is in respect to the California and New York laws that are widely practiced in the entertainment industry. It states that management is not licensed to be an employment agency and cannot seek or procure employment for an artist. The only exception is the procurement of a recording contract.

9.   You warrant and represent that (a) you are free to enter into and perform the terms of this agreement, (b) no other party is presently engaged to act as your personal manager, (c) you will not during the Term engage any other person or entity to render services similar to those to be rendered by us hereunder, (d) you have not heretofore nor will you hereafter assign or otherwise encumber any of the gross earnings that may be subject to our commission or other rights hereunder and (e) you shall at all times engage and utilize proper theatrical, booking or employment agencies to obtain engagements and employments for yourselves. You and we agree to indemnify, defend and hold each other harmless from and against any and all cost, loss, damage, liability or expense arising from a breach of any of the warranties, representations or agreements, made by each of you and us hereunder and agree to execute any and all documents and take any and all actions which are reasonably necessary to secure each of your and our respective rights under this agreement. In the event of any litigation between the parties, the prevailing party shall be entitled to recover its costs and attorneys fees.

10.   This constitutes the entire agreement between you and us regarding the subject matter hereof, and this agreement may only be modified pursuant to a written instrument signed by both you and us.

11.   Each of you and us has cooperated in the preparation of this agreement, and accordingly, in any construction to be made of this agreement, the same shall not be construed against any party on the basis that such party was the drafter.

Clause Eleven is a statement pertaining to the awareness of both parties of all clauses and their interpretations.

12.   You and we intend to enter a more formal agreement embodying the terms contained herein, as well as such other terms as are customary, in exclusive, worldwide personal management agreements of this type. Until such time, if ever, as that more formal agreement is signed, this agreement shall be legally binding contract between you and us with respect to the subject matter hereof.

13.   Promptly after the execution of this Agreement, you shall, at your sole cost and expense, use best efforts to engage throughout the Term a certified public accountant experienced in the entertainment industry (the "CPA") to act as your business manager and to collect all of the gross earnings payable to you pursuant to Paragraph 3(a) above. You acknowledge and agree that (i) you shall consult with us in good faith prior to engaging any such CPA, and (ii) such CPA shall abide by the terms and conditions of this Agreement regarding the payment of any and all monies or other consideration due to us hereunder.

Management is requiring that a CPA be engaged to collect funds. This helps to protect them from any alleged fiduciary irresponsibility. Also, they require that they take part in the engagement of the business manager.

Very truly yours,

SLICK MANAGEMENT, INC.

By: _____

        (an authorized signatory)

AGREED TO ACCEPTED:

THE DUMBBELLS

(individually and collectively)

_____   _____   _____
Heavyweight SS#   Middleweight SS#   Flyweight SS#

EXHIBIT "A"
CUSTOMARY GROSS EARNINGS EXCLUSIONS

(a)   "Recording Costs" – payments, advances, overrides and royalties payable to individual producer, engineers, musicians and vocalist, or the respective companies furnishing their services, as defined under any applicable agreement for your recording services, but specifically excluding advances, payments or other consideration retained for your personal use;

(b)   "Video Production Costs" – monies paid to you or on your behalf in connection with video or film productions featuring or incorporating your recorded performances, but specifically excluding advances, payments or other consideration retained for your personal use;

(c)   "Tour Support" – monies used to offset a deficit incurred in connection with any personal appearance of concert engagement or tour of yours (unless the relevant record company does not object to our commissioning same) and monies spent by Artist's record company on so-called "independent promotion" and "independent marketing", but specifically excluding advances, payments or other consideration retained for your personal use;

Clauses a, b, and c exempt all payments that will be used to offset recording costs, video production costs and touring expenses. However, if any money is leftover or designated for personal use, then commission will be due.

(d)   Costs incurred in connection with "sound and lights" facilities or similar or related production costs, such as the costs of video projection equipment for use during live appearances) as result of you concert or other appearances, including, without limitation, hiring such "sound and lights" facilities, the transportation thereof and travel and accommodation expenses of the personnel required to erect, dismantle, transport and operate such facilities;

(e)   Advances, fees, royalties and other costs incurred with regard to third-party engineers, producers and songwriters and/or music publishers rendering services to you, including, without limitation, artist, producer and engineer advances, fees and royalties incurred with regard to production, and/or producer agreement between you and any such third party(ies) and royalties payable to any writer(s) or others with regard to any publishing agreements(s) between you and any writer(s); and

(f)   Costs incurred in connection with "opening" acts, "support" acts and other performers employed or retained to appear before, with or after you at concert or other appearances of yours.

Conspicuously absent from exemption is the booking agency fees or any fees related to employing a public relations person for the tour. However it is understood that managers usually ask for their commissions prior to the agent's fee being paid

Clauses a through f are standard commission exemptions that honest managers are willing to forego their commissions on because of the high costs involved.

SUMMARY

1. A written agreement between an artist and personal manager is employed in the industry for protection. It is signed by both parties so that each is protected from the other.

2. In order to attain success, a trusting relationship is needed between an artist and the personal manager. However, the artist is always the boss.

3. The manager acts in a fiduciary capacity for the artist. This means that the relationship is one involving a confidence or a trust. The manager should never act in his or her self-interest.

4. Contracts need not be in writing to be valid. However, a dispute involving a verbal contract must rely on testimony by a witness in order to be resolved.

5. The four parts to any legal contract are: mutual consent, consideration, capacity, and legality.

6. Neither the artist nor the manager should sign a binding contract between one another without counsel.

7. The American Federation of Musicians lists guidelines as to what areas advice and counsel should be offered by the manager.

8. The contents of an artist/personal manager agreement should be fully understood by both parties, and all clauses should be clearly defined.

PROJECTS

1. Role-play a negotiating session between an artist and a personal manager.

2. Compose a fair agreement for both parties.

3. Locate (from local bands or attorneys) several artist/personal manager agreements and discuss their contents.

4. Survey local bands that claim to have managers and see if they have a written agreement.

5. Research *Billboard Magazine* for articles concerning artist/personal manager lawsuits and discuss the reported reasons for the suits.

CHAPTER THREE
LEGAL ASPECTS

"How to you know when an attorney is lying?"
"His/Her lips are moving!   (Popular joke)

By the end of this chapter you should be able to:

1. Explain the legal basis by which you can claim rights to a name.
2. Complete a name search.
3. Define trademark and servicemark.
4. Explain how to register a trademark or servicemark.
5. Discuss the rights that you are granted when you file for federal registration.
6. Explain what determines secondary meaning.
7. Define and discuss how to set up the various forms of business entities.
8. Discuss the basic tools used in bookkeeping.
9. Discuss the issues that should be negotiated in case of a performing group's breakup.

SELECTING A NAME

Naming a group or choosing a stage name is one of the most important decisions an artist will make. The name should be memorable, and should not allow your artist to be confused with any other artist. It would not be a good idea to call the group the Beetles, even though the name is spelled differently by the famous group. This would obviously confuse the public, the Beatles would probably sue you, and besides, it is not a very original idea.

Since the 1950's, the names of rock groups have gone through many changes. There were the so called "bird" groups of the early 1950's —the "Cardinals," "Orioles," and "Ravens"— that evolved from the rhythm and blues style of the 1930's and 40's. Then, in the mid-50's there were thousands of "doo-wop" groups. Their names were associated with things that were hip and topical at the time. Some examples are: "Cadillacs," "Teen Queens," "El Dorados," "Safaris," and "Shep and the Limelites." Some argue that there was a relationship between the name of the group and the style of music performed; however, with over 15,000 groups that cut at least one single at that time,1 there were many exceptions.

During the San Francisco era of the 1960's, group names took on a surrealistic tone. Names such as: "Ball Point Banana," "Blue Light District," "Dancing Food and Entertainment" and "Freudian Slips,"[2] were performing along side the more famous San Francisco bands. The "Disco" and the "Punk" styles of music in the 1970's spawned names that were easily associated with the sound of the styles (from "The Stylistics" to "The Clash").

Today, the names of groups are used to associate the group with the style of music being performed. Many heavy metal groups use macho names ("Iron Maiden," "Metallica"), black and dance performers use slick names ("Expose," "Pebbles"), and groups that consider themselves performers of the next important style use names like "Pearl Jam," "Creed" "10,000 Maniacs," "Gene Loves Jezebel," and "Faster Pussycat"[3]. Whatever your reason for choosing a certain name, remember . . . originality is most important.

In terms of the legal aspects, using someone else's name without permission is an infringement. The basis of the law is what is termed **"priority of use."[4] What matters is not who owns the name or who has registered the name, but who has established first use of the name or has used the name continuously.**

Trademark and Servicemark

A trademark is a brand name of a product. It can be used as the logo for a product or independently (ie: Coca-Cola). When it is used for a service, such as performing music, it is called a servicemark. In some instances, a servicemark acts like a trademark (ie: on an artist's t-shirt), and there are some legal differences between the two.[5] However, for the purpose of this discussion, it is only necessary to understand that rights to either are based on **use**.

The law also permits you to use a brand name on a completely different product, such as using Remington® on something different than a shaver. However, if the use causes a high degree of confusion to the public, the courts may not permit you to continue its use.

If you are a singer and your real name is Frank Sinatra, would you be able to use it as your stage name? Unfortunately, the answer is no. *The* (late) Frank Sinatra has "priority of use," and the using your own name would cause confusion.

There are two classes of federal trademark and servicemark registration. They are "Principal Registration" and "Supplemental Registration." A mark must be "distinctive" (as opposed to descriptive) to qualify for the Principal Register[6]. For example, the group Chicago's logo is very unique and distinctive and therefore qualifies. Registration on this register gives constructive notice to the public, which means that it satisfies the legal requirements as to notification, and gives the holder exclusive rights to the name[7].

Registration on the Supplemental Register does not give the user exclusive rights to the name nor does it give constructive notice to the public. An example of a common name that would be included on the Supplemental Register is "The Blues Band." The name is not distinctive and does not clearly describe any uniqueness in the product[8].

Completing a Search

After a name is selected and before it is used, a search must be conducted to insure that no one is currently using it. The procedure for conducting a search is as follows:

1. Check with the local newspapers, "underground" papers, rock and music magazines, the local musician's union, and local talent agencies for use of the name.

2. Check all of the national music and entertainment trade publications and organizations for use of the name.

3. Investigate record company and talent agency rosters for its use.

4. Check with international music and entertainment directories for its use.

5. Search the web, specifically the U.S. Government agency site: **www.ustpo.gov**

6. Check all databases and search engines. Go to online record store sites and enter the name. Check the domain name directories, such as, www.inter-nic.net.

7. If needed, employ a professional searching bureau to ascertain if the name has been registered with the U.S. Patent and Trademark office of any state bureau.

Even if a thorough search has been conducted, you can never be 100% sure that the name isn't being used somewhere by someone.[9]

If the name does appear in the course of your search, you should return to square one and come up with another name. There is an illustrious history of small-unknown acts that have successfully sued larger acts based on priority of use. If you believe that you'll only be successful if you use a particular name, you might try to buy the rights to that name from the current user, if you are convinced that they do, indeed, own the rights.

Registering for a Federal Trademark or Servicemark

If you are interested in filing for a federal trademark or servicemark, and you have completed your search, you should begin by using the name across state lines. You will have to be able to prove that you've done this. Proving it may be as simple as saving newspaper advertisements announcing the appearance in another state, or keeping actual contracts. You will also have to produce a drawing of the mark and some specimens. Then you must file for federal registration with the Patent and Trademark Office in Washington D.C. (If you don't live in a particularly large state and do expect to travel over the state line, then federal registration is best.) According to Stan Soocher, in a *Musician Magazine* article, the procedure for filing is expensive for the following reasons:

1. A considerable fee is required for each class in which a name is registered (ie. One fee for use on recordings, another for use on t-shirts, etc.).

2. Attorneys charge up to $600+ to complete the complicated federal filing procedure.

3. Companies that conduct searches for purposes of federal trademark registration charge about $300+ per search.[10]

The procedure for filing a federal registration is as follows:

1. File an application with the U.S. Patent and Trademark office. In order to file, you must be able to prove that you used the name across state lines. Keep copies of advertisements or contracts to use as proof (the process takes about a year).

2. In order to have the rights to the name, you must continue to use the name. Two years of nonuse constitutes abandonment.

3. After the fifth anniversary of the registration you must file an affidavit stating that the name has been used continuously.

4. Renewal must be completed every twenty years.[11]

Even though it is expensive, there are many benefits to obtaining a federal registration. Federal registration gives you the following rights:

1. You can sue someone for infringement in federal court.

2. It provides "constructive notice" so that any subsequent user cannot claim "no knowledge of your right."[12]

3. After the registration has been approved, you may use the symbol R to protect your name.

   * *U.S. government is proposing that all new registrations be submitted electronically*

Who Owns The Rights to the Name

The basis of the law is "**priority of use**." If the name is registered on the Supplemental Register (as opposed to the Principal Register), the first person or group to use the name may not have the right to use it anywhere at anytime. They may need to establish "secondary meaning." Secondary meaning is determined by four factors:[13]

1. The geographic region in which the user works.

2. The duration of the use of the name.

3. The drawing power of the user (or how big a star).

4. The extent of its use in advertising

Two artists may establish secondary meaning in two different geographic regions. If neither has the name federally registered then both artists may use the name in their respective geographic regions.

Continued use is the key to obtaining legal rights to a name. However, there is such a thing as **residual use** of a name. Residual use usually means that the name is still associated with an artist after they have stopped performing, but their products continue to sell. Acts, such as the "Beatles," have a residual use right to the name, and it has been continuously used by EMI-Capitol Records. For further information concerning trademarks and servicemarks, contact the U.S. Office of Patents and Trademarks or consult an attorney. Worldwide use of a name is a far more complicated issue, and an attorney should again be consulted.

STARTING YOUR OWN BUSINESS

Bands usually begin performing and making money before they become an actual business. They play the gig and split up the money. Expenses are covered before anyone is paid. If each member owns his or her own equipment and there is no overhead, this method of conducting business may continue indefinitely. However, when a band decides to purchase something as a band (usually a sound reinforcement system), and wishes to pay it off in credit installations, it is forced to make some decisions about becoming a legitimate business. Either one member (or a member's parent) becomes responsible for paying off the loan, or the band becomes a legitimate business entity.

The forms of business entities practiced in the most industries are: **proprietorship**, **partnership**, (some form of a) **corporation**, and a **limited liability company**.

Proprietorship

A proprietorship is the simplest and the easiest form of business to start because, by definition, it is a business conducted by one self-employed person who is the owner. The procedure for setting up a proprietorship is as follows:

1. File a "DBA" (Doing Business As) form (purchased at any stationery store) with the county clerk in the county you'll be conducting business. If you intend to use your own name (John Smith as opposed to John Smith Productions) completing a DBA form is not necessary.

2. You may have to publish a legal notice in the local newspaper stating that you're doing business under the name. Check with you local county clerk's office.

3. You should file Form SS-4 with the Internal Revenue Service to obtain an employer's tax I.D. number (even if you haven't any employees).

4. If you intend to sell (retail) goods, you must obtain a resale tax permit from the state tax authority.

5. Open a checking account in the company's name.

6. Contact your local county clerk for a free brochure explaining the specifics.

The advantage of a proprietorship is that you have complete control of any and all decisions made and make all the profit. However, you are personally libel for any accidents or suits that might occur and you also must absorb any losses. You are not protected from any creditor who may want to place a lien on you personal property. There are many tax issues involved and an accountant should be consulted.

Partnership

There are several types of partnership, ie: general partnerships, joint ventures, and limited partnerships.

1. General Partnership

A general partnership is an "association of two or more persons conducting business on a continuing basis as co-owners for profit"14 Each partner contributes property, service, and/or money to the business. Partners may also loan property to the business.

Each partner owns a part or interest in the whole partnership ("assets in common") and acts on behalf of the partnership. The entire general partnership (not an individual partner) is responsible for any law suit except where bodily harm or injury has occurred by an individual partner.

Many bands form partnerships when they begin to purchase equipment that is used by the entire group or is too expensive for an individual to buy. It's actually a good idea for a partnership to acquire some assets because all of the partnership's assets must be liquidated before creditors have access to any individual partner's personal property. The procedure for setting up a general partnership is similar to setting up a proprietorship. However, an attorney should compose the actual terms of the agreement.

2. Joint Venture

On many occasions in this industry, a group and an entrepreneur join together to complete a project (such as writing a song, or producing a master recording, etc.). When the project is completed, there is no reason for the relationship to continue. In these situations, the two or more people are conducting business for one purpose, and are actually partners for the business transaction. This is a joint venture. One party is contributing service and one party is contributing service or money.

3. Limited Partnership

A limited partnership is a vehicle for funding a business project. A general partner takes on the normal business responsibilities, and the limited partner contributes capital but takes no part in the management of the business and has no liability beyond his or her capital contribution.15 The limited partner acts as a backer to finance a project (usually for a limited time period). Limited partnerships are governed by state and federal security laws, and an attorney should be consulted before agreements are made.

Corporation

Most recording artists form one or more corporations to handle their business affairs. All contractual obligations are made through the corporation, who in turn, make the artist available for fulfilling the responsibilities of the specific deals.

A corporation is a separate business entity from the persons who manage it. Ownership is obtained by buying shares of stock in the corporation. Personal assets of individuals are thereby protected from business creditors.

Corporations are governed by a board of directors who are elected by the shareholders. The business affairs are managed by a group of officers, who are employees of the corporation hired by the board of directors.16 Or in other words:

Shareholders

ELECT

Board of Directors

WHO APPOINT

Officers

TO MANAGE

employees

There are two types of corporations: **private and public**. The stock of public corporations is traded publicly on one of the stock exchanges and anyone can buy shares in (and own a part of) the business.

Private corporations do not trade their stock on the open market. All the stock is held by shareholders that have some relationship to the business. The procedure for forming either type of a corporation is as follows:

1. A corporation charter, or a document that describes the business and the structure of the corporation must be filed in the state in which you plan to be incorporated.

2. By-laws for the corporation must be formed.

3. Several sets of taxes and fees must be paid.

When forming a corporation, an attorney should be retained. Usually a corporation immediately becomes an employer because it begins paying someone a salary, even if the only employee is the artist. Therefore, there are many legal obligations, such as tax laws and labor laws, which must be followed. An accountant should also be retained.

The Limited Liability Company (LLC)

the LLC has become very popular in the last few years because it allows members to enjoy the tax benefits of a partnership and the limited personal liability of a corporation. States vary as to the criteria for forming an LLC and an attorney should be able to set one up for well under $1000. An operating agreement must be signed by each member who will then be issued shares in the company.

Bookkeeping

Today, computer programs are extremely helpful in maintaining accurate financial records of all business transactions. Many programs complete several accounting procedures automatically. The basic tools used in bookkeeping are as follows:

1. **Checkbook** - It is essential to open a separate checking account under the company's name. All of the business accounts and cash disbursements should be accounted for by a check.

2. **Ledger** (monthly)- The ledger is a book containing all accounts and transactions are posted monthly.

3. **Cash disbursement record** - This is usually designed in the form of a monthly chart that shows how any cash is spent. Items usually include parking, tolls, taxi, etc..

4. **Accounts receivable** - This is a listing of all accounts from which the company receives money. It is usually posted monthly.

5. **Accounts payable** - This is a listing of all accounts the company owes money to on account, and makes payments to. It is usually posted monthly.

6. **Receipt file** - A place where receipts are kept.

7. **Balance sheet** - The balance sheet is a monthly account of the financial condition of the company. The debits and credits for the month must balance (be equal).

8. **Calculator** - "Don't leave home without it!"

9. If you cannot keep accurate records or hate to, hire someone who will!

GROUP BREAKUPS

There are several ways that groups breakup. If the group totally disbands, things are not quite as messy as when one of two members want to continue with new personnel, or when the remaining group members, and the group members who are leaving both want to use the group's name. If the group is under contract with a major label, things will become more complicated, as all the major labels contractually protect themselves against not recouping any owed advance money (money they have advanced the artist for recording expenses). They do this by requiring the continuing group (provided the record company accepts the new members) to recoup any remaining advances before they may collect any royalties. This is an important point and must be negotiated carefully (see Chapter Six). In any case, the best time to plan for a breakup is at the formation of the group. The following areas should be covered in the group's partnership agreement before anyone says "I DO!"

1. A clear procedure for changing, adding, or subtracting group members. This should include any "buy outs" or the division of any of the group's assets.

2. Who owns the rights to the group's name.

3. What rights does a leaving member have to income generated after s/he leaves.

4. How to deal with the record company should any changes in the group's personnel occur. This should include the right of approval of new members, recouping advances, key man clauses (the most important group member), and any other matters.

5. A procedure for the complete disbanding of the group and the dissolution of the partnership, its assets and liabilities.

Blondie Members Suing Each Other Over Name Use

Now that the band is back together and recording, two former members filed a complaint against the four current members in New York Supreme Court on July 23, 1998. The two allege that the defendants have entered into "unlawful appropriation and breach of fiduciary duty" in using the Blondie name and in making business decisions for the corporation without a vote. The defendants claim that the plaintiffs "...are seeking to win a free ride on the backs of defendants' current hard work and musical enterprise."[17]

SUMMARY

1. Choosing a group's name is one of the most important decisions a group makes.

2. Using someone else's name without permission may be an infringement. The basis of the law is "priority of use," or continued use, not who has registered the name.

3. A trademark is a brand name of a product. When it's used for a service it's a servicemark.

4. After a name is selected and before is used, a search must be conducted. If the name appears in the search, do NOT use it.

5. In order to file for a federal trademark or servicemark, you must first use the name across state lines.

6. Filing is expensive.

7. There are two classes of federal registration. Principal registration automatically gives constructive notice to the public, allows you to sue someone for infringement in federal court, and gives you the right to use the symbol R. Supplemental registration does not, and "secondary meaning" must be established.

8 When two or more people on the registered on the Supplemental Register are using the name, the person who establishes "secondary meaning" has the greatest rights to a name. Secondary meaning is determined by four factors: the geographic region in which the user works, the duration of the use of the name, the drawing power of the user, and the extent of the user's advertising.

9. The forms of businesses practiced in the music industry are: proprietorship, partnership, corporation, and limited liability company.

10. A proprietorship is a business conducted by one self-employed person who is the owner. A general partnership is an association of two or more persons conducting business on a continuing basis as co-owners for profit. A corporation is a separate business entity from the persons managing it. An attorney should compose any partnership or corporation agreements.

11. The basic tools used in bookkeeping are: checkbook, ledger, cash disbursement record, accounts receivable, accounts payable, receipt file, balance sheet, and a calculator.

12. Groups' breakups can be complicated issues. The best time to plan for a breakup is at the formation of the group.

PROJECTS

1. Choose an original name and conduct a mini-search.

2. Contact an established performing group in your area, and find out if they legally have a right to their name. What evidence do they have that assures them of the right? Did they establish secondary meaning?

3. Contact an established performing group in your area and find out what business entity they are conducting business. Do they have any employees and are they receiving legal treatment under the labor laws?

4. Contact an established performing group in your area and find out if they have made any provisions for changing members or totally disbanding.

5. Read a recording contract and discuss the parts dealing with breakups and disbandments.

NOTES

1. Barry Hansen. "Doo-Wop." <u>The Rolling Stone Illustrated History of Rock and Roll</u>. Random House, New York. 1980. pg. 84.

2. Ralph J. Gleason. <u>The Jefferson Airplane and the San Francisco Sound</u>. Ballantine Books, New York. 1969. pg. 331-333.

3. Top Pop Albums Chart. <u>Billboard</u>. 12 March 1988. pg. 72 & 75.

4. Stephen Bigger. "Entertainment Group Name Selection and Protection." <u>The Musicians Manual: A Practical Guide</u>. Beverly Hills Bar Assn., Beverly Hills, CA. 1986 pg. 1.

5. Ibid. pg. 2.

6. Sidney Shemel & M. William Krasilovsky. <u>This Business of Music</u>. Billboard Publications Inc., New York. 1985, pg. 337.

7. Ibid.

8. Ibid.

9. Op. Cit. <u>The Musicians Manual: A Practical Guide</u>. pg. 3.

10. Stan Soocher. "Protecting Band Names: A Legal Survival Kit." <u>Musician</u>. September 1987. pg. 45.

11. Op. Cit. <u>The Musicians Manual: A Practical Guide</u>. pg. 7.

12. Ibid. pg. 6.

13. Op. Cit. <u>Musician</u>.

14. Edward R. Hearn. "Forms of Business Entities To Use In Starting Your Own Business." <u>The Musicians Manual: A Practical Guide</u>. Beverly Hills Bar Assn., Beverly Hills, CA. 1986 pg. 11.

15. Ibid. pg. 13.

16. Ibid.

17. Dylan Siegler. "Former Blondie Members Sue Over Use of Band Name." Billboard 9 January 1999 pg. 22.

CHAPTER FOUR
Marketing the Artist

"There is no such thing as too much publicity. There's only not enough."
Diane Rapaport. Publicity: There's Never Enough. In The Musican's Business and Legal Guide

By the end of this chapter you should be able to:

1. Discuss the role of rock 'n' roll music in the popular culture marketplace.
2. Discuss the scope of today's market, including the prerecorded and live music domestic and international scene.
3. Describe the role of the artist in the marketplace.
4. Discuss how stardom is achieved.
5. Define positive deviance.
6. Discuss the process of de-labeling a star.
7. Describe the process of creating and managing an image.
8. List the contents of a press kit and describe their roles.
9. Define media mix.
10. Write a news alert and a news release.

THE MARKETPLACE

Since the 1960s, rock'n'roll music has become a major player in the popular culture marketing mix. As the war babies became of age and began representing the largest segment of the population, their consumer behavior became of interest to every leisure time activity marketer in business. It was actually the first Woodstock Music and Art Festival in August 1969, that convinced retailers to take serious notice of the buying habits of these young adults. By merging the behavior of flower children with mainstream marketing techniques, the potential for making money became a reality.

The record industry saw this potential as well. In fact, the potential was so great, that until around 1980, the record industry was considered inflation proof! According to R.I.A.A statistics, in every year until 1979, sales as well as software unit shipments increased. Up until very recently, thanks to the soundtrack recordings of Saturday Night Fever and Grease, sales and units shipped figures of 1978 were considered one of the industry's crowning achievements.

As these war babies reached middle age in the early 1980s, it was originally thought that they would "grow up," leave rock 'n' roll behind, and turn to recordings by Sinatra, Steve and Edie, and various cover artists. Surprise! A new generation gap never really evolved. Their listening habits did not change. As it became hip to be square, Mick and Keith, Steven Tyler, Roger Waters, and Bruce continued to rock. Metallica's following increased (in number as well as average age of their listeners), and in her 50s, Tina Turner recorded a very sexy mainstream AC album. As the alternative scene developed, white kids had a increasingly difficult time using music as a tool for rebelling (and also discovering a music that their parents did not enjoy). This dilemma did not hurt the industry. By the mid-1980s, sales of recorded music software in the U. S. began to rise again. Helped by the new software configuration (always a sure booster of catalog sales), the CD, the industry has increased sales each year to date. For an industry that measures its achievements quantitatively, this all adds up to success.

What does all this mean to the artist? As a product, the artist retails his/herself through two basic formats: the recorded product and the performance ticket. Just as the retail record store sells records to the consumer, the concert promoter sells tickets to the fan. Both markets play significant roles in the success of the artist. (The internet has yet to produce significant sales.)

The Scope of Today's Market

The Domestic Scene

Prerecorded Music

According to R. I. A. A. statistics, industry domestic shipments of prerecorded product topped $14 billion for the first time in 1999. This represented an increase of 6.2% from 1998 and a modest 3.2% net unit increase. Total units were down 7% in 2000. The configuration of choice is the CD, representing 83.2 cents of every dollar spent on prerecorded music at retail. (CD units were up only 0.4% in 2000). There is considerable advertising for the Digital Video Disk (DVD), however, in 2000 only 3.3 million units were shipped. Cassettes, cassette singles and CD singles produced dismail sales

In a 1999 study by 'Kids and Media at the New Millennium,' it was found that "children spend an average of almost 1.5 hours a day and 10 hours a week listening to CDs, tapes or radio." (It also stated that kids watch 19 hours of TV a week.) Based on the number of units sold, fifteen to nineteen year old comprise 12.6% of the market, and fifteen through twenty-nine years old make up almost 36% of the domestic buying power. This is down considerably from the past few years, as in 1996 they represented almost 45%. The big jump has come in the 45+ age group, now representing 24.7 cents of every dollar spent. Although virtually equal, males buy a shade more than females, and for the first time in the past ten years, only 44.5 cents of every dollar is used to purchase records at a record store.[1] Other discount stores, book stores, and the internet are starting to make a dent in pure record store sales.

Live Performance

It has been proven that the headlining artist makes more money touring to sellout audiences than through selling records. Today's tours have several "legs" and last twelve, eighteen, sometimes twenty-four months (more about touring in Chapter Nine). According to a *Amusement Business Magazine*, two top grossing domestic single concert shows by different artists were: The Rolling Stones, with Smashing Pumpkins, Dave Mathews Band, and Third Eye Blind, $3,680,635; and U2, $2,297,613[2]. In 2000, the average gross per show for Bruce Springsteen and the E Street Reunion was $1,674,465. Bands, like the Dave Mathews Band who tour constantly gross close to a hundred million. Even after expenses are deducted, it's easy to see that sellout stadium and arena touring is very lucrative.

The International Scene

Prerecorded Music

The international scene has expanded significantly. According to the International Federation of the Phonographic Industry (IFPI) 1999 statistics, the global music market was worth US$38.5 billion. Although the US represents approximately 38% of world sales it is down considerably from the 1970s, when the U. S. represented almost one-half. The second biggest world market was Japan, and South Korea and Indonesia showed the highest growth rates. It is important to note that Japan and the U. S. total one half of the world market. However, different countries have different methods of calculating sales and many countries do not include every type of retail outlet or distribution point in the statistics they submit. Consequently, "real" sales can and do vary greatly from what is reported. For the purposes of this book, it should be noted that with a bit less than two-thirds of the records being sold outside the U. S., it is very important for artists to become international stars. Although royalty rates are lower and currency exchange rates are very volatile, there is still a great deal of money made from international sales. For more information concerning international sales, e-mail: **info@ifpi.org**.[3]

Live Performance

In 1992, The Rolling Stones performed nine dates in Japan and grossed over $30 million (in U. S. currency)![4] Of course, The Stones only work for the most ethical promoters and in the most exclusive venues, however, there is a very lucrative and growing concert scene outside of the U. S. for many artists. In fact, according to Amusement Business Magazine, at the turn of the century, the global touring industry was moving toward $2 billion in annual gross revenues. Attendance for the year was at 44+ billion worldwide. It is estimated that the 2001 Backstreet Boys 115-date worldwide tour, will gross in excess of $250 million.[5] Statistically that is a gross of more than $2 million per date.

The Role of The Artist

American Pop Culture's need for heroes and icons is filled by rock music artists. Being a successful rock musician is literally a 24 hour job. Fans expect their fantasy to be fulfilled whether they see their favorite hero on stage or off. Today's artist is expected to hold his/her image even during off hours. Consequently, the artist's image must fit the lifestyle s/he leads.

For many reasons, being a rock star is a risky existence, especially before the perks associated with being a success are delivered. Pop musicians have been considered social deviants for many years. Not necessarily negative deviants, but deviants none the less. In fact, sociologist George Lewis used the term *positive deviant* to describe the musician. He defined one as having "behavior that deviates from the expected, but is not negatively valued."[6] Another sociologist, Howard Becker, used the terms legitimate occupations versus illegitimate careers.

There are the characteristics of the musician's behavior that make him/her perceived as being a deviant. Firstly, there are the work habits. A musician works when others (the fans) are off. A musician works at night, and sleeps during the day. A musician *plays* an instrument. Secondly, the social circle of a musician is very limited. Because s/he works nights, s/he is subjected to many occupational hazards. Most of his/her fans are either musicians or night people. Drugs and other abusively used substances seem to be more available after dark. Consequently, for some, the straight life is alien and unfriendly. Lastly, conforming to the routines of day people are often difficult. Because musicians need sleep as much as anyone else, banking, shopping, and attending to medical needs are often a hassle.

Stardom

What is a star and who determines who becomes labeled as one? Lewis defines a star as "a person whose productions are so much in demand that, to some extent at least, he is able to use distributors as his adjuncts."[7] However, in demand by whom, and how do these productions become in demand? Lewis continues, "his success as a star depends upon his 'playing with the market.'[8] And the star label "is bestowed upon certain people by a specific audience which intentionally wishes to bestow such a quality."[9] Consequently, one becomes labeled as a star by a quantitative measure, and hence a positive deviant.

What happens when the star no longer lives up to the audience's expectations? Is there any procedure for de-labeling the musician as a star? Few artists are able to handle both their audience generated image and their personal identity with much success. Much of the problem is due to the amount of insulation from the real world that occurs. It compounds the situation. Not only can some not distinguish between on and off stage personas, but there is "no appropriate institution for "de-labeling" the star."[10] The premature deterioration of Elvis is a good example of the worst case scenario. Unfortunately, Elvis did not surround himself with people who were sensitive to his needs as a star.

Creating the Image

What determines the image? It's obvious that the artist must feel comfortable with what is fabricated for him/her, but, isn't this determined by what the fans want or need? Shouldn't a good manager and PR team identify the market that is attracted to the music and develop the image accordingly? Capitalize on what the market needs to feel hip, and then exaggerate it and make it bigger than life.

For example, it isn't coincidental that every time Bruce Springsteen is photographed, he is wearing a faded pair of blue jeans. Or that Pearl Jam is in baggy shorts and flannel shirts. Or any number of rappers are in gold chains etc. It would be odd if it were any other way; as strange as if Keith Richards, while guest hosting The Tonight Show, came out in a three piece suit and sang "Spinning Wheel!"

What would be wrong with this picture? For one, the image would be totally inconsistent with Keith's image of the last twenty-five years. His fans trust him, buy his records, go to his concerts, and follow his career because he has been consistent over time. He has never "sold out" by conforming to society's middle of the road safeness. As a spokesperson for rock 'n' roll, he has gained the respect and loyalty of millions of people because of the consistency of his rebellious image.

Managing The Image

As mentioned earlier, stars are so much in demand (by fans) that insulation from them becomes, to many, a means of survival. This becomes a problem because the onstage image gets confused with the reality of life and some artists are not mature enough to keep the two separate. Also, fans are so demanding to see the artist as a larger than life fantasy, that they do not care to see the artist as a everyday human being. Therefore, by definition, it is impossible for the artist to live up to the expectation.

The artists that have control of the situation are the artists that do not allow themselves to be so insulated from the public that they lose sight of reality. They may be surrounded by bodyguards (ie. Madonna, Mick, Cher), however, they go about their lives in the environment of reality, compared to one constructed to fit their on stage persona (ie. Elvis).

The second problem is the difficult process of changing the image (if needed). Some artists, such as David Bowie, Madonna, and Miles Davis have done this fairly easily. For many, the consequence outweighs the risk. The artist's audience may feel alienated if the change is too great, however, the artist may feel trapped without the freedom of artistic experimentation. One may think that his/her fans are a great group of longhaired liberals, however, the need that a consistent image fills is actually very conservative.

De-labeling the Star

How can a manager and an artist create a positive image, manage the image through a prosperous career, and then successfully transform the artist back to a life of John Doe? There is no creative procedure. Getting in touch with his/her personal identity, not the fabricated identity, is the key. Avoiding burnout, rather than drinking oneself into oblivion, is the mature process of transformation.

Unfortunately, the music industry has never taken this task seriously. It is only recently that some members of the industry (and NARAS) have taken action to develop better health plans, detoxification centers, and old age residences for artists that either blew their "fortunes" or never really made it. For the time being, it is the responsibility of the manager and the artist to see that this transition (if needed) is completed successfully.

The Media Tools

The Press Kit

If it's hip, the press kit can still be one of the artist's most useful marketing tools. It establishes credibility by presenting the artist's accomplishments in an organized professional presentation. The kit must reinforce the image that was created to fit the needs of the audience, and contain a publicity angle. Lately though, some artists have lost interest in its use.

The publicity angle is some uniqueness about the artist. It must be newsworthy, fresh, informative and believable. For example, maybe one of the band members has played with someone famous, or the band has been politically active in their hometown. The angle must grab the attention of the press and eventually the fan. It must be consistent with the image and complement the music. Try to avoid trite sayings that describe characteristics of the band, which hype the same characteristics as every other band.

Ingredients

Every press kit should contain a **biography** (bio) of the artist (or band). It must be exciting and capture the essence of the artist's musical style as well as the most interesting characteristic of the artist (or band members). In a few short typewritten pages, it should shape the image. Important quotes may be tailored to the image desired and incorporated into the story. The bio should have a beginning, middle and an end.

The **8 X 10 black and white glossy** photo is another basic part of the kit. It may be a headshot of the artist or a full body one. A good publicity photo is the most difficult piece of the kit to get right. Like the bio, it must represent the image of the artist, look natural, and make one want to hear the music. The photo should also reproduce well for printing in a newspaper, so a picture with small details should not be considered. Most likely the photo will be cropped to fit in the available space in the newspaper. Therefore, the focal point of the photo must be kept in the center of the photo.

As many **newspaper clippings** as possible should also be part of the mix. They are important because the media generates them. They legitimize and support the artist's efforts. A good manager and PR person will concentrate on doing everything in his/her power to get the press interested in the artist and write or talk about the him/her and the music. Clippings are especially important for a new artist. If the artist has accumulated a number of good press clippings, the best ones may be pulled and included in an easy to read one page quote sheet.

Depending on the objective of the artist, other materials may be included. For example, a lyric sheet may be important. An audio recording of the artist's best material maybe requested by club owners, if the artist does not have a record contract. If the artist is particularly visual and his/her stage presence is a strong part of the act, a video may be important. A calendar showing how busy the artist is may be impressive to a prospective purchaser of talent. Flyers with space for the date, time and place of the engagement are also recommended.

The Webpage

In addition to being featured on record company web pages, most artists have their own web page. It is predicted that the value of the sites will become immeasurable to the artist. The obvious should be displayed on the page: calendar, tour itinerary, bio facts, fan club information, merchandise; however, it will also be useful to link the page other pages so that search engines can display the page when someone isn't necessarily looking for the artist by name. An example of this is the following: Suppose an artist is a left handed guitar player. Linking the artist's web page with the page on left handed guitar players (if one exists), then when someone clicks on the artist's name, their web page will be displayed. This is a useful tool to introduce the artist to a new audience without any major expense. Now there is no need to learn the programming language for developing a web site (html), a search on the net will reveal scores of professional web page designers and maintenance companies who will create a site for a reasonable cost.

The Media Mix

Print, radio and television make up the media mix. Compiling a media list is the job of the PR person working for the artist. A new artist must do the legwork his/herself. Today, media lists may be bought (either in hardcopy or on a disk), or are found in any number of industry sourcebooks and by surfing the net. However, names and addresses change often, and it is difficult to stay current. It's a jungle out there and compiling mailing labels and lists is very time consuming, so target the outlets carefully. Also do not forget the fan base. Keeping them informed is a well worth the effort.

The Campaign

Planning and managing a press campaign is a fulltime job. Being organized shortcuts wasting time. Staying focused on the objective of the campaign, and understanding what the media needs to do their job is essential. The key to getting any type of publicity is meeting deadlines. They are real.

There are several types of press releases employed. All releases must be on the artist's letterhead, typewritten and double-spaced. A news alert is a short announcement describing who, what, where, when, and why. It is usually sent to calendar listings and is direct and to the point. Figure 4.1 is an example.

News Alert Format

For Immediate Release (this is unnecessary)   Contact Person:_____

Date:_____   Address:_____

          _____

          Phone:_____

          Fax:_____

Title of Release: **Performance**

The Dumbells will be performing at the **Weightlifter Club** on **Sunday April 1, 2001 at 9PM. $9 admission fee**. Tickets will be sold at the door.

Figure 4.1

A **news release** is usually two or three paragraphs describing some newsworthy event that is accompanied by other materials, such as the press kit or a new recording. It offers the opportunity to expand on the artist's latest activities while focusing on the specific objective of the release. It should be written so that it anticipates questions the reader of the publication might ask and answers them (see Figure 4.2).

News Release Format

For Immediate Release (this is unnecessary)

Date:_____

Contact Person:_____

Address:_____

_____

Phone:_____

Fax:_____

Title of Release: **Performance**

The Dumbells will be performing at the **Weightlifter Club** on **Sunday April 1, 2001 at 9PM. $9 admission fee**. Tickets will be sold at the door.

The Dumbbells are a new alternative band. Musicians include: **Muscle Shoals on Guitar and Arm Strong on Drums**. *Barbelly Magazine* said **"power, sheer power!"** to describe their last gig.

Look for The Dumbbells **at Wimpy's and Celulite's on Easter weekend**.

Also, coming soon, The Dumbbell's first CD: **Lifting for Love** on Heavyweight Records.

Figure 4.2

If a great shot of the artist doing something creative or unique (newsworthy), then use a catchy **photo caption release** detailing what's happening in the photo. Since the goal of the picture is to catch the reader's eye, the caption should complement it by filling in the blanks that are missing about the artist's story.[11]

It is very important to create and follow a campaign **timetable**. Just as media centers adhere to deadlines, the publicity campaign must follow a organized routine. If your campaign is concentrating on a performance, the work begins three to four weeks prior to the gig. Get out a news alert so that it will have plenty of time to be published in various calendar listings. About two weeks before the performance send out a news release and begin hanging flyers where they will do the most good.

On the day of the show, make certain that those invited are on the guest list. Remember, one of the objectives is to generate press reviews, so reminder phone calls to the local reviewers is recommended. Immediately after the performance check all the local rags and other outlets and save all the reviews, good or bad. And don't ignore e-mail or the web, a following can easily be developed by publishing a hip web page linked to e-mail address. This legwork is extremely tedious, but a required activity . . .persevere![12]

New Media

In Chapter Six, a complete marketing campaign for an album that went multi-platinum. Study it and use it as a guide for creating your own campaign. Below is an example of how the web was used to create a buzz to introduce Christina Aguilera's first album.

CHATTING' A SINGER UP THE POP CHARTS
SELLING CHRISTINA

Stage One: Listening to teens

To see what, if anything, kids were already saying about Ms. Aguilera, Marc Schiller and Electric Artists monitored popular teen sites like **www.alloy.com**, **www.bolt.com** and www.gurl.com, as well as fan sites for teen acts like Britney Spears and Backstreet Boys. They picked up some early talk on "Genie in a Bottle" as well as a budding rivalry between Ms. Aguilera's fans and Ms. Spears.

Stage Two: Fueling buzz on "Genie"

Electric's team started to email information to the sites, newsgroups and individual fans they found during Stage One: "Does anyone remember Christina Aguilera – she sang the song from "Mulan," "Reflection"? I heard she has a new song out called "Genie in a Bottle." The team also lobbied big web sites like America Online to run features on Ms. Aguilera.

Stage Three: Gear up for the album

Electric's postings shifted emphasis to the album rather than the single "You've got to convince them to go from a $1.98 purchase to a $16 purchase." Also, key now was making sure the album cover was on the big retailers' web sites. That helps parents shopping for their kids remember the album's name.

Stage Four: Broaden the fan base

To promote her second single, Electric may target Mariah Carey and Whitney Houston fan sites. It's important to show that this was not Britney Spears, this was not a one shot thing.[13]

The Image Makers

The publicist must create a trust between s/he and his/her client. The artist puts his/her pubic image in the hands of the publicist and relies on the credibility of the publicist to do his/her work justice. What follows are a series of quotes by industry image makers. They are taken from an out of print book, *The Making of Superstars* by Robert Stephen Spitz.

Next to music, image is perhaps the most important aspect of recording artist's career. The way a particular artist looks and feels, thinks and reacts to situations plays heavily upon the way the public views that person and, many times, creates an appeal equally as important as the music. But unless the artist is so unique a talent or a personality before embarking on a recording career, it is up the publicist to create an image that will catch the public eye and lure them into giving this artist a chance to be heard.

Publicity is an art in itself, distinguished by those in the profession who have achieved credibility by creatively formulating an image within the bounds of reality from those who merely "hype" false praise. Robert Stephen Spitz.

My responsibility to my clients is to represent them accurately and to better translate their interesting points to the public. An artist does not know what makes him interesting to a magazine or to the public and that's what I'm there to tell him.

I think even the big acts need press all the time. A career should build. It's very hard for an artist to get a record company behind them when their record in five months old and they won't have another one coming out for three or four months.

Credibility is perhaps the most useful quality which a publicist can develop. I maintain my credibility by trying never to lie about the proportions of the act I'm publicizing. C. J. Strauss

Breaking a new artist by press is extraordinarily difficult. There is a certain amount of luck involved. First of all, the music has to be there. You cannot hype anything for very long that is either not musically valid or entertaining. But we'll try, though.

When conferring with a new artist, we spend a lot of time discussing the strong character points of an artist and how to bring them out.

I always strive to have our publicity department "bunch" things. We try to get as many things going on a particular artist in the hope that they will all break

around the same time. Concentration of that nature, I always find, inundates the public's awareness. If it's spread out over a year, publicity loses its effectiveness.

Bob Regehr

Basically, my job is to get my clients the best possible space in the best possible public showcases. I try to take the real part of my clients and build those aspects into publicity so that when they are in the public eye they don't fall short of the press which they received. I am careful not to overbuild an artist- especially a new artist- because people will become disappointed and turn off to them.

Pat Costello

Direct to Consumer Marketing

The web was designed for direct to consumer marketing. Most artists have well designed web pages that help to gather information about their fan base and buyers of their music and merchandise, and create databases to use in direct to consumer marketing. Independent music marketing firms create web campaigns (see above) and data bases, and contact the buyers of products, making use of the demographic information to alert these buyers of other products s/he may be interested in, or to the artist activities.

Some record companies are completing this task in- house, because it is a very effective tool for artists that are not very "radio friendly" but have a loyal fan base. As long as there is product in the marketplace, a marketing company can expand on the marketing tools.

SUMMARY

1. Since the 1960s, rock 'n' roll music has played a major role in the pop culture marketing mix.

2. Domestic shipments of prerecorded product topped $14 billion in 1999.

3. Many headlining artists gross over one million dollars at some arena shows.

4. In 1999, the U.S. accounted for more than 1/3 of the world sales of prerecorded music.

5. The artist's image must fit the lifestyle s/he leads.

6. Being a rock musician is a risky existence.

7. Musicians can be considered positive deviants because they exhibit behavior that deviates for the expected, but not in a negative way.

8. A star is a person whose productions are so much in demand that s/he is able to use distributors as his/her adjuncts.

9. His/her audience bestows the star label upon an artist.

10. There is no appropriate institution for de-labeling a star.

11. The fans' wants and needs determine the image that is created.

12. Many artists insulate themselves so much from their audience that they have trouble separate their stage image from real life.

13. It is a difficult process to change an image.

14. The press kit is still the main media tool in the industry.

15. A press kit should include a bio, glossy photo, newspaper clippings, and a quote sheet.

16. Two types of press releases are the news alert and the news release.

17. It is important to follow a press campaign a timetable to respect deadlines.

18. Direct to consumer marketing via the web is very useful to some artists.

PROJECTS

1. Compile a press kit.

2. Locate an artist that is performing live, and write a news alert and a news release announcing the event.

3. Choose an artist on tour and track the gross receipts for a leg of the tour.

4. Discuss the images of three current stars and determine if they are fabricated.

5. Formulate a marketing campaign for a local artist, including a timetable and the media mix.

6. Examine five different artist's web pages for ideas.

NOTES

1. "Our Greatest Hits". The Annual Report of the Recording Industry Association of America. 1997.

2. "Boxscore, Top 10 Concert Grosses." Amusement Business Magazine. As reported in Billboard Magazine. December 27, 1997.

3. "World Record Sales". Popular Music (1998), Vol. 16/No. 3. Pg. 311-313.

4. Ibid.

5. "Big Tour By Backstreet Boys Set." Billboard Magazine. December 9, 2000. p. 7.

6. George Lewis. "Positive Deviance: A Labeling Approach to the Star Syndrome in Popular Music." Popular Music and Society. Fall, 1980. p. 74.

7. Ibid.

8. Howard Becker. Outsiders. Free Press. Glencoe, Ill. 1963.

9. Op, cit. Lewis.

10. Ibid.

11. Veronique Berry. Guide To Independent Music Publicity. Audio & Video Labs, Inc. Philadelphia, PA. 1993.

12. Diane Rapaport. "Publicity: There's Never Enough." The Musician's Business and Legal Guide. Badlands Press

13. Erin White. "Chatting' a Singer Up the Pop Charts." The Wall Street Journal. October 5, 1999. p. B1

CHAPTER FIVE
The Transnationals

The world is our audience (Time Warner). *Think globally* (Sony).
A truly global organization (EMI). *Globalize local repertoire* (BMG). *Committed to meeting your life's ever-changing needs* (Vivendi, the parent to Seagram's Universal).[1]

By the end of this chapter you should be able to:

1. Describe a multi or trans national company.

2. Discuss, with examples, how they have become so powerful.

3. Discuss the "big five" transnationals that control the music industry and give examples of their music related and non-music related businesses.

The term multinational or transnational company is used to describe a company that conducts business on an international scale and who has a global presence. This mega-company may be headquartered on the other side of the globe, but is able to complete business transactions as if it lived right next store. It is truly international in its ability to look and behave as if its interest lies on the local level as well as all across the globe.

Globalization is the buzzword of its mission statement as exemplified in the slogans of several transnationals (see this chapter's title). Reading between the lines, the feeling that is generated is that the multinationals envision a world business community that is expanding, as it's becoming smaller. That is, more countries are participating in the trading of merchandise (enlarging the community), but new delivery systems and distributions channels are shortening the time it takes for products to arrive at their destinations.

The ownership of the multinationals that control the recording industry is also truly international. Two are located in Japan, one is in England, one in Germany, and ownership of one is still in the good old USA. This is a far cry from the pre-1980s, when Americans owned all but one.

Integration and Concentration

The five transnationals account for almost 90% of the world's record sales. They have become so powerful because they have created conglomerates that have expanded both horizontally and (or) vertically, and (or) because they have gained control of a specific segment of a business.

An example of **horizontal expansion** is when a record company buys another record company or merges with another company. Companies that once competed join forces to create an even larger company. An example of this is Sony's acquisition of CBS Records Group in 1988. Sony was and still is one of the largest electronics companies in the world. It had a label presence in its own country of Japan, but in order to take part in the profits of the worldwide sales of products that utilized its hardware, it needed to become a software company as well. Sometimes two companies are bought by a parent company of one and continue to compete. The parent company increases in size and revenue, but the companies continue to fight for home run hitting artists. An example of this is Bertelsmann's purchase of the RCA and Arista Music Groups. Philips also used a similar tactic when it purchased Polygram.

An example of a **vertical merger** is when a record company buys a distribution or Retail Company. It increases in size and decreases its expenses by owning another piece of the product merchandising chain (ie; producing and manufacturing, or distributing and retailing). EMI owns HMV music shops and Virgin Records, which brought with it the Virgin Megastores.

Concentrating on a specific segment of the entertainment industry and controlling every phase of that segment has also proven to be a profitable way of gaining market share. For example, if a company envisions itself as a media company, then its ownership will include: film, video, print, and record companies. It will share in all profits to the rights of the **video** of the **single** from the **soundtrack** of the **movie** of the book, as they are all part of its business. Time Warner is an example of this.

*The Big Five

All the information concerning the corporations was found on the individual corporation web sites.

Bertelsmann AG

Bertelsmann Foundation is headquartered in Germany. Its business areas include: book publishers and clubs; music labels and clubs; professional information; magazines and newspapers; television, film and radio; print and media services; online services, multimedia and E-commerce. BMG Entertainment represents 28.1% of its revenues, and the US represents 33.8%.

BMG is home to more than 200 record labels in 54 countries, the world's largest record club, the industry's most highly regarded distribution company, and the fastest growing music publishing company today.

Bertelsmann AG employs 76,000 people worldwide and is the world's third largest media company.

EMI Music Group

For over 100 years, EMI has been one of the world's leading music companies. Its record labels and music publishing businesses have worked with and represented some of the top recording artists and songwriters of all time. Today, the EMI Group operates directly in 45 countries, with licensees and distribution agreements in a further 26. EMI releases more than 1000 albums every year and has a roster of over 1500 artist from all around the globe.

EMI Music Publishing is one of the world's leading music publishers, controlling over a million copyrights spanning the whole musical spectrum.

EMI global market share is approximately 12.5% and it employs 10,000 people in 50 countries.

Sony Corporation

Sony Corporation of America, based in New York City, is a subsidiary of Corporation headquartered in Tokyo. Sony is one of the world's premier entertainment and electronics companies, providing top quality entertainment and electronic products and services to consumers around the world. Sony is poised to be the leading provider of digital content, service, and devises in the 21st century. Sony's principal US businesses include Electronics Inc., Sony Pictures Entertainment, Sony Music Entertainment Inc., and Sony Computer Entertainment of America. Its workforce numbers 190,000 employees worldwide, with 25,000 of those in the US.

In January 1988, Sony Corporation acquired CBS Records Group, known today as Sony Music entertainment Inc. CBS/Sony is today known as Sony Music Entertainment (Japan) Inc. In January, 1994, in acknowledgment of its worldwide growth and success, Sony Music Entertainment reorganized into four label groups: Epic Records Group, Columbia Records Group, Relativity Entertainment Group, and Sony Classical.

[AOL] / Time Warner Inc.

Time Warner Inc. is the world's leading media company. With an array of world-class brands and the best corporate and divisional management, Time Warner is helping transform the global information and entertainment landscape. Time Warner Inc. operates five businesses: the cable networks group, publishing, music, filmed entertainment, and cable systems.

The Warner Music Group's record labels – Warner Music International, Atlantic, Elektra, Rhino, London Sire Records, Warner Bros. Records and their affiliate labels – are home to over 1000 established stars and new artists worldwide.

Warner/Chappell was named Billboard Hot 100 Publisher of the Year in 1999 and controls over one million copyrights.

WEA Inc. is one of the largest distributors of recorded music in the world. In January 2000, America Online acquired Time Warner for about $100 billion in stock and cash (actual acquisition price may have been considerably less).

Vivendi/Seagram

Vivendi is world leader in utilities and a major player in communications. The company employs 275,000 people that contribute to improving the quality of life of its customer through environmental services and communications.

The Seagram Company Ltd., headquartered in Montreal, operates in four global business segments: music, filmed entertainment, recreation, and spirits and wine. Universal Music Group, the world's largest recorded music company, produces, markets and distributes recorded music throughout the world in all major genres, and it is engaged in music publishing. In 1998 Universal Music Group acquired Polygram, establishing it as the world largest music company. In June 2000, Seagram announced a strategic business combination with France's Vivendi and Canal+, which will culminate Universal's evolution into a fully integrated global leader in media, communications and entertainment. The company is listed as Vivendi Universal.

Table 5.1 illustrates the five multinationals that control the music business.

NAME	OWNERSHIP	COUNTRY	**LABELS OWNED AND/OR DISTRIBUTED
BMG	Bertelsmann AG	Germany	Artist, BadBoy, BMG, Classics, Imago, Jive, La Face, Logic Novus, RCA, Windham Hill
SONY	SONY	Japan	Sony Classical Group Columbia Records Group Epic Records Group Relativity Records Group
EMI	EMI	England	Blue Note, Chrysalis Capitol, EMI, EMI Classics, Parlophone, Priority, Virgin
UNI	Vivendi/Seagram	France	Decca Record Co., Deutsche Grammophon Interscope Geffen A&M, Island Def Jam Music Group, Jimmy & Doug's Farmclub.com, MCA Records, MCA Nashville, Motown Records Group, Phillips, Polydor, Universal Records Group, Verve Music Group
Warner Music Group	AOL/ Time Warner, Inc.	USA	Atlantic Music Group, Electra Entertainment Group, Rhino, Sire Records Group, Warner Bros. Records, Warner Music International

Table 5.1
*** For complete listing of labels visit the parent company web sites.*

The entertainment business is clearly an internationally owned industry. Table 5.2 illustrates many of the non-music businesses that each own.

Bertelsmann AG	Bertelsmann AG; Bertelsmann Book AG; Gruner + Jahr AG; RTL Group; Bertelsmann Arvato AG; Direct Group Bertelsmann; Bertelsmann Springer; Bertelsmann in the USA
SONY	Sony Electronics Inc; Sony Pictures Entertainment; Sony Computer Entertainment
EMI	EMI Electronics; HMV Group
Vivendi/Seagram	Generale des Eaux; Canal+; Societe Francaise de Radiotelephonie; Seagram Spirits and Wine; Universal Studios; Universal Recreation and Others
Time Warner	Cable Networks; Publishing; Filmed Entertainment; Cable Systems.

Table 5.2

It is obvious that the major players in the record industry are all tied to other businesses.

Lastly, Table 5.3 illustrates the role the music division plays in each conglomerate.

MUSIC SALES AS PERCENT OF TOTAL SALES:	
CONGLOMERATE	**MUSIC SALES**
EMI	100
Vivendi/Seagram	6-11
AOL/Time Warner	5-10
Bertelsmann	8-12
Sony	3-8

Table 5.3

SUMMARY

1. The term transnational company is used to describe a company that conducts business on an international scale and who has global presence.

2. The ownership of the transnationals that control the recording industry are truly international.

3. The five multinationals account for almost 90% of the world's record sales.

4. They became so powerful because they expanded horizontally and vertically and also took control of a specific segment of the industry.

PROJECTS

1. Visit the web pages of the big five and see who are the leaders of each division.

2. Research the big five and find out what percentage of their sales, revenue, and expenses the music division is of each.

NOTES

1. Robert Burnett. <u>The Global Jukebox</u>. Routledge Press. London, U.K. 1996. p. 8.

2. Big five web pages

CHAPTER SIX
The Record Company

Vice President/NYC

Manage & direct heavy metal, country, alternative & dance music sectors of international music recording & distributing company. Exercise final approval discretion on selection of talent. Identify promising artistic talent. Negotiate contract terms w. agents of artists, exercising final approval agreements. Coordinate with Company attorneys in foregoing task. Create broad plans & policies for achieving corporate financial & development goals established by management, including budget & sales forecasting. Conceive, supervise, coordinate & implement activities that create public awareness & demand for corporate products & artist, by way of advertising, sales campaigns, market analysis, & media exposure. Develop image strategies for recording artist, including supervision of artwork, photography, image consultants posters & packaging, editorial & label copy. Develop & exercise final discretion on methods to enhance career growth of Company artist, including finding & selecting material to be recorded & recordings to be released. Spvse & direct artists tour support, incl. market & venue selection, budgetary control & timing. Use all available mkt info to guide decision making. Hire & fire staff. Direct Company's outside recording studio activities, incl. studio selection, product & staff quality evalu. & cost oversight. Associate's degree, or foreign equiv. in Business Administration; 5 yrs. exp. in job. Exp. must be with internally distributed recorded media. At least 2 yrs. extensive exp. providing interntl. & domestic tour booking & supervision to groups playing 200 seat club to 15,000+ seat arena venues. Reqs. at 2 yrs. recording exp. as producer or exec. producer. 2 yrs. exp. in music publishing (finding & selecting material to be recorded). $200,000/yr.; 40 hr./wk. Resume in dupl. to CJ-112, Rm 501, One Main St., Brooklyn, NY 11201."

Classified ad. Billboard Oct. 19, 1991

By the end of this chapter you should be able to:

1. Discuss the role of the record company in the life of the artist.
2. Discuss the three types of financial advances offered to an artist.
3. Discuss, with examples, the three types of record companies in the industry, and the advantages and disadvantages of each.
4. Discuss the structure of a record company and the functions of the various departments.
5. Describe the internal path of a product thorough the various departments.
6. Discuss, in detail, the various ingredients in marketing campaign.
7. Describe, with examples, the costs of releasing a product and how to calculate royalties.
8. Calculate the artist's and the record company's share of royalty revenue.

This is it!

I've made it!

I'm one of the best!

These are the thoughts that run though the mind of an artist during his/her first visit to his/her record company as a royalty artist. After all, this is the stuff dreams are made of! It is truly one of the most exciting off stage appearances an artist makes. You feel like you're a part of one big happy family, and not only does everyone get along with each other, but everyone can't wait to help you deliver a hit. You envision a long association with the label as your career develops. Feeling a bit guilty, you repeat to yourself, "Boy, what did I do to deserve this life."

Record companies are tuned into this feeling and create slogans that help convince people that music and careers are as important as the bottom line of product sales. Arista Records has used the slogan "where careers are launched." With this slogan, Arista announces that their interest and intention is in discovering new talent and developing solid foundations for long and prosperous careers, rather than just being interested in releasing a bunch of records with the hopes that a few will make money and pay the bills.

Another example is CBS Records, now Sony. For years, CBS had the indignation to call itself "**THE** Music Company". The slogan positioned CBS as the knowledgeable company that recorded material that deserved to be recorded and classified as music, and the other labels didn't. Certainly CBS would have a hard time convincing most of us that everything they've released over the years should be considered great music. However, as a former artist with the company, this author recalls the feeling of being something special signed to CBS.

These assurances are very healthy for the artist and the manager. However, if all or even most of the above is true, why do two-thirds to three-quarters of the pop records released never recuperate their recording costs? And fewer become hits? Why do so many managers say that they do not feel secure in leaving the record company alone to run the show? Why do so many artists fail to sell records and are eventually dropped from the label's roster? Why do so many good records get lost in the shuffle? How can companies continue to operate with what might be considered such a dismal track record? These questions will be addressed later in this chapter when we look at the typical route of a new recording as it travels through the many departments of the company.

The Role of the Record Company

Choosing a label is by far the most significant business decision the artist and his/her manager make together. The record company plays many roles in the life of the artist. Two aspects of this relationship are most important. One is obvious and the other not. The obvious role a company plays is to produce, manufacture, release, promote, manage and distribute the artist's recorded product. And, through sales, generate income for the artist. Although it is not an easy task, it is the company's main function in the industry and an artist should expect these tasks to be carried out effectively and efficiently.

A subtler role is one of a financial backer. Through various types of financial "advances" which are charged against the artist's royalty account, the record company acts as a reservoir or bank for the artist to obtain funds.

Advances

The term advance is used to describe the loaning of money to a royalty artist (normally with interest charged), with the understanding that the money will be paid back to the company before any royalty checks are delivered to the artist. As we will learn in Chapter Seven, The Record Contract, record companies will seek every conceivable way to generate the revenue to recoup any of the expenses (including advances) that they have incurred. If permitted, they will "cross-collateralize" revenue generated into royalty accounts from past and future recordings, merchandising, endorsements, sponsorships, etc., to guarantee as many sources of revenue as possible. Therefore, the artist and manager should be careful not to over extend the debt to the company. Remember, because it is charged to the royalty account, it's the artist's money that is being spent. Three types of advances commonly given by the company are personal, production, and inducement advances.

Personal Advance

A personal advance is the lending of money to the artist for such needs as normal living and household expenses when there is insufficient revenue being generated by personal appearances and/or recording sales. The artist is loaned money to pay the bills and even though s/he is not obligated to pay back any of it (should the sales of the recording never reach their expected level), every precaution should be taken to see that the artist does not accumulate unnecessary personal expenses prematurely. Sometimes, personal advances are used to pay the salaries of employees. Again, the number of employees should be kept at a minimum until desperately needed.

Production Advance

A production advance is the lending of money by a company for the production of a recording. These expenses might include new instruments, or technical support items such as lighting, staging, or a rehearsal hall. Production advances are usually part of the all inclusive "recording fund" as are personal advances needed specifically during the recording process. This is discussed later in this chapter and in Chapter Seven.

Inducement or Bonus Advances

This type of advance is usually reserved for the established artist with a proven track record of successful sales. In some instances, in order to sign the artist, the record company becomes involved in a bidding war for the artist against another label, and the artist's manager seizes the opportunity to ask for a sum of money to be delivered upon signing. Although the adage "one in the hand is worth more than two in the bush" may be true, the artist and manager should be concerned with the longevity of the relationship with the company and what the company can accomplish to insure a successful career, rather than the fast buck!

Types of Record Companies

The simplest way to distinguish between record companies is by size: large vs. small. However, other terms are used in the industry, ie: major, independent, specialty, or boutique. Efficient companies come in all sizes, and hit artists have become enormously successful regardless of the size of the label. For example, the group U2 has recorded multi-platinum records for Island Records, once an independent label identified mostly with reggae music, and now part of Uni. Whitney Houston has done the same for Arista Records.

Major Labels

Major labels with their subsidiaries and associated labels, dominate the business and account for almost 90% of the records sold worldwide. Most major labels are owned by larger non-American transnational conglomerates whose businesses extend beyond the entertainment industry (see Chapter Five). As stated earlier, distinguishing a label as major does not relate only to size. A monster hit can launch an act into superstardom and increase the size and distinction or the label almost overnight.

A record label is considered a major label if it owns or controls the distribution of its releases and employs its own radio promotion force. Majors also distribute their subsidiary and associated labels, as well as other label's product. Using this definition of a major, there are five in the U.S. They are:

Record Company	Distribution Company
Sony Music Group	Sony Distribution
EMI Records	EMD Distribution
BMG Entertainment Group	BMG Distribution
Warners Music Group	WEA Distribution
Universal Music Group	Uni Distribution

Major labels offer the following advantages to their artists:

1. an in-house distribution network

2. an in-house promotion department

3. prestige

4. large financial resources

5. stability

However, there are disadvantages and they are:

1. the risk of getting lost among a large roster of talent

2. the possible lack of individual attention

3. the administration of the company may not be in total control of the company and may have to answer to the parent company which may have little involvement with the music and entertainment business

Independent Label

Although total independence in record companies is a thing of the past, we tend to classify any label that is not owned by one of the majors as an independent. Consequently, a label is considered an independent if it relies on another label for one or more of the following services.

Distribution - An independent label will rely on either a major label's distributor or an independent record distributor for distribution of their product.

Promotion - Depending on the size of the record label, the services of the distribution may also include a promotion staff.

Merchandising/Sales - same as above

Financial Resources - It is common for someone (or company) to give start-up money to a new independent label and financially back it for a period of time.

The **advantages** of an independent label to an artist are:

1. the strong possibility of receiving individual attention in all of the record company's departments

2. the possibility of becoming a big fish in a smaller pond and generating more publicity than they would on a major.

However, the **disadvantages** to an artist are:

1. the possibility of limited available resources

2. inadequate distribution network

3. less prestige

Specialty Label

Specialty labels usually release only one style of music. There are jazz, classical, folk, children, etc. specialty labels. The style of music need not be without financial success, as there are labels that move a great deal of urban, metal, dance, and new age music. Artist owned labels fall into this category as do many subsidiary labels of majors.

The **advantages** to an artist are:

1. the expertise of a company's staff in the genre

2. the ability to communicate easily with other artists in the same genre on the label.

The **disadvantages** might be:

1. a lack of financial resources

2. the inability to distribute to large chain record retailers

Boutique Label

Although it is not an "official" term, it is used to describe a midsize company that behaves like a major, but is more selective in its choice of artists. These companies usually have a higher percentage of hit makers within a smaller roster of artists. J, Arista, Jive, and DreamWorks Records are examples of three of these so-called labels. The advantages to an artist are obvious and many. The downside is very minimal, although it does not allow the artist to make very many excuses for poor selling records!

The Structure

Record companies are obviously in business to make money. Structurally there are two major divisions in any company. They are the creative division and the business/administrative division. Although the creative areas are concerned with making a profit, the tug or war between areas concerned primarily with the bottom line and areas concerned with the artistic merits of a release are common. In fact, in some a&r departments there is the distinction made between "pop product" that is released to rocket up the charts and disappear after one or two monster releases, and product with artistic quality that has the promise of longevity.

Figure 6.1 is a representation of the structure of a major record company. The departments or areas in italics represent the creative areas and the departments in plain text represent the business areas. At the top of the chart are the stockholders of the "parent company." They are the owners of the company and are the true "bosses." The company as a corporation may be a public company, with stockholders that invest capital through the purchase of shares on the open stock markets, or they may be private investors who purchase shares in return for financial

Structure of a Record Company

Stockholders of Parent Company
Chairman & Board of Directors
President of Parent Company
Label President
Vice Presidents of:

Artist Dev.	Manuf.	Bus. & Legal Aff.	A & R	Dist. & Merch.	Finance	Int. Op.	Promo.
1. *Per. Appear*	1. Press. Plants	1. Artist Cont.	1. *Artist Sign.*	1. Trans	1. Acct.	1. Commun.	1. *Radio*
2. *Tour Supp.*	2. Printing	2. Licenses	2. *Mech. Lic.*	2. Acct. Ser.	2. Inventory Control	2. Personnel	2. *Video*
3. *Career Dv.*	3. Duplication	3. Labor Agr.	3. *Prod. Coor.*	3. Sales	3. Royalty Payments	3. Phy. Pl.	3. *Field*
4. *Publicity*		4. Prod. Cont.	4. *Master Pur.*	4. Warehouse	4. Taxes		4. *Indie*
5. *Media Ser.*		5. Comp. Ads.	5. *Admin.*	5. POP Ads.			
		6. Copyright & Patent		6. Co-op Ads			
		7. Ent. Law		7. Invtry			

Marketing
1. *Prod. Dev.*
2. *Artwork/ Graphics*
3. *Ads*

LEGEND
Creative Areas = Italics
Business Areas = Plain

Table 6.1

support. As with any corporation, the board of directors is directly responsible to the stockholders and is represented by their chairperson. The board of directors receives their information concerning operations of the (parent) company from the president of the company. The operations of the record label is represented to all of the above by the label president. S/he is in the hot seat! If the entertainment business is newly acquired or only a small part of the central operations of the parent company, then the label president's ability to communicate the successes and failures of the label becomes crucial to its future.

Under the label president are the senior vice presidents and vice presidents of each department. Their job is to make the president look credible, responsible, and in control. The chart describes, in outline form, the functions of each department. What follows is a short synopsis of each of the department's responsibilities.

Artist Development

The activities of this department involve increasing the artist's (not necessarily his/her product) recognition in the marketplace, including short and long term career development, and publicity.

Artists and Repertoire

Until the mid 1960's, when the industry superstars began employing independent producers, the a&r department would discover the talent, pick the songs to be recorded, and produce the records. Everything was completed "in house" and the "head" of a&r was considered the most important person in the company. Mitch Miller, who was responsible for the careers of Doris Day, Tony Bennett, and others, was head of a&r at Columbia Records in the 1950's and considered the most influential person in the industry.

Presently, a&r still play a significant role in the musical direction of the company. They discover artists, locate material to be recorded, match artists with producers, and deem the recorded product acceptable for release. Although still considered to be the most creative department in the company, an independent producer completes the actual production of the record. Consequently they are not active in the actual recording or mixing of the recording. The administration of the department keeps track of the budget of each recording session.

Because the large umbrella category known as popular music is subdivided into narrow- casted "micro" formats (such as metal, urban, rap, dance, new age, etc.), each department usually employs a specialist to discover artists, and direct activities in his/her area of expertise. Although being a musician is not a qualification for the position, these are the few **MUSIC** people left in a company.

Business and Legal Affairs

Although separate departments in names, these two departments work closely in contracting various agreements that concern the revenue flow of the company. These include artist agreements, licensing agreements, labor agreements, and any regulatory agreements that involve income and expenditures. These departments employ the people that wear the suits (and/or high heels) to work and make the important but not glamorous bottom line decisions. Artists and managers tend to question the rationale of many of their decisions.

Distribution and Merchandising

These two departments also work closely in servicing the branch distributors, tracking inventory, and servicing point of purchase promotional vehicles for in-store display. Because *Billboard Magazine* has introduced "Soundscan," a computerized sales tracking device for servicing their charts, retail sales have taken on greater industry significance.

Finance

Again an important but non-glamorous department that accounts for every penny that the company spends and receives. These people tend not to have decision making power outside of consulting with the administration and business affairs to offer the most cost effective options for the company.

Internal Operations

This department has the greatest variety of responsibilities, from paper clips to personnel to telephone and data processing systems to tropical plants to kosher meats for the kitchens. Their goal is the most cost effective efficient operation of the company.

Marketing and Promotion

The marketing department is an umbrella department with several areas that are responsible for the integrity of the recorded product once it has been delivered to the company by the producer, and the a&r department has pronounced it acceptable for release. They design a marketing campaign for the record that includes the visual concept for the cover artwork, print advertising, point of purchase displays, and any merchandise that will be sold in conjunction with the release.

A great number of companies separate the marketing and promotion departments with individual vice presidents for each. Promotion departments are also separated by radio formats, with National Directors leading the staff in each. Promotion departments live and die by airplay, and are responsible for completing the radio and video portions of the campaign.

The decision to employ free-lance or independent experts for any of the marketing plan's responsibilities is made by this department's vice president.

Manufacturing

The goal of this department is attaining the most cost-effective efficient method of product duplication possible.

Product Flow

The following describes the internal path a product takes from the time the master is delivered, and the a&r department decides to "sign off" on the recording as being "commercially acceptable," and all necessary forms and releases have been completed. In Figure 6.2, the diamonds represent decisions that must be addressed, and the rectangles represent actions. The diagram represents the linear flow of the product but does not represent simultaneous actions completed by separate departments.

Product Flow Chart

```
START
  │
  ▼
Is Product                        From A& R to Marketing
Commerically                           │
Acceptable for  ──YES──►  Has product campaign been  ──YES──►  Has single  ──YES──►  Single released and
airplay and               developed, graphics and             been chosen?          promotion and publicity
sales?                    video completed?                        │                 begins and video is
  │                            │                                 NO                 delivered
 NO                           NO                                  │                      │
  │                            │                                  ▼                      │
  ▼                            ▼                               Choose                    │
Record                    Campaign completed                  single                     │
or remix                  and video shot                                                 ▼

Release                    Is record        ──YES──►  Has feedback  ──YES──►  Is record
another      ──NO──►       a hit?                      been positive?          moving up
single and                    │                            │                  the charts?
fine tune                     ▼                            NO                      │
campaign                  $UCCE$$                           │                     NO
                                                            ▼                      │
                                                       Increase                    ▼
LEGEND                                                 promotion             Increase
◇ Decision                                             and                   promotion
▢ Activity                                             publicity             and/or
                                                                             publicity;
                                                                             ads and POP
```

Table 6.2

Is the Product Commercially Acceptable for airplay and sale, and the first single chosen?

This is the most important decision made and it's a&r's responsibility. The term "**commercially acceptable**" is the term used in the recording contract that allows the record company to make a release decision based on just the technical integrity of the recording. It allows the company to censor the recording. They may feel the lyrics may offend a certain segment of society and if aired, have a negative effect on sales, or they may deem the lyrics as obscene. The company may feel that the recording sounds too much like a previously copyrighted work and may be bordering on infringement. Whatever the "problem" with the recording, the term commercially acceptable allows the company the legal freedom to hold back a release for reasons beyond a recording's technical inefficiencies. Recently, several record companies have required the legal department to review (and sign off on) the lyrics on all material scheduled for release. As also stated in the recording contract chapter, artists are very skeptical about this term and should be. However, very few artists (if any) have the term substituted in the contract.

Choosing the first single to be released is also an a&r decision. It is the manager's responsibility to make certain that the right song is selected. Major battles are fought everyday over this decision, and a good manager persuades a&r to make the right choice. Sometimes the company's administration is involved with the choice, and managers find themselves trying to persuade a president that the record s/he really wants as the single is the same record the manager and artist wants.

There is quite a bit of paperwork involved in delivering the master recording to a&r for release. The names and social security numbers of each performer on the record must be submitted and a host of other forms completed. For example, the federal government is very concerned that foreigners do not replace working citizens of the USA. Various labor union forms must also be completed. All expenses pertaining to the actual recording and other debits to the recording fund must be accounted for. The manager and artist's accountant and attorney should review all expense statements as well as other "official" documents.

Has product Campaign Been Developed, Graphics and Video Completed?

The actual marketing campaign has many facets that must be coordinated by the product manager responsible for the project. Figure 6.3 represents a plan for the campaign.

SPOOKS INTERNATIONAL MARKETING PLAN

"The dictionary defines a spook as a ghost: a spector. A secret agent or a spy. To spook someone is to haunt them, to startle them in some way as to cause momentary disturbance and shock. It's a word loaded with hidden meanings, one that can be derogatory and celebratory. Spooks is a word that holds numerous connotations: a word that refuses to be limited to just one definition.

ALBUM TITLE: S.LO.S.O.S.

U.S. ALBUM RELEASE DATE: JULY 11, 2000

INTERNATIONAL RELEASE DATE: FALL 2000

Record Company:
Artemis Records/Sheridan Square Entertainment
130 Fifth Avenue
7th FloorSuite 7
New York, New York 10010

(212) 433-1800 Main Phone
(212) 414-1703 Main Fax
Dave Lory: Marketing
Dlory@artemisrecords.com E-mail

Leslie Hoeflich: Promotion
(212) 433-1841 Direct Line
ihoeflich@artemisrecords.com E-mail

Management:
Rising Entertainment
90 Nassau Street

New York, New York10038

(212) 385-1022 Main Phone
(212) 267-1053 Main Fax
Jeff Burroughs: Manager
jefburroughs@aol.com E-mail

Spooks International Marketing Plan
May 2000 / Page 2

BAND MEMBERS: (The Spooks consist of four MC's and one Vocalist)

Ming-Xia	(Lead Vocalist)
Mr. Booka-T	aka Bookaso
Water Water	aka Aqua Dinero
Hypno	
J.D.	aka Vengence

TRACK LISTING:

1. Other Script	(3:52)	9. Karma Hotel	(5:00)
2. Mission	(3:35)	10. Safe House	(4:42)
3. Things I've Seen	(4:33)	11. Something Fresh	(4:14)
4. They Don't Know	(4:18)	12. Swindley's Maracas	(4:58)
5. I Got U	(4:04)	13. Bitch Blood	(4:43)
6. Flesh Not Bone	(3:57)	14. Murder	(4:12)
7. Sweet Revenge	(5:00)		
8. Deep Cutz	(4:12)		

FIRST SINGLE: Things I've Seen

              b-sides: Things I've Seen (Radio edit)(3:30)
                                Apple Peaches
                                Yes
                                I Believe

Remixes:
1. Things I've Seen (Philip Steir's Spooktacular Bomb Mix-Edit)   (3:54)
2. Things I've Seen (Philip Steir's Spooktacular Bomb Mix)   (5:19)
3. Things I've Seen (Philip Steir's Spooktacular Bomb Mix Instrumental)   (5:18)
4. Things I've Seen (Boris & Beck Mix-Edit)   (3:48)
5. Things I've Seen (Boris & Beck Mix-Dub)   (8:27)

Additional Recorded b-sides:

1. Hit and Run (Japanese Extra Track)

Spooks International Marketing Plan
May 2000 / Page 3

TOOLS AVAILABLE:
Bio
EPK
Video (Things I've Seen)
(9) Color Group Slides
(3) Black and White Photos
Stickers with Logo
18" x 24" Color Poster
24" x 36" Posterboards
Double-sided Flats
12" Vinyl
Ad Matte(s)
Radio Ad
TV Ad
Fliers
Turntable Slipmat

OVERVIEW:

Spooks come armed with intelligence, insight, inspiration and the desire to shake up the status quo with a sound and a fury that is unmistakably their own. They are all over the map and hard to pin down musically. The group has a broad range of influences from U2, Potishead, Bjork and Cold Crush Brothers to James Brown, Earth, Wind and Fire and RadioHead. Our goal is to build a career and identity for Spooks instead of the quick out-of-the-box hit single artist. Spooks is one group that throws out the playbook and creatively colours outside of the so-called urban music lines. With this in mind we need to create a real fan base and allow the group to change throughout their career path. Spooks is an innovative definition for a new era in hip hop.

OBJECTIVES / BASIC MARKETING STRATEGIES:

Our initial marketing strategy is to build a vibe. This can include handing out fliers where fans of this band would hang out (i.e. cool clothing shops, concerts, cafes, etc.) along with cassette samplers or teasers of the first single. This should also include images of the band/album/commercial single cover art. Keep in mind that this band will be an artist that will cross many genres (i.e. R&B, Hip Hop, Rock, Alternative, Pop) so our marketing strategies need to cover these basis from the beginning while building the vibe.

Spooks International Marketing Plan
May 2000 / Page 4

OBJECTIVES / BASIC MARKETING STRATEGY (Cont.):

Additional areas to build a vibe prior to going to radio is to service the vinyl to clubs along with the turntable slipmat and see if we can get some action there. This along with the previously mentioned street marketing ideas can have a huge impact once we go to radio.

Prior to going to radio, placing trade and consumer advertising beginning with just the logo and name of SPOOKS will further the interest and also keep the mystery which the band likes. You could do a series of ads beginning with just the logo and name of the group and then adding information each time updating the ad. The third ad could hit prior to the street date of the commercial single and also tag other information like the album street date or promotional visits, etc.

Servicing the EPK to press, radio and retail will be an important tool in describing what SPOOKS are all about.

RETAIL:

As we mentioned in our basic plan above, we can tie in retail with flyers, posters like the ads mentioned to get the curiosity going. In store airplay we believe will work on this single more than most as the hook is so catchy.

The band is very intelligent, charming and personable and doing walk throughs and in store appearances is something they are very at ease with doing. They win people over quickly this way.

RADIO:

Although the group can not understandably do acoustic sessions per say, they can do impromptu singing on the air. The interviews that the group have done so far in the US always go longer than expected because the DJ's have been having such a great time with them on-air. They have great personalities and are never short on something to say.

PRESS:

Because the band is so intelligent and have a message, they provide for a great interview. They can be split up or do interviews as a group. Photo shoots are not a problem in fact we ask for them. Imaging is so important for the band themselves and this project, we encourage this and want your market to have what you need to properly market the group in your territory.

In the event that the photo shoots come out great, please make sure that we can have the rights so we can use on a worldwide basis.

Spooks International Marketing Plan
May 2000 / Page 5

INTERNATIONAL TIME LINE
(Subject to Change)

2000:

April - June 3:	North America
June 4 -10:	UK/European Promotion Trip
June 11 - August 31:	North America
July 11:	U.S. Album Release date
September:	UK/European Promotion Trip
October - December:	North America

2001:

January:	International Promotion

SPOOKS PHASE II MARKETING PLAN

Album Title:
Selection Number: In-Store Date: List Price: Shipped to date:
Management: Booking Agent:
S.I.O.S.O.S. : VOLUME 1
751039-2, 4 (explicit); 751040-2 (clean)
July 11, 2000
$16.98 cd, $10.98 cs
65,000
Chuck La Vallee @ Eagle Coast/Deluxe Entertainment 310.444.5588
Cara Lewis @ William Morris Agency 212.903.1316

TARGET MARKETS

PRIMARY:	SECONDARY:
• San Diego	• Philadelphia
• Los Angeles	• Indianapolis
• San Francisco	• New Orleans
• Sacramento	•Las Vegas
• Boston/Providence	• Miami
	• Tucson
	• DC/Baltimore

The Primary markets will utilize all marketing materials and promotions. We will focus on all indie record stores and lifestyle accounts to distribute value-added materials. These five cities will be the focus for the in-store play contests and strong college marketing.

The Secondary target markets will be used primarily for retail marketing. The focus will be to set up added-value promotions and create good visibility in the stores. Both the primary and secondary markets would be possibilities for radio time buys if seen fit.

SALES

CIMS Listening Post   (9/11 - 9/30)

- Nationwide in 50 key indies Will also provide stores with postcards, posters, added-value samplers and in-store play CDs. RED ASRs and UMRs will focus on getting displays and securing in-store play.

- Also will work on possible contests

Added Value samplers to indie stores   (Aug/Sept)

- 5000 samplers are already made to be distributed in indie stores in target markets. RED will assist in distributing. Artemis will be providing signage. All samplers will be stickered with radio request lines and album information.

- SF: Amoeba, Mod Lang

- DC/Balt.: Record & Tape traders, Soundgarden, DCCD

- LA: Moby Disc, Bionic (all stores), Rhino , Sound Spectrum, Aron's, Fingerprints, Benway, Salzers

- SD: Off The Record, Lou's Records

MARKETING

- Seattle: Cellophane Square, Sonic Boom, Orpheum
- NC: Schoolkids
- MN: Electric Fetus
- AZ: Zia
- New Orleans: Tower New Orleans
- Philadelphia: Plastic Fantastic
- Indianapolis: LUNA Music
- Sacramento: Penny Lane, Dimple

In-store Play Contest   (Sept/Oct)

- Prize money available. Stores are called randomly over a 2-4 week period. The clerk is asked what is playing in the store. If it is Spooks, they win money.

RADIO

The single for Phase 11 is "Swindley's Maracas/Flesh Not Bone"

Mixshow Independent   (8/28 - 9/25)

- Jay Boone has been hired to work along with Paris and Antra staff for 4 weeks before commercial add date.
- 12" features 4 versions of both songs: Original, Edit, Instrumental and Acapella.

Urban and Crossover Independents   (9/18-11/20)

- Independents will be hired to work "Swindley's Maracas/Flesh Not Bone" to commercial radio.
- CD Pro features 3 versions of "Swindley's Maracas": Original, Edit and Instrumental; and 2 versions of "Flesh Not Bone°: Original and Instrumental
- CD Pro will be shipped 9/1

Impact Date for Commercial Radio   (9/13 –8/14)

Add Date for Commercial Radio   (10/2)

Trade Advertising   (Oct TBA)

- Trade ads will be prepared to be used around and after add date.

Contests   (TBA)

- Prize money is available for contests on supportive stations

Lifestyle Marketing   (Aug-Sept)

- A mailing of full-length CD was sent to 120 lifestyle stores nationwide that are featured in PAPER magazine. All stores were followed up and many are distributing samplers in addition to playing CD in-store
- Will also target bars, open-mic hip-hop nights and comedy clubs in our focus markets to play CD in between acts. Tent cards will be produced to put on tables in these locations.

PlayJ sampler   (Sept)

- MP3 on 100,000 samplers distributed in colleges around the US.

Radio Buys   (Sept/Oct)

- These will a possibility of happening in our focus markets of New Orleans, San Diego, Boston, Providence, Sacramento, Los Angeles and San Francisco. If seen fit, we will run these after good radio play or touring.

College Marketing   (Sept-Nov)

- **"The Making Of Music" TV Special (Sept).** Spooks will have a 5 minute feature on this show where they will showcase parts of the EPK and video. This is broadcast to over 2000 schools with an audience of 320,000 college students plus an additional 3.5 million home through local cable. This will run approx 20 times in the month of September. We will also have postcards handed out at these colleges with a retailer tagged. College Fest (Oct 14&15). Samplers, stickers and flyers will be handed out to the 40,000 students attending the festival in Boston.
- **CMJ Festival (Oct** 19-22). Samplers and stickers will be handed out at compatible shows during the NYC festival.
- College Reps (continuous). 10 Artemis college reps will continue on setting up displays, securing in-store play and promoting band to college radio and local outlets.

Merchandise   (avail Sept)

- Stickers, Posters and Postcards will be reprinted to be distributed by street teamers, college reps and in retail stores. CD samplers, videos, singles and 12"s will be utilized for value-added promotions by RED and Artemis staff.

Street Teams   (current)

- The Artemis-run Spooks street team is in effect now. There are currently over 150 kids that are being supplied with stickers, flyers and posters. These will be used for record store displays, lifestyle accounts and compatible shows.

INTERNET
Song and Video Downloads   (Aug-Dec)

- Both "Things I've Seen" and "Swindley's Maracas" are featured downloads on MTV.com and other sites such as Rioport.com, Sonicnet.com, Sputnik7.com and more. "Swindley's," "Flesh Not Bone," and "Things I've Seen (Philip Steirs Mix)" will be offered for downloads on music and lifestyle sites.

Street Team   (Sept-Dec)

- The Spooks street team and college reps will be hitting hip-hop, lifestyle and college websites promoting the album, plus any radio play and tour info.

College Marketing   (Sept-Oct)

- Will have an online retailer tagged on 5-10,000 postcards promoting the "Making Of Music" TV special.

Group Emails   (current)

- Emails will continue to be sent to stores, radio stations and fan lists about any radio, press and tour information. Will look into sending emails to people who have purchased similar artists.

PUBLICITY

Press will concentrate on regional exposure around tour dates, including dailies, weeklies, fanzines and local TV and follow the radio and/or international story to build further.

ARTIST DEVELOPMENT INTERNATIONAL

Opening for Spearhead @ Wetlands in NYC	(8/15)
Opening for Spearhead @ Wetlands in NYC	(8/16)
Opening for Slum Village @ SOB's in NYC	(8/29)
EUROPEAN PROMOTIONAL TOUR	(10/7-21)
Germany	(10/13-15)
France	(10/18-19)
Holland	(10/20-21)

Additional countries confirmed to visit on this trip but still being routed one day each are Switzerland, Belgium and Sweden. We will also probably have a few UK days in there as well before it's over.

Figure 6.3

The timetable is vital to a campaign. The timetable for releases must create and maintain a momentum for airplay and product sales. The timetable for the introduction of the items in the marketing campaign must keep the public aware of the product. Carefully, study the mix and the timetable for the introduction of the items in the marketing campaign in Figures 6.3 and 6.4. The prerelease campaign for the product in Figure 6.4 had a hefty $500,000 price tag (in 1991 dollars) attached to it. Capitol Records decided that it was not going to leave the fate of this record to chance.

MC HAMMER "TOO LEGIT TOO QUIT" CAMPAIGN

- Promotional video clips for 12 of the album's 17 songs
- Two long form videos
- Second TV Blitz December 15-22
- Paramount film "The Addams Family" November 22 release will feature four Hammer tunes, including "Addams Groove" which will be the film's prerelease in-theater, radio, and TV ad campaigns
- "Hammerman" cartoon show continues to get support
- Mattel introduced two Hammer dolls into Barbie's celebrity friend line
- HBO special "Influences: James Brown & Hammer"
- Saturday Night Live and The Arsenio Hall show appearances
- New Pepsi commercial with Hammer and Too Legit Too Quit in background
- World tour planned

from *Billboard Magazine* October 26, 1991 Pg. 1

Figure 6.4

Videos are considered integral part of the marketing campaign. In fact, according Denisoff in his book "Tarnished Gold," in 1984, 68% of survey respondents indicated that they purchased the record after viewing it on MTV, and only 63% of respondents indicated that they purchased the record after listening to it on the radio. MTV claimed that it was the number one vehicle for record recognition among buyer (over radio). However, this is no longer true. Recent studies show that overwhelmingly, radio is the first contact that buyers have to new product. In fact, it was reported in Billboard Magazine in August, 1997 that according to Strategic Record Research, 80% of record buyers said that radio influenced them to buy the record. Seeing the video only influenced 43% of the record buyers.

MTV has literally cornered the market on video presentation. The station was launched nationally on August 1, 1981 and used a very narrow format. It was heavily criticized for not airing black music videos, but has since become a leading outlet for rap artists. John Sykes, the first Vice President of Programming, said that MTV was like an art gallery. The station aired videos in the same manner as a gallery hangs paintings, and the station does not take responsibility for a video's quality. Concentrating on rap and heavy metal artists, it saw the need for an outlet for adult contemporary artists. A second channel was launched, VH-1, specifically as an outlet for softer, adult contemporary artists. MTV is a worldwide network that caters to the needs of the individual markets.

By the mid 1980s, MTV was offering the major record company's money and advertising spots, for the rights of first refusal on a percent of the company's video releases. The station was willing to pay for exclusivity, and the record company's jumped at the chance to generate income to help defray some of the cost of video production. It was a bold move on MTV's part because radio has never been willing to or has ever paid a dime for records. It was a brilliant decision and they were the only outlet at the time that could afford to make the offer. It secured the station's position as number one and killed the competition.

Although music video sell-through is growing, videos are still essentially a promotional vehicle for a record, and acceptance for airing by MTV, VH-1, or the M2 Channel is crucial. If the MTV networks for airplay do not accept a video, its potential viewing audience is dramatically reduced. MTV is so powerful that it is estimated that the combination of all the other outlets for airing videos does not equal the strength of a regular rotation airing on MTV. The network has purchased the BET channel as well.

Has A Single Been Chosen?

Choosing the first single to be released off of a record is not a scientific process. Companies usually have a weekly meeting to decide what is to be released and when. Obviously, the a& r department plays the biggest role in the decision, but company administrators also like to get their egos in on the decision. In fact, Clive Davis, former president of Arista Records (and now head of J Records), has been involved in choosing singles and editing down album cuts for single release since his reign as President of Columbia Records over thirty years ago. Release meetings may also include personnel from the marketing and merchandising departments.

A fierce battle can occur if the artist's manager and the a&r department do not agree on the release schedule of the singles. It is the manager's responsibility to convince the a&r department that the single s/he and the artist want to be released, is the same single that they have chosen. If the manager muscles the company and wins the battle but the project loses priority status, the artist may lose the war as the company's interest in the project may be jeopardized. Consequently, the strength of the manager's persuasive skills may be of extreme importance.

Is the Record Moving Up the Charts?

The record industry measures success quantitatively. How high up the charts did it go? How much airplay did it receive? And ultimately, how many records did it sell. Therefore the goal of any marketing campaign is to sell records. The key to the bottom line of project is for a salesclerk to answer "yes" when asked by a customer if the record is in the store.

Record companies believe that airplay is the key to exposure. Many industry studies have shown a strong correlation between heavy radio listeners and buyers. Airplay is the job of the promotion department.

Record promotion is handled either in-house by the company's staff field promotion people, or by an independent record promotion person hired by the company or the artist's manager. Independent promotion people are hired when, either the record has a specific sound or style to it they may need exposure on specific radio stations before other stations will air it, or the record receives a heavy priority within the company and the "indies" are called in to increase its success potential.

Independent promotion people claim to have an above average success rate for airplay on stations that play the particular style of music that they claim is their expertise. They claim to deliver hits, and if successful, can charge a very high fee to "work" a record. Lately, a new procedure for obtaining airplay has taken place. Radio stations have been selling airtime to indie promo men (not secretly), and indies have been charging record companies for the right to get a shot at airplay. Although the process appears to be legal, its implications are not.

So what happens if the record isn't "growing legs" with the marketing plan's tactics? Does the manager scream at the record company to get "on" the record? Does the promotion department hire a few "indies" to work the record? If the promotion department doesn't do enough to increase the record's airplay, does the manager hire an indie? Does the artist increase his/her publicity activities? Does the manager start calling radio stations to try to increase airplay? Does someone hound MTV for more exposure? Do the company's field merchandising staff push for in-store airplay? The answer is one or all of the above.... plus anything else that can be thought of. Few singles have ever received a second chance to become a hit. Fewer artists have ever been given priority status in a company after recording a "dog."

Has Feedback Been Positive?

The old adage, "any publicity is better than no publicity" is still true. However, lukewarm feedback does a record little good. Although it has been reported that less than eight percent of record buyers are influenced by record reviews, the industry still enjoys positive responses. Because the company has relatively little control of the media, the marketing campaign spends a great deal of the artist's money giving free publicity paraphernalia to whom it considers influential people. Their stamp of approval gives the record and the artist credibility, and once they publicly announce their approval of artist's work, additional positive responses are expected. If feedback has not been positive, the record company should alter the promotional and publicity activities to induce the kind of feedback that is needed. This usually requires additional financial commitments by the company, which, of course, is ultimately the artist's money.

Is the Record A Hit?

This is really the third time the same question has been voiced in the chart, and doing all that can be done to make the record a success can not be emphasized too strongly. If the record still has not grown its own legs, it is probably time to release another single and fine tune the campaign. If the artist's manager was very insistent on the choice of the first single and it was a dog, no matter what the reason was (ie; lack of promotion), his/her power is now diminished and a& r will have the upper hand in choosing this one. Hopefully this new activity will generate action on the chart.

The flow chart has illustrated the path of the product through the marketing department, including the responsibilities of the publicity and artist development departments. The product manager monitors the record through the sales, merchandising, and distribution departments to make certain that all facets of the marketing campaign are completed.

Where the Money Goes

Keeping track of the recording budget during the recording is the responsibility of the a & r administration department. Record companies use a *Recording Authorization Form* to keep track of the expense. Each line item is estimated at the time the recording proposal is submitted. When the budget is approved by the Vice President of A & R, the artist and manager or producer must seek to have budget re-approved if additional funds are needed. Therefore, estimates should be made as accurately as possible. Some of the typical expense categories found in most *Recording Authorization Forms* are listed below. They are:

- producer fee
- artist advance
- AFM payment
- AFTRA payment
- travel/hotel
- per diem
- Studio time
- mixdown time
- engineer fee
- tape
- rental instruments
- misc.
- unforeseen expenses

For example, let's assume the studio time for an initial recording of a rock group is estimated as requiring 200 hours of studio time (24 track) @@$250 per hour including the mixdown and engineer. Tape costs are additional, and 200 hours might use 15 rolls of two inch wide tape. This would bring the entire studio bill to $50,000. AFM and AFTRA payments to a four member group might be $5000 plus additional studio musicians and instrument rental is another $2000. The producer might have a fee of $40,000 plus accommodations for everyone is another $7500, and miscellaneous expenses could equal $5000. The bottom line of the Recording Authorization form could read $100,000 without any waste. Additional money might also have been spent on recording one or several videos totally $200,000, plus additional advance incentive money of $75,000. Therefore it would not be outrageous for a new artist to be in debt to the record company for approximately $300,000 on the day the record is released.

Remember these expenses are all charge-backs that are recoupable out of the artist's royalty account and paid back or credited to the record company out of record sales before the artist realizes any royalty checks. Consequently, the artist and his/her manager should be very interested in the number of records (units) that must be sold in order to bring the artist's royalty account out of the red and back to zero. Or, in other words, what is the **break-even** sales point.

To understand this, let's use the example that the artist's royalty rate is 12% of the retail list price (superstars may demand a 15 + rate). Let's use a retail list price of $16.98 and multiply this figure by 12%. The answer is $2.04. $2.04 will be credited to the artist's royalty account for every record sold. To find the break-even point we need to calculate how many $2.04 (or albums sold) will equal $300,000. So by dividing $300,000 by $2.04 we arrive at 147,059 albums (units) must be sold in order for the artist's royalty account to break-even.

$16.98 (retail list price)
$\underline{\text{x .12}}$ (royalty rate)
$ 2.04

$300,000 divided by 2.04 = 147,059 units

Although this is an incredible number of records to sell before the artist sees any royalties, the calculations are a bit more complex than this, and the number of records that need to be sold is even greater. We need to calculate various account allowances and adjustments. For example,

Packaging Allowances are deducted from the royalty base as a percentage. The record company may seek a package or container allowance as high as 25%. A long standing pet argument of this author's has been the packaging allowance. Isn't normal packaging just part of the cost of manufacturing records? If an artist doesn't ask for anything out of the ordinary, why must a packaging allowance be debited to the royalty account? Wouldn't a similar example be if you were charged extra for the standard tires on a new car? If the artist is going to be charged, shouldn't the record company give the artist the right to shop for packaging by an independent company? However, attorneys say that packaging allowances are nonnegotiable.

Record Companies also have charged a **CD Reduction rate** of 20% through a New Media Reduction Clause in the contract. However, for this example, let's assume a 25% packaging allowance, and not calculate the CD reduction rate.

The **Free Goods Allowance** is usually 15%. Stated another way: "of every 100 albums shipped, 15 will be royalty fee." Some companies add a clause that states that they will pay on 85% of the records shipped and some companies use 90%. When attorneys approach this clause with the argument that it replaces the free goods allowance clause, some companies deny it. Executing both clauses would allow the record company to pay 85% of 85% (which has occurred) before the packaging allowance! For this example let's assume 15%.

The industry is not standardized on its use of several contractual terms. For example, some companies do not use the term wholesale price, but choose to use the term "normal retail channels." **Royalty base** is another confusing term. For our purposes, we'll define it as **the percentage of the retail list price that remains after all allowances and deductions, on which the royalty rate is based**.

Now we can calculate the artist's royalty amount more accurately by using the royalty base and the royalty rate figures. If we subtract 25% for packaging and 15% for free goods from a royalty base retail list price of $16.98, the answer is $10.18. The artist's royalty rate is 12% of the retail list price, however, to calculate, we must multiply 12% by the adjusted list price of $10.18. The artist's royalty rate is really $1.22 on every record sold. Now if we divide $300,000 by $1.22 we arrive at **245,902 albums (units)** must be sold in order for the artist's royalty account to break-even.

The calculation is as follows:

1. **retail list price x (royalty base or 100% - allowances) = adjusted retail list price**

2. **adjusted retail list price x artist royalty rate = royalty per unit**

3. **royalty account debit / royalty per unit = break´even number**

Although we will not go into other scenarios here, there could be further allowances deducted from the original royalty base. For instance, a breakage allowance, a CD reduction rate, and/or a "Special Marketing Discount" is common, or the addition of a producer's cut in an "all in deal."

The Record Company's Share

Using a wholesale price of $10.70 and subtracting the $1.22 royalty to the artist per unit, there remains $9.48 that the record company receives. Out the remaining $9.48 manufacturing costs, distribution costs, mechanical royalties, and union benefits must be paid.

Let's use as an example a ten-song recording, and the record company will pay a 25% percent reduction from the statutory rate, currently at $.08 per song, on negotiated mechanical licenses, which equals $0.6. Add to this a manufacturing cost of *$1.50 (or less). Subtract the $2.30 from $9.48 and the company is left with $7.18.

By law, record companies must contribute to two American Federation of Musicians (AFM) funds. They must contribute about $.05 to the Special Payments Fund, and about $.03 to the Music Performance Trust Fund. The record company may also have to contribute a lump sum to the vocalists' union, the American Federation of Television and Radio Artists (AFTRA). For our example let's assume that it contributes $2000, which we will compute in a moment. If we subtract $.08 from the remaining $7.18, we are left with $7.10.

---

* Some estimates are as low as 50 cents.

If we multiply $7.10 x 245,902 (the number of units that must be sold for the artist to break-even) we arrive at $1,745,904.20. Now subtract the $2000 AFTRA payment and we have $1,743,904.20 as the amount the record company receives. However, this is not all profit for the company. Promotion and advertising expenses must be subtracted from this, as well as a portion of the general overhead and operating costs.

Figure 6.6 illustrates where the money goes from the sale of a recording ($16.98 list price was used). With about 90% of the records released never regaining their recording costs, superstars have a big job in the record business. They must deliver the multi-platinum sellers that pay the bills for all the "stiffs." Always remain aware that record companies are in the business for one reason, **to sell records**!

(Please note that all calculations were simplified for illustration purposes.)

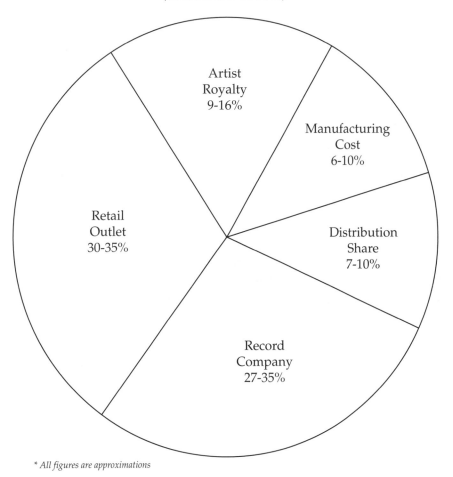

Financial Cuts on a Recording
($16.98 Retail List Price)*

Artist Royalty 9-16%

Manufacturing Cost 6-10%

Retail Outlet 30-35%

Distribution Share 7-10%

Record Company 27-35%

* All figures are approximations

Figure 6.6. Adapted from Country Music Association March 1981 and Neil Strauss, "Pennies That Add Up to $16.98, NY Times, 7/5/95, Pg. C11.

SUMMARY

1. The relationship of the artist and his/her record company is a business relationship and an emotional one.

2. The record company manufactures, releases, promotes, and distributes the artist's works, but also acts as a financial backer.

3. The three types of advances given to an artist under contract are: personal advance, production advance, and bonus advance.

4. The types of record companies include: major, independent, specialty, and boutique.

5. The major record companies own their own distribution networks.

6. A record company has a creative division and a business/administrative division.

7. Record companies demand master tapes that are "commercially acceptable".

8. A product flows through the record departments in an organized manner.

9. The artist's royalty account is credited after all record company expenses are met.

PROJECTS

1. Set up a record company in class and ask individual students to list the responsibilities of each department.

2. Create a listening party in class. Have students listen to a new release and as they represent various departments of the company, formulate a marketing plan.

BIBLIOGRAPHY

Brabec, J. & Brabec, T. *Music, Money, and Success*. Schirmer Books. New York, 2000.

Denisoff, R. Serge. *Tarnished Gold*. Transaction Books, Inc. New Brunswick, 1987.

Strauss, Neil. "Pennies That Add Up to $16.98." *New York Times*, July 5, 1995.

Wadhams, Wayne. *Sound Advice*. Schirmer Books. New York, 1990.

CHAPTER SEVEN
The Recording Contract

"Astute artist attorneys recognize that having key record company executives excited by an artist's music and committed to breaking the artist in the marketplace is far more important than specific contractual guarantees, particularly if the guarantees being requested are of dubious practical value."

Michael J. Pollack, V.P. and General Counsel, Arista Records.

Billboard Magazine. July 23, 1988.

By the end of this chapter you should be able to:

1. Intelligently discuss every clause of the example agreement in this chapter.

2. When given a different example contract, transfer what you have studied in this chapter to the corresponding clauses of the new contract, and discuss its content.

3. Discuss the current royalty and mechanical rates negotiated in new artist recording contracts.

The brass ring.

The major leagues.

The big time.

The beginning.

All these phrases describe what securing a long-term royalty artist recording contract from a nationally distributed label means to an artist. It also means that the artist is no longer just a local or regional phenomenon. In fact, it is the most important goal of any new artist, and the payoff to years of practicing, rehearsing, and also performing in the endless number of beer joints and at nondescript fraternity parties. It is a payoff. A payoff that very few musicians ever receive.

However, it is also the beginning. It's the beginning of a career. It is the chance to be idolized by the hometown musicians. This is the chance for the artist to be respected by his or her parents and relatives. But most importantly, it is the chance for the artist to perform original material in his or her own unique style, and not be required to work another job to pay the bills!

Then why do so many artists blow their chance? Industry estimates say that from two-thirds to three-quarters of the pop recordings released never regain their recording costs. Consequently, many artists are dropped by labels after only one release, and play out their "careers" performing their "hit" in hotel cocktail lounges. Actually a "stiff" is not always the artist's fault. However, the consequence is the same.

When selecting an artist for a long-term royalty agreement, what does a company look for? What is the selection criteria used by a company's a&r staff? How does an a&r rep. judge the value of the artist in the marketplace six to nine months (the minimum amount of time needed to negotiate a contract with a major label and complete the recording of an album) after he or she is convinced that the artist is worthy of a deal?

These are some of the usual answers. "Intuition!" "It's just a feeling I have about the artist and the songs." "You can feel the electricity in the air when he or she performs." "He or she is a unique talent." None of this offers any insight for the unsigned musician. However, some helpful criteria might be:

1. charisma — The magnetic quality of a personality.

2. stage-presence — The artist's command of an audience.

3. uniqueness — Is the artist new or different?

4. worth in the marketplace — Is the artist and his or her music a saleable commodity? And for how long?

There are basically three ways a new artist may attempt to secure a recording contract. They are:

1. The artist makes a demo recording and the manager or an attorney tries to secure a deal (shops the demo).

2. The artist locates a producer and makes a demo recording and the producer (or the production company) shops the demo (an all-in deal).

3. The artist, with or without a producer, makes a master recording and shops the master.

When securing a recording contract, it is generally not a good idea for an artist to be tied to a producer (as a third party). The producer will insist on final control over the production of the recording, and any attempt by the artist to nurture a relationship with the company may be hindered.

The following is an actual first draft recording contract submitted to a new artist by a major recording company. Included are my editorial comments. Although it is not written to be grossly unfair to either side, upon examination, any competent attorney would not allow his or her client to sign it without serious negotiations.

This deal differs from the contract that would generally be offered by an independent label. If an independent label agreed to sign the artist, the contract would most likely be a per recording commitment which is also known as a "step deal." The step deal could encompass either a single-to-single contract based on sales, or a single-to -album commitment. However, it would probably not include much, if any, advance money.

Some new artists believe the recording contract is an agreement "written in stone" and demand that every word be negotiated. Obviously both sides must feel comfortable with the language, not only for the financial aspects, but also more importantly, because the contract should be the basis for a long-term relationship. Although it provides the guidelines for this relationship, one cannot contractualize the strong company commitment that is necessary for the artist to succeed. (Alanis Morissette recently noted in her July 23, 2001 keynote address at the 2001 Plug.In Conference that "the number of records that are released commercially each year in the U.S. exceeds 30,000 and less than 1/3 of 1% of those releases sell enough to generate a royalty check for the artist.") Therefore, everything is negotiable.

RECORDING CONTRACT FORM

AGREEMENT made as of this ____ day of _____, 200__, by and between _____, {address} (hereinafter "Company"), and _____ {address} (hereinafter "you").

*Many attorneys suggest that the **definitions** section of the contract, in this case **Section 19**, be read and understood before trying to understand the rest of the agreement.*

1. SERVICES.

1.01   During the term of this Agreement (the "Term") you will render your exclusive services as a performing artist for the purpose of making Master Recordings for Company, you will cause those Master Recordings to be produced, and you will Deliver those Master Recordings to Company, as provided in this Agreement. (You are sometimes called "the Artist" below; all references in this agreement to "you and the Artist," and the like, will be understood to refer to you alone.)

Your obligations will include furnishing the services of the producers of those Master Recordings and all other third parties rendering services in connection with those Master Recordings, subject to the terms of this Agreement, and you will be solely responsible for engaging and paying them.

This agreement is known as an "all in royalty" deal, meaning that the artist will supply the producer for the recordings and is responsible for paying him or her. Therefore the royalty rate reflects this.

2. TERM.

2.01   The Term shall consist of an Initial Period and of the Option Periods (defined below) for which Company shall have exercised the options hereafter provided. The Initial Period and each Option Period are each hereafter sometimes referred to as a "Contract Period". The Initial Period shall commence on the date hereof and shall continue until the earlier of the dates referred to in paragraphs (a) and (b) immediately below:

(a) the date twelve (12) months after the Delivery to Company, as defined in paragraph 19.09 below, of the fully equalized, digital tape Masters to be used in manufacturing the Phonograph Record units to be made for distribution in the United States from the last Master Recordings made in fulfillment of your Recording Commitment for the Contract Period concerned under Article 3 below; or

(b) the date nine (9) months after the initial commercial release in the United States of the Album required to be delivered in fulfillment of your Recording Commitment for the Contract Period concerned; but will not end earlier than one (1) year after the date of its commencement.

Clause 2.01 describes the contract period of the term of the agreement, which in this case reads twelve months. However, the beginning of the term occurs on the earlier of the two dates describe in (a) or (b).

2.02

(a) You grant Company _____ (___) separate options to extend that Term for additional Contract Periods ("Option Periods") on the same terms and conditions, except as otherwise provided herein. Company may exercise each of those options by sending you a written notice not later than the expiration date of the Contract Period which is then in effect (the "Current Contract Period"). If Company exercises such an option, the Option Period concerned will begin immediately after the end of the Current Contract Period and shall continue until the earlier of the dates referred to in paragraphs 2.01 (a) and (b) above.

(b) Notwithstanding anything to the contrary contained in this Article 2, if Company has not exercised its option to extend the Term for a further Contract Period as of the date on which the Current Contract Period would otherwise expire, the following shall apply:

(i) You shall send Company written notice (an "Option Warning") that its option has not yet been exercised.

(ii) Company shall have the right to exercise such option at any time until the date ten (10) business days after its receipt of the Option Warning (the "Extension Period").

(iii) The Current Contract Period shall continue until either the end of the Extension Period, or Company's notice (the "Termination Notice") to you that Company does not wish to exercise such option, whichever is sooner.

(iv) For avoidance of doubt, nothing herein shall limit Company's right to send a Termination Notice to you at any time, nor limit Company's right to exercise an option at any time if you fail to send Company an Option Warning in accordance with (i) above.

Record companies negotiate from the position that, the more option periods to extend the contract, the better. It gives them an easy way to move to the option periods. However, if the artist is unsuccessful, a longer contract will not force the record company to allow the artist to record, or release any product.

In the third line of 2.02a after "sending you a notice," the phrase 90 days, or 60 days, or at least 30 days prior to the expiration date may be inserted. The artist should have the right to know whether the record company is going to exercise the option period before it expires, in order to have time to shop for another deal. Usually, record companies are not willing to change this clause.

In (b) (i) the responsibility is on the artist to notify the company that they have not exercised the option, and then they have ten days to rectify the situation. However, if you fail to send the notice, the company can still drop you!

3. RECORDING COMMITMENT.

3.01   Your Recording Commitment hereunder is as follows. During the Initial Period you shall record and you shall deliver to Company one (1) Album. During each Option Period you shall record and you shall deliver to Company one (1) Album. The Albums delivered hereunder in fulfillment of your Recording Commitment are sometimes referred to collectively herein as the "Committed Albums" and individually as a "Committed Album". The Committed Albums are sometimes herein called the "First Album", the "Second Album", the "Third Album", the "Fourth Album", the "Fifth Album" and the "Sixth Album", respectively, in order of their Delivery to Company.

This contract is really a one-album deal.

3.02   You shall deliver to Company the Album constituting your Recording Commitment for a Contract Period no later than ninety (90) days after the commencement of that Contract Period.

It would better serve the artist if the three-month period was longer, and extended to, for example, at least five months

4. RECORDING PROCEDURES.

4.01   You shall designate and submit to Company for Company's approval the producer of each of the Masters, all other individuals rendering services in connection with the recording of those Masters, the Musical Compositions or other Selections or materials which shall be embodied in those Masters, the studios at which those Masters shall be recorded, and the dates of recording of those Masters (the "Recording Elements"). You shall also prepare and submit to Company in writing for Company's approval a recording budget for those Masters in such detail as Company shall require (the "Recording Budget") at least fourteen (14) days before the planned commencement of recording. You shall advise Company of the content of each medley before it is recorded. Company shall not be deemed to be unreasonable in rejecting any request to begin recording any Album which is a part of the Recording Commitment within six (6) months after the Delivery of a prior Album under this agreement. The scheduling and booking of all studio time will be done by Company. No recording sessions shall be commenced nor shall any commitments be made or costs incurred hereunder with respect to any Masters until and unless Company shall have approved in writing each Recording Element and the Recording Budget for those Masters. If Company shall disapprove the Recording Budget submitted by you, then Company's decision shall be final.

This agreement is known as an "all in royalty" deal, meaning that the artist will supply the producer for the recordings and is responsible for paying him or her. Other costs are also your responsibility.

4.02

(a) You shall notify the appropriate Local of the American Federation of Musicians in advance of each recording session.

(b) You will comply with the following procedures in connection with the requirements of the U.S. Immigration Law:

(1) Before each recording session:

(i) You will require each background instrumentalist, background vocalist, and other person to be employed in connection with the session to complete and sign the EMPLOYEE INFORMATION AND VERIFICATION ("employee") section of a U.S. Immigration and Naturalization Service Employment Eligibility Certificate (Form I-9), unless you have already obtained such a Certificate from the person concerned within the past three (3) years;

(ii) You will complete and sign the EMPLOYER REVIEW AND VERIFICATION ("employer") section of each such Certificate; and

(iii) You will attach copies of the documents establishing identity and employment eligibility which you examine in accordance with the instructions in the employer section.

If any such person is engaged during a session you will comply with subsections (i) through (iii) above, with respect to that person, before (s)he renders any services.

(2) You will not permit any such person who fails to complete the employee section, or to furnish you with the required documentation, to render any services in connection with Recordings to be made under this agreement.

These clauses that use the terms employer and employee allow the record company to maintain its copyright claim as the artist is employed on a "work for hire" basis.

(3) You will deliver those Certificates and documents to Company promptly, and in no event later than the Delivery of the Recordings concerned.

(4) You will comply with any revised or additional verification and documentation requirements of which Company advises you in the future.

(c) As and when required by Company, you shall allow Company's representatives to attend any or all recording sessions hereunder.

(d) You shall timely supply Company with all of the information Company needs in order: (i) to make payments due in connection with such Recordings; (ii) to comply with any other obligations Company may have in connection with the making of such Master Recordings; and (iii) to prepare to release Phonograph Records derived from such Master Recordings. Without limiting the generality of clause (ii) of the preceding sentence:

(A) You shall furnish Company with all information Company requires to comply with its obligations under Company's union agreements, including, without limitation, the following:

(1) If a session is held to record new tracks intended to be mixed with existing tracks (and if such information is requested by the American Federation of Musicians), the dates and places of the prior sessions at which such existing tracks were made, and the AFM Phonograph Recording Contract (Form "B") number(s) covering such sessions;

(2) Each change of title of any composition listed in an AFM Phonograph Recording Contract (Form "B"); and

(3) A listing of all the musical selections contained in Recordings Delivered to Company hereunder; and

(B) You will furnish Company with all of the immigration control documentation required by subparagraph 4.01(b) above, at the same time as the AFM or AFTRA session reports, tax withholding forms, and other documentation required by us in order to make the payments to the session musicians and other employees concerned, if any.

(e)

(i) All Master Recordings shall be recorded under Company's current Phonograph Record Labor Contract with the AFM; all musicians who render services in connection with the recording of such Master Recordings (including instrumentalists, if any) will be paid by Company, on your behalf, the scale set forth in the said Labor Contract; and Company, on your behalf, shall pay the required contributions to the Pension Welfare Fund.

(ii) All AFTRA members whose performances are embodied in the Master Recordings will be paid by Company, on your behalf, the rates applicable under the current AFTRA Code of Fair Practices for Phonograph Recordings. Company shall, on your behalf, if necessary, also pay to the AFTRA Pension and Welfare Fund any contribution required to be made under the AFTRA Code based on compensation to other performers whose performances are embodied on the applicable Master Recordings recorded hereunder.

(iii) The foregoing representations and warranties are included for the benefit, respectively, of the AFM, AFTRA, and the AFM and AFTRA members whose performances are embodied in the applicable Master Recordings, and for the benefit of Company, and may be enforced by AFM and/or AFTRA or their respective designees, as the case may be, and by Company.

(iv) You shall furnish or shall cause the applicable Producer to furnish Company with copies of all union contracts and/or union session reports so that all payments may be made by Company, on your behalf, in a timely fashion to the proper parties thereunder; and if you fail to do so with the result that Company is required to pay any penalty sum for making a late payment under the applicable union agreements, such payments shall be a direct debt from you to Company which, in addition to any other remedy Company may have, Company may recover from any monies otherwise payable to you.

4.03

(a) You shall deliver to Company the Masters promptly after their completion. All original session tapes and any derivatives or reproductions thereof shall be delivered to Company concurrently, or, at Company's election, maintained at a recording studio or other location designated by Company, in Company's name and subject to Company's control. Each Master shall be subject to Company's approval as commercially and technically satisfactory for the manufacture and sale of Phonograph Records, and, upon Company's request, you shall re-record any Musical Composition or other Selection until a Master commercially and technically satisfactory to Company has been obtained.

Every artist would love to change the phrase to only technically satisfactory. The issue is creative control and the record company will not give it up. However, superstars may be able to negotiate this, thereby giving the record company only the right to make certain that it is acceptable for airing on radio, but a new artist would not stand a chance

(b) You shall Deliver to Company fully mixed, edited, and unequalized and equalized Master Recordings (including but not limited to a final two-track equalized tape copy), commercially satisfactory to Company for its manufacture and sale of Phonograph Records, and all original and duplicate Master Recordings of the material recorded, together with (i) the multi-track tape and three (3) safety copies thereof; (ii) all necessary licenses and permissions; (iii) all materials required to be furnished by you to Company for use in the packaging and marketing of the Records, including without limitation, complete "label copy" information with respect to such Master Recordings; such "label copy" shall include, without limitation (A) the title, recording dates, timing, publisher(s) songwriter(s), performer(s) and composer(s) of each musical composition embodied on the Master Recordings; (B) the producer(s) thereof; and (C) any other credit and information that is to appear on the labels, liners and packaging of Records embodying such Master Recordings; (iv) all "sideman" and any third party clearances and consents, including, without limitation, all written consents in connection with Embodied Copyrighted Materials (as defined in paragraph 13.04(a) below), together with your written warranty and representation, in a form satisfactory to Company, that you have obtained for Company the unrestricted right to exploit the Master Recording(s) concerned; (v) a document, in a form satisfactory to Company, signed by the producer of the Master Recording(s) concerned which confirms Company's ownership of such Master Recording(s) in accordance with the provisions of Article 6 hereof; (vi) all mechanical and first-use licenses for each musical composition embodied in the Master Recording at the rate specified herein; and (vii) all liner notes, approved artwork, and credits for all configurations of records.

(c) You further agree to irrevocably direct in writing the person who has possession of any and all tapes of masters or digital masters recorded hereunder that all such tapes and masters are Company's property and that such person shall be obligated to deliver such tapes and masters to Company upon its written request.

4.04   Each Master shall embody the Artist's performance as the sole featured artist of a single Musical Composition previously unrecorded by the Artist and shall be recorded in its entirety in a recording studio. No Masters shall be recorded in whole or in part at live concerts or other live performances unless an authorized officer of Company agrees to the contrary in writing. Each Committed Album shall embody no fewer than forty (40) minutes in playing time and containing no fewer than eight (8) and no more than ten (10) Musical Compositions unless Company otherwise agrees to the contrary in writing. You shall not record or deliver hereunder, nor shall Company be obligated to accept, Masters constituting a Multiple Album. However, if you shall do so and Company shall accept those Masters hereunder, then, at Company's election, for the purpose of calculating the number of Masters recorded and delivered hereunder, those Masters shall be deemed to be only one (1) Album. Masters delivered hereunder shall not contain selections designed to appeal to specialized or limited markets including, but not limited to gospel, Christmas and/or children's music.

The record company will not accept a recording of a live performance, or any old recording as fulfilling the recording commitment. Only compositions recorded specifically for the commitment will be considered.

4.05   Any Masters which are not recorded or delivered in all respects in accordance with the terms hereof shall not, unless Company otherwise consents in writing, apply towards the fulfillment of your Recording Commitment. Furthermore, if Company shall make any payments with respect to any Master which shall not have been recorded or delivered in all respects in accordance with the terms hereof, you shall, upon Company's demand, pay to Company the amount thereof and Company may, without limiting Company's other rights and remedies, deduct that amount from any monies payable by Company hereunder or any other agreement between you and Company or Company's affiliates.

4.06   If you or the Artist shall for any reason whatsoever delay the commencement of or be unavailable for any recording sessions for the Masters, you shall, upon Company's demand, pay Company an amount equal to the expenses or charges paid or incurred by Company by reason thereof. Company may, without limiting Company's other rights and remedies, deduct that amount from any monies payable by Company hereunder or under any other agreement between you and Company or Company's affiliates.

Company may, at its election, discontinue any recording sessions for the Masters if in Company's judgment the Recording Costs incurred or to be incurred will exceed the approved Recording Budget or if the Masters being produced will not be satisfactory.

This clause allows the record company to pull the plug if the recording budget is exceeded or the company anticipates that the budget will be exceeded. However, the question is, exceeded by how much? One dollar? One thousand dollars? Obviously the record company wants the project finished and will allow the master to be delivered over budget.

5. RECORDING COSTS.

5.01   Company shall pay the Recording Costs of the Masters recorded at recording sessions conducted in accordance with the terms hereof in an amount not in excess of the Recording Budget approved by Company in writing. If the Recording Costs of any Masters shall exceed the Recording Budget approved by Company, you shall be solely responsible for and shall promptly pay the excess. If, however, Company shall pay the excess, you shall, upon Company's demand, pay to Company the amount thereof and Company may, without limiting Company's other rights and remedies, deduct that amount from any monies payable by Company hereunder or under any other agreement between you and Company or Company's affiliates. You shall be solely responsible for and shall pay any payments to any individuals rendering services in connection with the recording of the Masters which exceed union scale unless the excess and the recipient thereof shall have been specified in the Recording Budget approved by Company. You shall also be solely responsible for and shall pay any penalties incurred for late payments caused by your delay in submitting union contracts forms, report forms, or invoices or other documents. If, however, Company shall pay any excess not approved by Company or any penalties, you shall, upon Company's demand, pay Company the amount thereof, and Company may, without limiting Company's other rights and remedies, deduct that amount from any monies payable by Company hereunder or under any other agreement between you and Company or Company's affiliates.

5.02   Recording Costs shall mean and include all union scale payments (including "excess" scale payments) made to the Artist, all payments made by Company to any other individuals rendering services in connection with the recording of the Masters, all other payments which are made by Company pursuant to any applicable law or regulation or the provisions of any collective bargaining agreement between Company and any union or guild, all amounts paid or incurred for studio or hall rentals, tape, engineering, editing, instrument rentals and cartage, mastering, mixing, re-mixing, "sweetening", transportation and accommodations, immigration clearances, trademark and service mark searches and clearances, "sample" clearances any so-called "per diems" for any individuals (including the Artist) rendering services in connection with recording of the Masters and for Company's A&R employees attending recording sessions hereunder, together with all other amounts paid or incurred by Company in connection with the recording of the Masters. Recording Costs shall be recoupable from royalties payable by Company hereunder or under any other agreement between you and Company or Company's affiliates. The costs of metal parts other than lacquer, copper or equivalent masters, and payments to the AFM Special Payments Fund and the Music Performance Trust Fund based upon record sales (so-called "per-record royalties"), will not be recoupable from your royalties or reimbursable by you.

5.02 conveys that the artist will receive AFM union scale for recording his or her own record. At the rate or approximately $250+ per three hour session per musician, substantial money can accumulate fairly quickly. All costs are considered advances and recoupable.

5.03   If packaging for Phonograph Records hereunder contains special elements or requires additional fabrication costs (e.g., for embossing, die-cutting, special ink or paper, additional color separations requested by you, etc.) such that Company would incur manufacturing or fabrication costs in excess of Company's standard per-unit costs without such special elements or costs, or if the origination costs of the artwork embodied in such packaging exceeds Company's standard artwork origination costs (such standard manufacturing, fabrication and origination costs are collectively referred to herein as "Standard Packaging Costs"), and provided you have requested or consented to such special elements or additional fabrication costs, the excess above Company's Standard Packaging Costs ("Special Packaging Costs") may be deducted from any monies (other than mechanical royalties) required to be paid by Company pursuant to this Agreement. (Nothing contained herein shall be deemed to require Company to utilize any artwork elements which would cause Company to incur any Special Packaging Costs.)

Special packaging costs are the artist's responsibility.

6. RIGHTS.

6.01   All Master Recordings recorded during the Term which embody the performances of the Artist, from the inception of the recording thereof, shall, for purposes of copyright law, be deemed "works-made-for-hire" for Company by you, the Artist, and all other persons rendering services in connection with those Master Recordings. Those Master Recordings, from the inception of the recording thereof, and all Phonograph Records and other reproductions made therefrom, together with the performances embodied therein and all copyrights therein and thereto throughout the Territory, and all renewals and extensions thereof, shall be entirely Company's property, free of any claims whatsoever by you, the Artist, or any other person, firm, or corporation. Company shall, accordingly, have the exclusive right to obtain registration of copyright (and all renewals and extensions) in those Master Recordings, in Company's name, as the owner and author thereof. If Company shall be deemed not to be the author of those Master Recordings or those Master Recordings are deemed not to be "works-made-for-hire", this agreement shall constitute an irrevocable transfer to Company of ownership of copyright (and all renewals and extensions) in those Master Recordings. You and the Artist shall, upon Company's request, cause to be executed and delivered to Company transfers of ownership of copyright (and all renewals and extensions) in those Master Recordings and any other documents as Company may deem necessary or appropriate to vest in Company the rights granted to Company in this Agreement, and you and the Artist hereby irrevocably appoint Company your attorney-in-fact for the purpose of executing those transfers of ownership and other documents in your names. Without limiting the generality of the foregoing, Company and any person, firm, or corporation designated by Company shall have the exclusive, perpetual and worldwide right to manufacture, sell, distribute and advertise Phonograph Records embodying those Master Recordings under any trademarks, trade names or labels, and to lease, license, convey or otherwise use or dispose of those Master Recordings by any method now or hereafter known in any field of use and to perform publicly Phonograph Records and other reproductions embodying those Master Recordings, all upon such terms as Company may approve, or Company may refrain from doing any or all of the foregoing.

This clause allows the company to file the SR Copyright Registration form as owner.

7. MARKETING.

7.01

(a)

(i) Company and any person, firm or corporation designated by Company shall have the perpetual right throughout the Territory to use and to permit others to use the Artist's name (both legal and professional, and whether presently or here-after used by the Artist), likeness, other identification and biographical material concerning the Artist, and the name and likeness of any producer or other person rendering services in connection with Master Recordings recorded by the Artist during the Term for purposes of trade and advertising. Company shall have the further right to refer to the Artist during the Term as Company's exclusive record-ing artist and you and the Artist shall in all your and the Artist's activities in the entertainment field use reasonable efforts to cause the Artist to be billed and advertised during the Term as Company's exclusive recording artist. The rights granted to Company pursuant to this paragraph with respect to the Artist's name, likeness, other identification and biographical material concerning the Artist shall be exclusive during the Term and nonexclusive thereafter. Accordingly, but with-out limiting the generality of the foregoing, neither you nor the Artist shall authorize or permit any person, firm, or corporation other than Company to use during the Term the Artist's legal or professional name or the Artist's likeness in connection with the advertising or sale of Phonograph Records.

The artist may not want to guarantee that he or she will be able to secure this information for everyone on the recording. The phrase "with artist's approval" should be added to the entire 7.01(a)(i).

(ii) Company will make available to you for your approval any pictures of the Artist or biographical material about the Artist which Company proposes to use for advertising or publicity in the United States during the Term of this Agreement. Company will not use any such material which you disapprove in writing within five (5) days from the time such materials are made available to you, provided you furnish substitute material, satisfactory to Company in its sole and reasonable discretion. This subparagraph will not apply to any material pre-viously approved by you or used by Company. No inadvertent failure to comply with this subparagraph will constitute a breach of this Agreement, and you will not be entitled to injunctive relief to restrain the continuing use of any material used in contravention of this subparagraph. You shall have the right to submit photographs, likenesses and biographical material of Artist and your submission of same shall constitute your approval thereof.

(b) Neither you or the Artist shall render any services or authorize or permit your or the Artist's name or likeness or any biographical material concerning you or the Artist to be used in any manner by any person, firm or corporation in the advertis-ing, promoting or marketing of blank magnetic recording tape or any other product or device primarily intended for home use, whether now known or hereafter developed, which may be used for the fixation of sound alone or sound together with visual images.

7.02 During the Term of this Agreement, with respect to audio Records manufactured for sale in the United States, Company shall not without your consent:

(a) License Master Recordings made under this Agreement for commercials other than commercials for Phonograph Records hereunder. This restriction will apply after the Term for the following: (i) political, religious or hygiene related advertisements; and (ii) all other commercials if Artist's account is in a fully recouped position;

(b) License Master Recordings made under this Agreement for featured use in a motion picture, television program or video game, provided that Artist's account is in a fully recouped position. This restriction will apply during and after the Term (regardless of recoupment) for NC-17 and X rated productions;

(c) Use Master Recordings made under this Agreement on premium Records or other commercial tie-ins to promote the sale of any product or service other than Records or other derivatives of the Master Recordings, which bears the name of the sponsor for whom the Record is produced. This restriction shall also apply after the Term of this Agreement;

(d) Commercially release "out-takes" on Phonograph Records or otherwise exploit such recordings ("out-takes" are preliminary unfinished versions of Master Recordings made under this Agreement). This restriction shall also apply after the Term of this Agreement;

(e) Couple during any one (1) year period more than three (3) Master Recordings made hereunder with recordings not embodying your performances, except promotional samplers (including those sold to the general public for less than full price), institutional samplers and programs for use on public transportation carriers and facilities;

Company shall undertake to inform its affiliates outside of the United States of the restrictions contained in this paragraph 7.02. Company shall use commercially reasonable efforts to correct its failure to comply with the immediately preceding sentence following its receipt of your notice of such failure. No inadvertent failure to comply with this paragraph shall constitute a breach of this Agreement, and you shall not be entitled to injunctive relief to restrain the sale of any Record released in contravention of this paragraph. The provisions of this paragraph 7.02 shall not apply to any Master Recordings which are not Delivered within ninety (90) days after the time prescribed in Article 3 or if you have breached any of your other material obligations hereunder.

In sentence two, the word "reasonable" could be changed to "best".

7.03 If Company determines during the Term hereof to edit or remix any Master Recordings made under this agreement for use on an Album, it will accord you a period of seven (7) days in which to do that work in accordance with Company's requirements unless that delay would interfere with a scheduled release. After Company has afforded you such first opportunity to edit or remix, Company may edit or remix the Master Recording concerned, provided that you may reasonably approve such remixed or edited version. Unless you notify Company that you disapprove such remixed or edited Master Recordings within five (5) business days after Company offers you the opportunity to approve such version it will be deemed approved. This paragraph will not apply to editing necessary for the release of Singles (including radio edits), Long Play Singles or non-disc configurations, or to eliminate material which in the reasonable good faith opinion of Company's legal counsel is likely to constitute a defamation, libel or violate or infringe upon any right, including, without limitation, the right of privacy of any person. An inadvertent failure by Company to comply with the requirements of this paragraph shall not be deemed a breach of this agreement. Any costs incurred in connection with the re-editing or remixing shall be deemed Recording Costs in connection with the project concerned, provided that such costs shall not reduce the applicable Recording Fund if the costs are incurred after satisfactory Delivery of the Album concerned.

7.04

(a)

(i) Company will commercially release each Album recorded and delivered in fulfillment of your Recording Commitment hereunder in the United States within six (6) months after Delivery of the Album concerned if the Album is delivered between January 1, and September 30, of a given year or within eight (8) months after Delivery of the Album concerned if the Album is Delivered after September 30, of a given year. If Company fails to do so you may notify Company within forty five (45) days after the end of the applicable period concerned, that you intend to terminate this Agreement unless Company releases the Album within ninety (90) days after Company's receipt of your notice (the "cure period"). If Company fails to commercially release the Album in the United States before the end of the cure period, you may terminate the Term of this Agreement by giving Company notice within thirty (30) days after the end of the cure period. On receipt by Company of your termination notice, the Term of this Agreement will end and all parties will be deemed to have fulfilled all of their obligations hereunder except those obligations which survive the end of the Term (e.g., warranties, re-recording restrictions and obligations to pay royalties). Your only remedy for failure by Company to release an Album will be termination in accordance with this paragraph. If you fail to give Company either of those notices within the period specified, your right to terminate will lapse.

This is the release commitment which "allows" you to terminate the agreement if the recorded material is not released. The company, of course, will own the recordings and not revert their ownership back to the artist.

(ii) The running of the six (6) month and the ninety (90) day periods referred to in paragraph 7.04(a)(i) will be suspended (and the expiration date of each of those periods will be postponed) for the period of any suspension during such periods of the running of the Term of this Agreement under paragraph 17.01.

7.05 Company will commercially release each Committed Album hereunder in the United Kingdom , Canada, France, Germany, and Italy, (the "Foreign Release Territories") within one (1) year after the date such Album was released in the United States . If Company does not release the applicable Committed Album in a particular Foreign Release Territory(ies) within the applicable time period, then you may give Company notice within forty five (45) days following the expiration of one (1) year period of such failure to release such record in the particular Foreign Release Territory, and Company shall have a period of sixty (60) days following the date of such notice to cure such failure. If Company does not cure such failure within said sixty (60) day period, you shall have the option, which may be exercised by giving Company written notice within forty five (45) days following the end of such sixty (60) day period, to require Company to enter into an agreement with a licensee designated by you, which licensee is actually engaged in the business of manufacturing and distributing Records in the particular Foreign Release Territory concerned, authorizing such licensee to manufacture and distribute Records derived from the Master Recordings not released in accordance with this paragraph 7.05 in the applicable Foreign Release Territory. Fifty (50%) percent of all revenues actually received by Company under the licenses referred to in this paragraph 7.05 will be credited to your royalty account under this Agreement. Each such license agreement will provide for such compensation for the license as you negotiate with the licensee, and will contain such other provisions as Company shall require, including but not limited to the following:

These are the term of any straight licensing deals with a foreign company should the company exercise their right to do so. The revenue will be split evenly between the company and the artist.

(a) The licensee will be required to deliver to Company all consents required by Company, and all agreements which Company may require for any third party to look to the licensee, and not to Company, for the fulfillment of any obligations arising in connection with the manufacture or distribution of Records under the license. The licensee will also become a first party to any agreements or funds required pursuant to any union agreements to which Company is a party. The license agreement will not become effective until the licensee has complied with all that provisions of this subsection 7.05(a).

(b) The licensee will make all payments required in connection with the manufacture, sale or distribution, by parties other than Company, in the applicable Foreign Release Territory of Records made from those Master Recordings after the effective date of the license, including, without limitation, all royalties and other payments to performing artists, producers, owners of copyrights in musical compositions, and any applicable unions and union funds. The licensee will comply with all applicable rules and regulations covering any use of the Master Recordings by the licensee.

(c) No warranty or representation will be made by Company in connection with the applicable Master Recordings, the license or otherwise. You and the licensee will indemnify and hold harmless Company and its licensees against all claims, damages, liabilities, costs and expenses, including reasonable counsel fees, arising out of any use of the Master Recordings or exercise of such rights by the licensee.

(d) Company will instruct its licensee in the applicable Foreign Release Territory not to manufacture Records derived from the Master Recordings licensed to the licensee. If the licensee notifies Company of such manufacture, Company will instruct its licensees to discontinue it, but neither Company nor its licensees shall have any liability by reason of such manufacture occurring before Company's receipt of such notice and Company shall have no liability by reason of such manufacture at any time.

(e) Each Record made under the license will bear a sound recording copyright notice identical to the notice used by Company for initial United States release of the Master Recording concerned, or such other notices as Company shall require, but those Records will not otherwise be identified directly or indirectly with Company.

(f) Company shall have the right to examine the books and records of the licensee and all others authorized by the licensee to manufacture and distribute Records under the license, for the purpose of verifying the accuracy of the accountings rendered to Company by the license.

(g) The licensee will not have the right to authorize any other party to exercise any rights without Company's prior written consent.

(h) Company and its licensees will have the continuing right at all times to manufacture and sell recompilation Albums in the Foreign Release Territory concerned which may contain the Master Recordings. A recompilation album is an Album, such as a "Greatest Hits" or "Best Of" type Album, containing Master Recordings previously released in different Album combinations.

For purposes of computing each of the one (1) year and sixty (60) day periods described in this paragraph 7.05 the period between October 15 and January 15 shall not be counted.

7.06

(a) A "qualifying recompilation Album", in this paragraph 7.06, means an Album, such as a "Greatest Hits" or "Best of" Album, consisting of: (i) Master Recordings made and/or released under this Agreement or otherwise recorded by you and previously released in different Album combinations; and (ii) two (2) new Master Recordings (the "New Recordings" below) of at least two (2) Compositions, made expressly for initial release in that Album and not applicable in reduction of your Recording Commitment.

(b) Within thirty (30) days after Company's release of a qualifying recompilation Album on top line Records sold Through Normal Retail Channels in the United States, Company shall pay you an Advance of one hundred thousand dollars ($100,000) less the Recording Costs for the New Recordings. No other Advance shall be payable in connection with the New Recordings. The Advance, if any, shall be payable to you promptly following the Delivery of such New Recordings. If your royalty account is in an unrecouped position (i.e., if the aggregate of the Advances and other recoupable items charged to that account at the time of payment of that

Advance exceeds the aggregate of the royalties credited to that account at the end of the last semi-annual royalty accounting period), the Advance payable under the first sentence of this paragraph shall be reduced by the amount of the unrecouped balance.

(c) If Company releases in the United States a qualifying recompilation Album consisting of Master Recordings hereunder, the selection of Master Recordings to be embodied on such Album(s) shall, during the term, be subject to your written consent (not to be unreasonably withheld), provided that all Master Recordings which have been previously released as a Single in the United States shall be deemed approved by you. If you and Company cannot agree as to all Master Recordings to be included, then such Album shall include all agreed-upon Master Recordings, and Company and you shall then alternate selection to fill the Album, with Company selecting first and determining in its sole discretion when such Album will be deemed filled. During the Term, Company will have the right to release one (1) recompilation Album after the third Album released in the United States during the Term. After the Term Company will have the right to release one (1) recompilation Album.

These clauses discuss a "best of " release and what material will constitute its contents. The advance or royalty account credit of $100,000 is negotiable.

7.07

(a) In preparation of the initial release in the United States of each Album of the Recording Commitment, the following procedure shall be followed:

(i) Company shall obtain your approval regarding the proposed Album cover layout and the picture or art to be used on the Album cover, in accordance with this paragraph 7.07. The proposed Album cover shall be made available to you at Company's offices for review and comment. Unless otherwise provided in this paragraph 7.07, Company shall make such changes in the artwork as you reasonably request.

(ii) Company shall not be required to make any changes which would delay the release of the Album beyond the scheduled date or which would require Company to incur Special Packaging Costs. Any premium charges incurred to meet the release schedule because of delays in approval by you shall constitute Special Packaging Costs.

(b) In preparation for the initial release in the United States of each Album of the Recording Commitment, if you request to prepare the Album packaging layout and/or the pictures or art to be used in connection with the Album, and if Company agrees in writing to such request, then you shall have the right to produce and deliver to Company, as applicable, such Album packaging layout and pictures or art, but only on the following conditions:

(i) Your plans for the proposed artwork shall be discussed with Company's Executive Vice President, Marketing, or his or her designee, before it is produced and a budget shall be assigned for artwork costs.

(ii) You shall produce the artwork in accordance with plans approved by Company and shall deliver "camera-ready" artwork to Company, in the form of mechanicals and art (including, without limitation, pre-separated film and chromes of the original artwork) conforming to Company's specifications, together with all licenses and consents required in connection with it, not later than sixty (60) days before the scheduled release date of the Album. If any of the aforesaid materials have not been delivered to Company within that time, Company shall have the right to prepare and use its own artwork without further consultation with you, and Company shall not be obligated to make any payments to you or any other Person to whom you have incurred any obligation in connection with any artwork produced for the Album concerned.

(iii) You shall deliver to Company, together with the artwork, an itemized statement of the actual costs paid by you in connection therewith. Company shall reimburse you promptly after Company's acceptance of the artwork and the aforesaid statement of costs in the amount of those costs, provided such costs do not exceed the approved budget therefore. If Company in Company's sole discretion shall elect to reimburse you for costs in excess of the approved budget, such excess shall constitute Special Packaging Costs.

(c) All matters relating to Company's trademarks or to notices or disclosures deemed advisable by Company's attorneys, and any matter other than the Artwork (i.e., the artwork to be used for the front cover of the initial United States release of each Committed Album) shall be determined in Company's sole discretion. Company shall not be deemed unreasonable in rejecting any requested change upon the advice of Company's attorneys.

(d) Company shall have the right to reject any artwork which is not commercially satisfactory in Company's reasonable judgement. Company shall not be deemed unreasonable in rejecting any artwork or Record packaging which includes so-called "commercial tie-ins", endorsements, advertising or marketing materials in respect of anything other than Records of the Artist's performances hereunder, or which Company anticipates would require Company to incur Special Packaging Costs. Company shall not be deemed unreasonable in rejecting any artwork which Company deems patently offensive or which, in the judgment of its attorneys, might subject Company or Company's licensees to liability for any reason. If Company accepts the artwork, all engraving and manufacturing costs in excess of the amount specified above shall be reimbursed by you on Company's request; all such excess amounts not reimbursed by you shall constitute Advances and may be recouped by Company from any monies becoming due to you.

You may "prepare" special packaging, however, veto power is with the company.

(e) You shall act as an independent contractor in all arrangements you make with other Persons in connection with the production of the artwork; you shall not purport to make any such arrangements as Company's agent or otherwise on behalf of Company.

(f) This paragraph 7.07 shall apply only to Albums Delivered within the time prescribed in Article 3 and initially released in the United States during the Term, and only if you are not otherwise in default under this Agreement.

7.08   It is hereby expressly agreed that, as between you, Artist and Company, Company shall exclusively own and control all materials comprising the artwork (including, without limitation, art, photographs, graphic designs, etc.) and other items created or used in connection with the exploitation of Phonograph Records hereunder (the "Art Materials"), including, without limitation, all copyrights and the right to secure copyright throughout the world and in perpetuity.

7.09   Company hereby agrees to spend not less than _____-Thousand ($_____) Dollars in connection with its promotion and sales and marketing activities for each Album Delivered hereunder in fulfillment of your Minimum Recording Commitment. The costs for videos, tour support and independent promotion will be among the items drawn from such marketing budget. Except as set forth in the following sentence, all sums paid or incurred by Company in connection with independent marketing and publicity of Phonograph Records hereunder, including the sums set forth in the preceding sentence, shall be deemed to constitute Advances hereunder. Only fifty (50%) percent of all sums paid or incurred by Company in connection with the independent promotion of Phonograph Records hereunder shall constitute Advances. Company shall endeavor to consult with you with respect to its marketing expenditures, including its independent promotion expenditures, provided, Company's inadvertent failure to do so shall not constitute a breach hereof.

Clause 7.09 discusses the promotional campaign finances and is negotiable. If it is necessary to use indie promo guys, the artist, will have "no" say in who, when, or where, but will be responsible for half of the expenses incurred! The entire clause needs to be clearly negotiated.

8. ADVANCES.

8.01   All monies paid to you or the Artist or on your or the Artist's behalf or to or on behalf of any person, firm or corporation representing you or the Artist, other than royalties payable pursuant to this Agreement, shall constitute Advances hereunder. You agree that the Advances hereunder include the prepayment of session union scale as provided in the applicable union codes, and you and Artist agree to complete any documentation required by the applicable union to implement this sentence.

8.02

(a) Conditioned upon your full performance of all your obligations hereunder, Company shall pay you the following amounts, which shall constitute Advances hereunder. With respect to each Album recorded and delivered hereunder in fulfillment of your Recording Commitment, the amount, if any, by which the sum designated below as the "Recording Fund" exceeds the Recording Costs for that Album:

(i) For the First Album, the Recording Fund shall be _____ thousand Dollars ($_____).

(ii) For the Album recorded during the first Option Period, the Recording Fund shall be the Formula Amount, but no less than _____ hundred and _____ thousand Dollars ($_____) and no more than _____ hundred and _____ thousand Dollars ($_____).

(iii) For the Album recorded during the second Option Period, the Recording Fund shall be the Formula Amount, but no less than _____ hundred and _____ thousand Dollars ($_____) and no more than _____ hundred and _____ thousand Dollars ($_____).

For the Album recorded during the third Option Period, the Recording Fund shall be the Formula Amount, but no less than _____ hundred _____ thousand ($_____) Dollars and no more than _____ hundred and _____ thousand Dollars ($_____).

For the Album recorded during the fourth Option Period, the Recording Fund shall be the Formula Amount, but no less than _____ hundred and _____ thousand Dollars ($_____) and no more than _____ hundred and _____ thousand Dollars ($_____).

For the Album recorded during the fifth Option Period, the Recording Fund shall be the Formula Amount, but no less than _____ hundred thousand Dollars ($_____) and no more than _____ hundred thousand Dollars ($_____).

Possibly a graduated scale which would look something like below would be appropriate. Remember that all figures are negotiable.

	Minimum	Maximum
Albums Delivered during the first Option Period:	$200,000	$400,000
Albums Delivered during the second Option Period:	$225,000	$450,000
Albums Delivered during the third Option Period:	$250,000	$500,000
		etc.

The "Formula Amount" for a particular Album recorded and Delivered hereunder in fulfillment of your Recording Commitment shall mean an amount equal to sixty-six and two-thirds (66 2/3%) percent of whichever of the following amounts is less: (A) the amount of the royalties, after the retention of reserves (which, solely for purposes of this calculation, shall not exceed twenty [20%] percent), earned by you hereunder from Net Sales through Normal Retail Channels in the United States on which royalties are payable hereunder ("USNRC Net Sales") of the immediately preceding Album delivered hereunder in fulfillment of your Recording Commitment; or (B) the average of the amounts of such royalties so earned by you hereunder on the two (2) immediately preceding Albums delivered hereunder in fulfillment of your Recording Commitment. In either case, the amount of royalties with respect to any preceding Album shall be computed as of the end of the month in which occurs the date which is twelve (12) months following the initial commercial release in the United States of the preceding Album concerned. Notwithstanding the foregoing, with respect to any applicable Album which is not delivered to Company within the applicable period provided for in paragraph 3.02 above, the Recording Fund for that Album shall be reduced by ten (10%) percent of the otherwise applicable Recording Fund for each month (or portion thereof) until that Album is delivered; provided, however, Company shall not reduce the applicable Recording Fund below the actual Recording Costs for the Album concerned.

This fairly lengthy definition of the "Formula Amount" (and the calculations) is fine if the first recording sold well. If it didn't and the artist is really looking to get it together for the next shot, there may not be sufficient money in the account for these calculations.

(b) The Advance payable to you in connection with the First Album pursuant to paragraph 8.02(a)(i) shall be payable as follows: (i) _____ thousand Dollars ($_____) promptly following the complete execution hereof and (ii) the balance of the Advance (less all Recording Costs), if any, promptly following delivery to and acceptance by Company of the First Album.

(c) Each Advance payable to you pursuant to paragraph(s) 8.02(a)(ii)-(vi), if any, shall be made as follows:

(d) Upon Company's receipt of your notice that the recording of the Album concerned has actually commenced, Company shall pay you a portion of the applicable Advance equal to fifteen (15%) percent of the applicable minimum Recording Fund specified in subparagraph 8.02(a); and

If the advance is indeed used to finance the recording, then initial percent payment most likely need to be higher. Company shall pay you the balance of the Advance (less all Recording Costs), if any, promptly following delivery to and acceptance by Company of such Album.

What does "promptly" mean.........thirty days......six months??

8.03

(a) The aggregate amount of the compensation paid to (each of) you under this agreement shall not be less than the "Designated Dollar Amount" (as defined below) per Fiscal Year. "Fiscal Year", in this paragraph, means the annual period beginning on the date of commencement of the Term, and each subsequent annual period through the seventh such annual period, during the Term. [You hereby warrant and represent that all payments made to you under this agreement during each Fiscal Year shall be distributed equally among you.]

If (each of you has) (you have) not received compensation equal to the Designated Dollar Amount under this agreement for a Fiscal Year, the company shall pay (each of) you the amount of (any) (the) deficiency before the end of that Fiscal Year; at least forty (40) days before the end of each Fiscal Year you shall notify the company if (each of you has) (you have) not received compensation equal to the Designated Dollar

Amount under this agreement for that Fiscal Year, and of the amount of the deficiency. Each such payment shall constitute an Advance and shall be applied in reduction of any and all monies due or becoming due to you under this agreement. The company may not withhold or require you to repay any payment made to you pursuant to or subject to this paragraph 8.03.

As used in this paragraph 8.03, the "Designated Dollar Amount" shall be:

Nine Thousand Dollars ($9,000) for the first Fiscal Year of this agreement;

Twelve Thousand Dollars ($12,000) for the second Fiscal Year of this agreement; and

Fifteen Thousand Dollars ($15,000) for each of the third through seventh Fiscal Years of this agreement.

If in any Fiscal Year the aggregate amount of the compensation paid to you under this agreement exceeds the Designated Dollar Amount, such excess compensation shall apply to reduce the Designated Dollar Amount for any subsequent Fiscal Years.

(d) You acknowledge that this paragraph is included to avoid compromise of the company's rights (including the company's entitlement to injunctive relief) by reason of a finding of applicability of California law, but does not constitute a concession by the company that California law is actually applicable.

These are the "play or pay" clauses. They state that if the company pays you these amounts, they have fulfilled their requirements of the agreement and they do not have to allow you to record, finance a recording, or do anything! In fact, in 8.03(b) the responsibility it put on you to notify them if you did not receive compensation. Unfortunately, this is standard language.

9. ROYALTIES.

9.01   Company will pay you an "all-in" royalty, during the term of copyright in the country concerned of Masters embodied in Phonograph Records delivered hereunder computed at the applicable percentage indicated in the Royalty Schedule below, of the applicable Royalty Base Price in respect of Net Sales of such Phonograph Records (other than Audiovisual Records) consisting entirely of Master Recordings recorded under this Agreement during the respective Contract Periods specified below and sold by Company or Company's licensees through Normal Retail Channels:

Be careful, normally "NRC Net Sales" in layman's terms is approximately the wholesale price.

ROYALTY SCHEDULE

UNITED STATES

Master Recordings made during the:	Albums	Singles	Long Play Singles
Initial Period			
First Option Period			
Second Option Period			
Third Option Period			
Fourth Option Period			
Fifth Option Period			

On albums, any figure starting around 24% would be standard. On singles 18%.

FOREIGN

Territory	All Records
Canada	% of the otherwise applicable rate set forth in the United States Royalty Schedule above in respect of Net Sales through Normal Retail Channels in the United States of the particular record concerned (i.e., Albums, Singles and Long Play Singles), without regard to any escalations.

Eighteen percent on albums and thirteen percent on singles.

All EU countries, Austraila, New Zealand and Japan	% of the otherwise applicable rate set forth in the United States Royalty Schedule above in respect of Net Sales through Normal Retail Channels in the United States of the particular record concerned (i.e., Albums, Singles and Long Play Singles), without regard to any escalations.

About the same in these countries as well.

Rest of World	% of the otherwise applicable rate set forth in the United States Royalty Schedule above in respect of Net Sales through Normal Retail Channels in the United States of the particular record concerned (i.e., Albums, Singles and Long Play Singles), without regard to any escalations.

Twelve percent for albums and nine percent for singles elsewhere.

The royalty rates set forth in this paragraph 9.01 are sometimes referred to herein as your "basic royalty rate(s)".

9.02 Notwithstanding anything to the contrary contained in the Royalty Schedule hereinabove, and with respect to each Album Delivered in fulfillment of your Recording Commitment hereunder, the royalty rate applicable to USNRC Net Sales of top-line Albums pursuant to the terms hereof shall be the royalty rate specified in the Royalty Escalation Schedule below.

ROYALTY ESCALATION SCHEDULE

Album recorded in fulfillment of the Recording Commitment for the:	USNRC Net Sales of top-line Albums (determined in accordance with Company's standard accounting procedures).
Initial Period	500,000 1,000,000
First Option Period	500,000 1,000,000
Second Option Period	500,000 1,000,000
Third Option Period	500,000 1,000,000
Fourth Option Period	500,000 1,000,000
Fifth Option Period	500,000 1,000,000

All negotiable!

9.03

(a) The royalty rate on Phonograph Records sold through direct mail or through mail order operations (including, without limitation so-called "record clubs") shall be one-half (?) of the otherwise applicable royalty rate if manufactured and sold by Company, and an amount equal to one-half (?) of the Net Royalty from the sale of those Phonograph Records if manufactured and sold by Company's licensees.

The 50% rate may be negotiated to a higher rate.

Secondly, a provision may be inserted that allows a percentage of "bonus" and "free" records to be accounted as records sold. There is the possibility that a hot album becomes one of the free intro-ductory albums to hundreds of thousands of club members. The artist shouldn't be totally penal-ized for this.

(b) The royalty rate on Phonograph Records sold via telephone, satellite, cable, point of sale manufacturing or other means of direct transmission, now known or hereafter devised (herein collectively, "Electronic Transmission") shall be seventy-five percent (75%) of the otherwise applicable royalty rate if sold by Company and an amount equal to one-half (1/2) of the Net Royalty from sale of those Phonograph Records if sold by Company's licensees. Notwithstanding the foregoing, with respect to any Records sold via Electronic Transmission by Company or its licensees, Company shall have the option (which Company may exercise in its sole discretion) to pay to you in lieu of any royalty otherwise payable in connection with such Records, the same dollars-and-cents royalty payable hereunder for the equivalent Record (or, if no such equivalent Record exists, a comparable Record) in audio-only compact disc configuration at the time of transmission.

This is one of the few clauses that indirectly refers to the Internet. It is far too vague and needs negotiation.

9.04   The royalty rate for the use of any Master as described in clause (a), (b), or (c) of this sentence will be one-half (?) of the basic royalty rate that would apply if the Record concerned were sold through Normal Retail Channels: (a) any catalog Phonograph Record sold by Company's special products operations or those of the distributor of the Records concerned (herein collectively "SPO's") to educational institutions or libraries, or to other SPO clients for their promotion or sales incentive purposes (but not for sale to the general public through Normal Retail Channels); (b) any Record sold by Company or Company's principal licensee in the country concerned in conjunction with a television and/or radio advertising campaign, during the calendar semi-annual period in which that campaign begins and the next two (2) such periods; and (c) any non-catalog Phonograph Record created on a custom basis for SPO clients. The royalty on any Record described in clause (c) will be computed on the basis of the SPO's actual sales price less all taxes and Container Charges. In respect of any Master Recording leased by Company to others for their distribution of Phonograph Records in the United States, Company will pay you fifty (50%) percent of Company's net receipts from Company's licensee. ("Net receipts", in the preceding sentence, means receipts as computed after deduction of all copyright, AFM and other applicable third party payments.) If another artist, a producer, or any other Person is entitled to royalties on sales of such Records, that payment will be divided among you in the same ratio as that among your respective basic royalty percentage rates.

This clause establishes the rate on special products to special customers.

9.05

(a) The royalty rate on any Budget Record or any "picture disc" (i.e., a disc Record with artwork reproduced on the surface of the Record itself) will be one-half (?) of the applicable basic royalty rate prescribed in paragraph 9.01. The royalty rate on any Mid-Priced Record will be seventy-five percent (75%) of the otherwise applicable basic royalty rate prescribed in paragraph 9.01. The royalty rate on any Record sold for distribution through military exchange channels shall be three-quarters (3/4) of the otherwise applicable basic royalty rate prescribed in paragraph 9.01. The royalty rate on any soundtrack Record will be seventy (70%) percent of the otherwise applicable basic royalty rate prescribed in paragraph 9.01 (provided, however, that on Masters licensed by Company for use on a soundtrack Record, the royalty rate shall be an amount equal to fifty (50%) percent of Company's net receipts received from such use). The royalty rate on any Record which is not an Album, Single or a Long-Play Single will be sixty (60%) percent of the applicable basic Album royalty rate prescribed in paragraph 9.01.

Negotiate separately!!

(b) The royalty rate on a Multiple Album will be one-half (?) of the applicable basic Album royalty rate prescribed in paragraph 9.01, if the Royalty Base Price of that Album is the same as the Royalty Base Price applicable to the top-line single-disc Conventional Albums marketed by Company or its Licensee in the territory where the Album is sold at the beginning of the royalty accounting period concerned. If a different Royalty Base Price applies to a Multiple Album, the royalty rate prescribed in the preceding sentence will be adjusted in proportion to the variance in the Royalty Base Price (but will not be more than the applicable Album royalty rate prescribed in paragraph 9.01). That adjustment of the royalty rate will be made by using the following formula:

(X divided by Y) multiplied by Z = adjusted royalty rate. (Subject to the parenthetical limit in the second sentence of this subparagraph.)

("X" represents the Royalty Base Price for the Multiple Album concerned; "Y" represents the Royalty Base Price for such top-line single-disc Records in the Multiple Album multiplied by the number of disc Records in the Multiple Album concerned; and "Z" equals the otherwise applicable basic royalty rate.)

(c) The royalty rate on any compact disc Record will be one hundred (100%) percent of the rate which would otherwise be applicable under this Agreement.

At least they are being fair by now including the standard configuration in the industry.

(d) The royalty rate on any New Media Record will be seventy (70%) percent of the rate which would otherwise be applicable hereunder; provided, in the event Company adopts a general policy applicable to the majority of artists signed exclusively to Company which provides for a royalty rate reduction with respect to Records in a particular New Media configuration more favorable to such artists than the royalty rate reduction provided herein, you shall receive the benefit of such general policy, on a prospective basis only.

In this clause the company is protecting itself from being omitted from an new "way" to receive product and digital downloading would be included here. The 70% can be negotiated.

9.06

(a) Except as otherwise specifically set forth herein, on Masters licensed by Company on a flat-fee or a royalty basis for the sale of Phonograph Records or for any other uses, the royalty rate shall be an amount equal to fifty (50%) percent of the Net Flat Fee or Net Royalty, as applicable, from such exploitation of the Masters.

(b) To the extent permissible at law, you hereby assign to Company all right, title and interest in and to any and all royalties or other payments to which you are or may become entitled to receive (herein "Your Share") under the Audio Home Recording

Act of 1992, as it may be amended (the "Act"), or any implementing or similar legislation requiring the payment of copyright royalties in connection with the sale of recording devices or blank tapes or any other recordable device (e.g., digital audio tape, DCC). Upon receipt by Company of such royalties or payments, Company shall credit your royalty account with one hundred (100%) percent of Your Share of such royalties or payments received. In order to effectuate the foregoing, you shall execute and deliver to Company a letter of direction address to the Register of Copyrights of the U.S. Copyright Office and you agree to execute and deliver to Company any other document or documents as may be reasonably necessary to cause the payment to Company of Your Share of such royalties or payments. It is expressly understood and agreed that except as provided above in this paragraph 9.06(b), Company shall be entitled to retain for its own use and benefit any royalties or payments received by Company pursuant to the Act.

Another reservoir to recoup advances.

9.07   Notwithstanding anything to the contrary contained herein, on Audiovisual Recordings, the royalty rate shall be as follows:

(a) On Audiovisual Records manufactured and sold by Company's licensees, in the United States or elsewhere shall be an amount equal to fifty (50%) percent of the Net Receipts from the sale of those Audiovisual Records. On Audiovisual Records manufactured and sold by Company, the royalty rate shall be computed in accordance with the provisions of this Article 9 applicable to Conventional Albums, except: (i) on sales of Audiovisual Records in the United States the royalty rate pursuant to paragraph 9.01(a) above shall be deemed to be ten (10%) percent; (ii) on sales of Audiovisual Records outside of the United States the royalty rate shall be deemed to be five (5%) percent; and (iii) the Royalty Base Price of Audiovisual Records shall be as prescribed in paragraph 19.23 below.

(b) On Audiovisual Recordings licensed or otherwise furnished by Company for exploitation other than on Audiovisual Records, the royalty rate shall be an amount equal to fifty percent (50%) of the Net Receipts from that exploitation.

(c) The following amounts will be charged in reduction of all royalties payable or becoming payable to you under this paragraph 9.07:

(i) All royalties and other compensation which may become payable to any Person for the right to make any uses of copyrighted Musical Compositions in Audiovisual Records; and

(ii) All payments to record producers, directors or other Persons which are measured by uses of Audiovisual Records or proceeds from those uses, whether such payments are to be computed as royalties on sales, as participations in revenues, or in any other manner. (The amounts chargeable under the preceding sentence will not include non-contingent advances, but will include payments - including payments in fixed amounts - which accrue by reason that such sales, revenues, or other bases for computation attain particular levels.)

9.07 is the section that discusses the use of video in sync with recorded music. Major will pay a royalty based on "net sales" in the U.S., or by components of Major outside the U.S. All the percentages are negotiated by the attorneys.

9.08   Notwithstanding anything to the contrary contained in this Article 9:

(a) In respect of Joint Recordings, the royalty rate to be used in determining the royalties payable to you shall be computed by multiplying the royalty rate otherwise applicable by a fraction, the numerator of which shall be one (1) and the denominator of which shall be the total number of royalty artists whose performances are embodied on a Joint Recording. The term "Joint Recording" shall mean any Master Recording embodying the Artist's performances and any performances by another artist with respect to which Company is obligated to pay royalties.

This clause refers to coupling the artist with another artist. This clause needs to be negotiated and the artist needs to receive final veto power as to who s/he is coupled with. The formula must reflect the artist's status compared to other artists on the recording. If the artist is the biggest star on the recording the formula should reflect the receipt of the largest piece of the pie!

(b) The royalty rate on a Phonograph Record embodying Master Recordings made hereunder together with other Master Recordings will be computed by multiplying the royalty rate otherwise applicable by a fraction, the numerator of which is the number of Selections embodying Master Recordings made hereunder and contained on the particular record concerned and the denominator of which is the total number of Selections contained on such Record. The royalty rate on an Audiovisual Record containing a Audiovisual Recordings made hereunder and other audiovisual works will be determined by apportionment based upon actual playing time on the Record concerned.

(c) No royalties shall be payable to you in respect of Phonograph Records sold or distributed by Company or Company's licensees for promotional purposes, as cut-outs, at close-out prices, for scrap, at less than inventory cost or at fifty (50%) percent or less of the Record's highest posted wholesale price (whether or not intended for resale), as "free", "no charge" or "bonus" Records (whether or not intended for resale), to Company's employees or those of Company's licensees and their relatives, or to radio stations. In connection with the foregoing, you and Company hereby agree that (subject to additional short-term special programs) distributions of Phonograph Records on a "no-charge" basis shall be deemed to be as follows:

(i) With respect to Albums, fifteen (15%) percent of such Records are deemed distributed on a "no-charge" basis; and

(ii) With respect to Singles, twenty-three (23%) percent of such Records are deemed distributed on a "no-charge" basis.

(The calculation of Records deemed distributed on a "no-charge" basis pursuant to the foregoing clauses (i) and (ii) shall be deemed applicable, and such Records shall not be royalty-bearing, regardless of whether or not any such records are in fact invoiced to customers on a "no-charge" basis.)

(d) If records derived from the Masters are sold to distributors or others for less than Company's highest posted wholesale price, or at a discount therefrom, but for more than fifty (50%) percent of such wholesale price, then, for purposes of this paragraph, a percentage of such records shall be deemed non-royalty bearing records, which percentage shall be an amount equal to the percentage of such lesser amount or the applicable discount.

(e) Company may elect from time to time to compute and pay you royalties hereunder on a royalty base different than the Royalty Base Price provided herein, as long as such computation does not materially affect the net amount of royalties otherwise payable to you at that time hereunder.

All negotiable.

10.   ROYALTY PAYMENTS AND ACCOUNTINGS.

10.01   Company shall send to you statements for royalties payable hereunder on or before October 1st for the semi-annual period ending the preceding June 30th and on or before April 1st for the semi-annual period ending the preceding December 31st, together with payment of royalties, if any, earned by you hereunder during the semi-annual period for which the statement is rendered, less all Advances and other charges under this Agreement. Company shall have the right to retain, as a reserve against charges, credits, or returns, such portion of payable royalties as shall be reasonable in Company's best business judgment. With respect to Albums sold hereunder, Company's reserve shall not exceed thirty-five (35%) percent of the number of such records shipped, unless Company reasonably believes a particular release justifies a higher reserve. With respect to Singles sold hereunder, Company's reserve shall not exceed fifty (50%) percent of the number of such records shipped, unless Company reasonably believes a particular release justifies a higher reserve. Reserves shall be fully liquidated no later than the end of the fourth full accounting period following the period in which such reserve was initially established. Records returned will be apportioned between royalty-free records and records on which royalties are payable in the same proportion as such records were shipped to customers. You shall reimburse Company on demand for any overpayments, and Company may also deduct the amount thereof from any monies payable to you hereunder. Royalties paid by Company on Phonograph Records subsequently returned shall be deemed overpayments.

This clause sets out the accounting periods of the royalty statements, in this case they are semi-annual periods. The continuation is standard.

10.02   No royalties shall be payable to you on sales of Phonograph Records by any of Company's licensees or distributors until payment on those sales has been received by Company in the United States. Sales by a licensee or distributor shall be deemed to have occurred in the semi-annual accounting period during which that licensee or distributor shall have rendered to Company accounting statements and payments for those sales.

10.03

(a) Royalties on Phonograph Record sales outside of the United States shall be computed in the national currency in which Company's licensees pay to Company, shall be credited to your royalty account hereunder at the same rate of exchange at which Company's licensees pay to Company, and shall be proportionately subject to any withholding or comparable taxes which may be imposed upon Company's receipts.

Language should be inserted that asks that a foreign account be maintained in case payments are blocked by the government or for any reason.

(b) If Company shall not receive payment in United States dollars in the United States for any sales of Phonograph Records outside of the United States, royalties on those sales shall not be credited to your royalty account hereunder. Company shall, however, at your written request and if Company is reasonably able to do so, accept payment for those sales in foreign currency and shall deposit in a foreign bank or other depository, at your expense, in that foreign currency, that portion thereof, if any, as shall equal the royalties which would have been payable to you hereunder on those sales had payment for those sales been made to Company in United States dollars in the United States. Deposit as aforesaid shall fulfill Company's royalty obligations hereunder as to those sales. If any law, ruling or other governmental restriction limits the amount a licensee can remit to Company, Company may reduce your royalties hereunder by an amount proportionate to the reduction in Company's licensee's remittance to Company.

10.04

(a) Company will maintain books and records which report the sales of Phonograph Records, on which royalties are payable to you. You may, but not more than once a year, at your own expense, examine those books and records, as provided in this paragraph 10.04 only. You may make those examinations only for the purpose of verifying the accuracy of the statements sent to you under paragraph 10.01. All such examinations shall be in accordance with GAAP procedures and regulations. You may make such an examination for a particular statement only once, and only within two (2) years after the date such statement is rendered by Company under paragraph 10.01 (each such statement shall be deemed rendered when due unless you notify Company to the contrary in writing within 60 days after the applicable due date specified). You may make such an examination only during Company's usual business hours, and at the place where Company keeps the books and records to be examined. If you wish to make an examination you will be required to notify Company at least thirty (30) days before the date when you plan to begin it. Company may postpone the commencement of your examination by notice given to you not later than five (5) days before the commencement date specified in your notice; if Company does so, the running of the time within which the examination may be made will be suspended during the postponement. If your examination has not been completed within three (3) months from the time you begin it, Company may require you to terminate it on ten (10) business days' notice to you at any time; Company will not be required to permit you to continue the examination after the end of that ten

(10) business day period. You will not be entitled to examine any manufacturing records or any other records that do not specifically report sales or other distributions of Phonograph Records on which royalties are payable to you. You may appoint a certified public accountant to make such an examination for you, but not if (s)he or his/her firm has begun an examination of Company's books and records for any Person except you unless the examination has been concluded and any applicable audit issues have been resolved. Such certified public accountant will act only under a Letter of Confidentiality which provides that any information derived from such audit or examination will not be knowingly released, divulged or published to any person, firm or corporation, other than to you or to a judicial or administrative body in connection with any proceeding relating to this Agreement.

Several clauses may be inserted in 10.04(a). Language should be included that allows an accountant to postpone the examination of the artist's statements until he or she completes the present audit, should one be in progress.

The artist should negotiate for more time before the audit must begin, and less time to give notice.

(b) Notwithstanding the penultimate sentence of paragraph 10.04(a), if Company notifies you that the representative designated by you to conduct an examination of Company's books and records under paragraph 10.04(a) is engaged in an examination on behalf of another Person ("Other Examination"), you may nevertheless have your examination conducted by your designee, and the running of the time within which such examination may be made shall be suspended until your designee has completed the Other Examination, subject to the following conditions:

(i) You shall notify Company of your election to that effect within fifteen (15) days after the date of Company's said notice to you;

(ii) Your designee shall proceed in a reasonably continuous and expeditious manner to complete the Other Examination and render the final report thereon to the client and Company; and

(iii) Your examination shall not be commenced by your designee before the delivery to Company of the final report on the Other Examination, shall be commenced within thirty (30) days thereafter, and shall be conducted in a reasonably continuous manner.

(The preceding provisions of this paragraph 10.04(b) will not apply if Company elects to waive the provisions of the penultimate sentence of paragraph 10.04(a) which require that your representative shall not be engaged in any Other Examination.)

10.05   If you have any objections to a royalty statement, you will give Company specific notice of that objection and your reasons for it within two (2) years after the date such statement is rendered by Company under paragraph 10.01 (each such statement shall be deemed rendered when due unless you notify Company to the contrary in writing within 60 days after the applicable due date specified). Each royalty statement will become conclusively binding on you at the end of that two (2) year period, and you will no longer have any right to make any other objections to it. You will not have the right to sue Company in connection with any royalty accounting, or to sue Company for royalties on Records sold during the period a royalty accounting covers, unless you commence the suit within that two (2) year period. If you commence suit on any controversy or claim concerning royalty accountings rendered to you under this agreement in a court of competent jurisdiction (as provided in paragraph 23.09 below), the scope of the proceeding will be limited to determination of the amount of the royalties due for the accounting periods concerned, and the court will have no authority to consider any other issues or award any relief except recovery of any royalties found owing. Your recovery of any such royalties will be the sole remedy available to you or the Artist by reason of any claim related to Company's royalty accountings. Without limiting the generality of the preceding sentence, neither you nor the Artist will have any right to seek termination of this Agreement or avoid the performance of your obligations under it by reason of any such claim.

Negotiate to extend the time to voice an objection and bring suit. Also it should be made clear that the terms of this clause are as stated unless there is fraud (which means there was intent to deceive), then a legal suit would be filed that introduce other remedies.

10.06   Company shall have the right to deduct from any amounts payable to you hereunder that portion thereof as may be required to be deducted under any statute, regulation, treaty or other law, or under any union or guild agreement, and you shall promptly execute and deliver to Company any forms or other documents as may be required in connection therewith.

10.07   Each payment made by Company to you or the Artist under this Agreement, other than union scale payments under Article 5 hereof, shall, at Company's election, be made by a single check payable to _____. All payments herein are contingent upon Company receiving properly completed W-9 and/or 1001 IRS tax forms, as applicable.

11.   MUSICAL COMPOSITION LICENSES.

11.01   You hereby grant to Company and Company's designees an irrevocable non-exclusive license, under copyright, to reproduce each Controlled Composition on Phonograph Records and to distribute those Phonograph Records in the United States and Canada.

11.02   Mechanical royalties shall be payable for each Controlled Composition on Net Sales of Phonograph Records and at the following rates:

(a)

(i) On Phonograph Records sold in the United States, the rate (the "United States Mechanical Rate") for each Controlled Composition embodied thereon shall be equal to seventy-five (75%) percent of the minimum statutory royalty rate (without regard to playing time) provided for in the United States Copyright Act which is applicable to the reproduction of Musical Compositions as of the date of the delivery of the first Master hereunder embodying the Controlled Composition in question.

[(ii) Notwithstanding anything to the contrary contained in the foregoing paragraph 11.02 (a)(i), with respect to USNRC Net Sales of all Phonograph Records in fulfillment of the Recording Commitment, the United States Mechanical Rate otherwise payable under paragraph 11.01(a)(i) above shall escalate to eighty-seven and one-half (87 ?%) of the United States Mechanical Rate on such sales in excess of five-hundred thousand (500,000) units and to one hundred (100%) of the U.S. Mechanical Rate percent on such sales in excess of one million (1,000,000) units.]

(b) On Phonograph Records sold in Canada, the rate (the "Canadian Mechanical Rate") for each Controlled Composition embodied thereon shall be equal to seventy-five (75%) percent of the prevailing rate agreed upon by the Canadian recording industry and the Canadian music publishing industry or its mechanical collection representative which is applicable to the reproduction of Musical Compositions as of the date of delivery to Company of the first Master hereunder embodying the Controlled Composition in question or, if earlier, as of the date that is sixty (60) days prior to the date upon which that first Master was required to be delivered hereunder; provided, however, in no event shall the Canadian Mechanical Rate be greater than the applicable United States Mechanical Rate.

11.03   Notwithstanding the foregoing:

(a)

(i) The mechanical royalty rate for a Controlled Composition contained on a Mid-Priced Record or a Budget Record shall be three-fourths (3/4) of the United States Mechanical Rate or the Canadian Mechanical Rate, as applicable. The mechanical royalty rate on a Controlled Composition, which is a copyrighted arrangement of a public domain work, shall be one-half (?) of the United States Mechanical Rate or the Canadian Mechanical Rate, as applicable. No mechanical royalties shall be payable on any Phonograph Records for which no royalties are payable pursuant to Article 9 above. No mechanical royalties shall be payable on any Controlled Composition having a playing time of less than ninety (90) seconds.

(ii) If ASCAP or BMI accords regular performance credit for any Controlled Composition which is an arranged version of a public domain work, the Mechanical Royalty rate on that Composition will be apportioned according to the same ratio used by ASCAP or BMI in determining the performance credit. Company will not be required to pay you at that rate unless you furnish Company with satisfactory evidence of that ratio.

(b) The maximum aggregate mechanical royalty rate for all Selections, including Controlled Compositions, contained on a Phonograph Record for sales in the United States or Canada shall be the product of (1): the United States Mechanical Rate (as set forth in paragraph 11.02(a)(i) above) or the Canadian Mechanical Rate, as applicable, for the first Master recorded in connection with the particular Album or EP project concerned and (2): eleven (11) for Albums (containing one (1) or more discs or the tape equivalent), five (5) for EPs, three (3) for Long-Play Singles and two (2) for

Singles, regardless of the number of Selections contained thereon. If the aggregate mechanical royalty rate applicable to all of the Selections embodied on any Phonograph Record hereunder shall exceed the applicable maximum aggregate royalty rate set forth above for that Phonograph Record, then the aggregate mechanical royalty rate for the Controlled Compositions, if any, contained thereon shall be reduced by an amount equal to such excess. If the aggregate mechanical royalty rate applicable to all of the Selections embodied on that Phonograph Record shall, even as reduced in accordance with the immediately preceding sentence, still exceed the applicable maximum aggregate mechanical royalty rate for that Phonograph Record, then you shall, upon Company's demand, pay Company an amount equal to the additional mechanical royalties payable as a result of that excess and Company may, in addition to all of Company's other rights or remedies, deduct that amount from any monies payable by Company hereunder or under any other agreement between you and Company or Company's affiliates.

11.04 Company will compute Mechanical Royalties on Controlled Compositions as of the end of each calendar quarter-annual period in which there are sales or returns of Records on which mechanical royalties are payable to you. On the next May 15th, August 15th, November 15th, or February 15th, Company will send a statement covering those royalties and will pay any net royalties which are due. Mechanical Royalty reserves maintained against anticipated returns and credits will not be held for an unreasonable period of time; retention of a reserve for two (2) years after it is established will not be considered unreasonable in any case. If any overpayment of mechanical royalties is made to any Person you will reimburse Company for it; Company may also recoup it from any payments due or becoming due to you. If Company pays any mechanical royalties on Records which are returned later, those royalties will be considered overpayments. If the total amount of the mechanical royalties which Company pays on any Record consisting of Master Recordings made under this agreement (including mechanical royalties for Compositions which are not Controlled Compositions) is higher than the limit fixed for that Record under subparagraph 11.03(b), that excess amount will be considered an overpayment also. Paragraphs 10.04 and 10.05 will apply to mechanical royalty accountings.

11.05 You shall, upon Company's request, cause the issuance to Company and Company's designees of mechanical licenses to reproduce on Phonograph Records Selections which are not Controlled Compositions and to distribute those Phonograph Records in the United States and Canada. Those mechanical licenses shall be at rates and on terms no less favorable to Company and Company's designees than those contained in the standard mechanical license issued by the Harry Fox Agency, Inc. or any successor with respect to Phonograph Records distributed in the United States and by CMRRA or any successor with respect to Phonograph Records distributed in Canada; provided, however, in no event shall those rates exceed one hundred (100%) percent of the applicable minimum statutory rates set forth in paragraph 11.02 above. You shall also, upon Company's request, cause the issuance to Company and Company's designees of mechanical licenses to reproduce Selections on Phonograph Records hereunder and to distribute those Phonograph Records outside the United States and Canada on terms no less favorable to Company and Company's designees than those generally applicable to Phonograph Record manufacturers in each country in question. The obligation to account and pay mechanical royalties on sales of Phonograph Records outside of the United States shall be that of Company's licensees.

11.06   If the copyright in any Controlled Composition is owned or controlled by a person, firm or corporation other than you, you shall cause that person, firm or corporation to grant to Company and Company's designees the same rights as you are required to grant to Company and Company's designees pursuant to this paragraph.

11.07   You hereby grant to Company and Company's designees at no fee, royalty, or other cost to Company or Company's designees, the irrevocable, non-exclusive, worldwide right to reproduce and publicly perform each Controlled Composition on Audiovisual Recordings, to distribute Audiovisual Records embodying those Audiovisual Recordings, and to otherwise exploit in any manner and through any media those Audiovisual Recordings. You shall, upon Company's request, cause the issuance to Company and Company's designees, at no fee, royalty, or other cost to Company or Company's designees, the irrevocable, non-exclusive, worldwide right to reproduce and publicly perform each Selection which is not a Controlled Composition on Audiovisual Recordings and to distribute Audiovisual Records embodying those Audiovisual Recordings, and to otherwise exploit in any manner or media those Audiovisual Recordings. If Company or Company's designees shall pay any such fee, royalty, or other cost, you shall, upon Company's demand, pay Company the amount thereof, and Company may, in addition to all of Company's other rights and remedies, deduct that amount from any monies payable by Company hereunder or under any other agreement between you and Company or Company's affiliates. Without limiting the generality of the foregoing, it is understood and agreed that Company's rights under this paragraph 11.07 include the right to reproduce and publicly perform, at no fee, royalty or other cost to Company or Company's designees, Controlled Compositions and Non-Controlled Compositions in television and/or radio commercials advertising Phonograph Records made hereunder.

11.08   Any assignment, license or other agreement made with respect to Controlled Compositions shall be subject to the terms hereof.

12.   AUDIOVISUAL RECORDINGS.

12.01   Upon Company's request, you shall cause the Artist to appear for the making of Audiovisual Recordings embodying the Artist's performances on the following terms:

(a) Company shall designate the Musical Compositions which shall be embodied in the Audiovisual Recordings (Company shall consult in good faith with you with respect to such designation; provided, Company's inadvertent failure to so consult shall not be deemed a breach hereof). You and Company shall mutually designate the director, storyboard and script of each Audiovisual Recording. You and Company will mutually designate the producer of the Audiovisual Recordings, all other individuals rendering services in connection with the production of the Audiovisual Recordings, and the locations at and the dates on which the Audiovisual Recordings shall be produced. Provided you are in compliance with your material obligations hereunder, with respect to each Committed Album hereunder, Company agrees to produce one (1) Audiovisual Recording embodying a Master contained on the applicable Committed Album.

(b) Company shall pay the Audiovisual Production Costs in an amount not in excess of a written budget approved by Company in writing. The Audiovisual Production Costs shall mean and include all minimum union scale payments made by Company to the Artist in connection with the production of the Audiovisual Recordings, all payments which are made by Company to any other individuals rendering services in connection with the production of the Audiovisual Recordings, all other payments which are made by Company pursuant to any applicable law or regulation or the provisions of any collective bargaining agreement between Company and any union or guild (including, without limitation, payroll taxes and payments to union pension and welfare funds), all amounts paid or incurred by Company for studio, hall, location or set rentals, tape, film, other stock, engineering, editing, instrument rentals and cartage, transportation and accommodations, wardrobes, immigration clearances, any so-called "per diems" for any individuals (including the Artist) rendering services in connection with the production of the Audiovisual Recordings, together with all other amounts paid or incurred by Company in connection with the production of the Audiovisual Recordings. To the extent permissible under applicable union agreements, you and Artist hereby waive any right to be paid union scale payments in connection with the production of Audiovisual Recordings. The Audiovisual Production Costs shall constitute Advances hereunder and shall be recoupable as set forth in paragraph 12(f) hereof.

(c) The Audiovisual Recordings shall be produced in accordance with the rules and regulations of all labor unions and guilds having jurisdiction over the production thereof.

(d) You shall cause the Artist to fully cooperate with Company and Company's designees and to perform to the best of the Artist's ability in connection with the production of the Audiovisual Recordings.

(e) If the Audiovisual Production Costs exceed the budget approved by Company in writing as a result of any cause which is within your or the Artist's control, or if you or the Artist shall for any reason whatsoever delay the commencement of or not be available for any scheduled appearance by you or the Artist relating to the production of the Audiovisual Recordings, you shall, upon Company's demand, pay to Company an amount equal to the expenses or charges paid or incurred by Company by reason thereof. Company may, without limiting its other rights and remedies, deduct that amount from any monies payable by Company hereunder or under any other agreement between you and Company or Company's affiliates.

(f) One Hundred (100%) percent of the aggregate amount of Audiovisual Production Costs shall be recoupable from any and all monies payable to you from the exploitation of Audiovisual Recordings hereunder. Fifty (50%) percent of the Audiovisual Production Costs for each Audiovisual Recording may be recouped from your royalties on sales of Records which do not reproduce visual images or other exploitations of audio Master Recordings ("audio royalties").

12.02 Company shall be the sole owner of all worldwide rights in and to each Audiovisual Recording (including the worldwide copyrights therein and thereto). Without limiting the generality of the foregoing, it is understood and agreed that Company's rights to use your name and the name, likeness, and other identification of the Artist and biographical material concerning the Artist in the Audiovisual Recordings are set forth in Articles 6 and 7 hereof, wherein the terms "Master Recordings" and "Phonograph Records" shall include Audiovisual Recordings and Audiovisual Records, respectively.

Section Twelve should cover "covered videos" only. The company is requiring full ownership yet they are asking the artist to not only pay for the production costs, but also allow 50% of the cost of each video to be recouped from your audio royalty account! Tough negotiations are necessary and a new artist may have to accept this.

13. WARRANTIES, REPRESENTATIONS AND COVENANTS.

You hereby warrant, represent and covenant that:

13.01   You have the right and power and capacity to enter into this Agreement, to grant the rights granted by you to Company hereunder, and to perform all of the terms hereof, and you have not done and shall not do anything that will impair Company's rights hereunder. Without limiting the generality of the foregoing, no Musical Composition or any other material recorded by the Artist shall be subject to any re-recording or other restrictions.

Add the sentence "Except those listed below:" and then list all prior recordings made for other record companies, as the artist may have recorded for another label.

13.02   During the Term you and Artist shall become and remain members in good standing of any labor union or guilds with which Company may at any time have an agreement lawfully requiring your or the Artist's membership.

13.03

(a) All recording sessions for the Masters shall be conducted in all respects in accordance with the terms of the AF of M Phonograph Record Labor Agreement, of the AFTRA Code for the Phonograph Industry, and of the agreements with all other labor unions and guilds having jurisdiction over the recording of the Masters.

(b) The information supplied by you pursuant to paragraph 4.03(b) above constitutes an accurate and complete listing of all individuals, vocalists, musicians and other performers whose performances are in fact embodied in such Masters and a corresponding description of the specified vocal, musical and/or other performances actually performed by each such person and embodied on such Masters.

13.04

(a) Your and Artist's names, masters, Selections embodied on masters and/or materials supplied to Company by you hereunder will not violate or infringe upon any common law or statutory right of any person, including, without limitation, any contractual rights, copyrights, rights of privacy, rights of publicity, trademark rights and rights to trade names. Neither you nor Artist shall "interpolate", "quote from," "sample", "borrow" or otherwise adapt any copyrighted music, copyrighted spoken words, copyrighted sounds, copyrighted words, copyrighted selections and/or copyrighted sound recordings (including, without limitation, any sounds accompanying copyrighted audiovisual works) owned or controlled by third parties in Masters ("Embodied Copyrighted Materials") without having first obtained the written consent of the applicable copyright proprietors of such Embodied Copyrighted Materials, and your failure to obtain such written consents shall be deemed a material breach of this Agreement; provided, always, that if Company, in the exercise of its reasonable business judgment, believes that Embodied Copyrighted Materials exist without such written consent from the applicable copyright proprietors, Company may withhold monies and/or royalties otherwise payable to you hereunder in amounts reasonably related to potential third party liability as a result thereof.

(b) You are the sole owner of the professional name(s) "_____" and no other Person has or will have the right to use such name in connection with Records during the Term other than Company. You shall not use a different name in connection with Records unless you and Company mutually agree in writing. You agree that Company may cause a search(es) to be instituted to determine whether there have been any third party uses for Record purposes of such name. Company may cause a federal application to USA federal registration of the name to be made in your favor for Record and/or entertainment purposes. You and Artist agree that, with respect to each such name, any and all amounts expended by Company pursuant to this paragraph will be deemed Advances. If the aforesaid search(es) indicate(s) that such name should not be used, Company and you shall mutually agree upon a substitute name for Artist. Nothing contained herein shall release you from your indemnification of Company in respect of Company's use of such name.

13.05

(a) There are no recordings embodying the Artist's performances which have not heretofore been commercially released in the Territory on Phonograph Records.

(b) Neither you nor Artist has heretofore granted any rights in and to any Controlled Composition to any music publisher or any other person.

Add the sentence "Except those listed below:" and then list all prior recordings made for other record companies, as the artist may have recorded for another label.

13.06   Neither you nor the Artist shall at any time, directly or indirectly, give or offer to give any consideration of any kind to any radio or television station or network, to any employee thereof, or to any person, firm, or corporation controlling or influencing that station or network's programming for the purpose of securing the broadcast or promotion of any Phonograph Records hereunder.

13.07   Except as otherwise specifically provided herein, Company shall have no obligation hereunder or otherwise to pay any person, firm, or corporation any amounts in connection with the exercise of any of Company's rights hereunder, including, without limitation, Company's rights with respect to the recording or exploitation of Master Recordings.

13.08   Artist has reached the age of majority prior to the date hereof.

13.09   You and Artist hereby waive any so-called "moral rights" you may have in the Masters and Records produced hereunder.

13.10   The Masters shall be free of any and all liens or and encumbrances.

13.11   Company's knowledge of facts which if true would constitute a breach of any warranty, representation or covenant made by you hereunder shall not impair or otherwise affect Company's entitlement to indemnification pursuant to paragraph 20 below or its other remedies hereunder.

[DRAFTING NOTE: IF NEITHER GRANTOR NOR ANY MEMBER OF ARTIST IS, AT THE TIME OF EXECUTION, A CLAIFORNIA RESIDENT, ADD THE FOLLOWING, AND DELETE BRACKETS WHERE APPROPRIATE:

10.11   Grantor warrants and represents that, as of the date hereof, neither Grantor nor [any member of] Artist is a resident of the Sate of California. Grantor shall notify PRI immediately in the event that Grantor and/or [any member of] Artist becomes a resident of the State of California.]

14. RECORDING RESTRICTIONS.

14.01   During the Term neither you nor the Artist shall enter into any agreement or make any commitment which would interfere with your or the Artist's performance of any of the terms hereof nor shall the Artist perform for or render services in connection with the recording of any Master Recordings for any person, firm, or corporation other than Company. After the expiration or termination of the Term, the Artist shall not, prior to the later of the following dates, perform for any person, firm or corporation other than us, for the purpose of making Phonograph Records or Master Recordings, any Selection which shall have been recorded hereunder or under any other agreement between you and Company or Company's affiliates: (a) the date five (5) years subsequent to the date on which that Selection shall have been last delivered to Company in a Master Recording recorded hereunder, or (b) the date three (3) years subsequent to the expiration or termination of the Term (the later date in respect of any Selection being hereinafter sometimes referred to as the "Restriction Date"). Notwithstanding the foregoing, if any Selection recorded hereunder is not released on Records as of the date which is one (1) year after the expiration of the Term hereof, the Restriction Date for such selection shall be one (1) year after the expiration of the Term hereof.

If possible, negotiate fewer years.

14.02   Neither you nor the Artist shall at any time manufacture, distribute, sell or authorize the manufacture, distribution, or sale by any person, firm, or corporation other than Company of Phonograph Records embodying (a) any performance rendered by the Artist during the Term or (b) any performance rendered by the Artist after the expiration or termination of the Term of a Selection recorded hereunder if that performance shall have been rendered prior to the Restriction Date applicable to that Selection. Furthermore, neither you nor the Artist shall record or authorize or knowingly permit to be recorded for any purpose any such performance without in each case taking reasonable measures to prevent the manufacture, distribution, or sale at any time by any person, firm, or corporation other than Company of Phonograph Records embodying that performance. Specifically, but without limiting the generality of the foregoing, if during the Term the Artist performs any Selection or if after the Term the Artist performs any Selection prior to the Restriction Date applicable thereto, neither you nor the Artist will authorize or knowingly permit that Selection to be recorded unless pursuant to a written contract containing an express provision that neither that performance nor the recording thereof will be used directly or indirectly for the purpose of making Phonograph Records. Upon Company's request, you shall promptly deliver to Company a copy of the pertinent provisions of each such contract and you shall cooperate fully with Company in any controversy which may arise or litigation which may be instituted relating to Company's rights pursuant to this paragraph.

14.03

(a) During the Term, the Artist will not render any musical performances (audiovisual or otherwise) for the purposes of making any motion picture or other audiovisual work ("Picture", below) for any person, firm or corporation other than us, and no other person, firm or corporation other than Company will be authorized to produce, distribute, exhibit, or otherwise exploit any Picture which contains any musical performance (audiovisual or otherwise) by the Artist, without an express written agreement providing that:

(i) the Picture concerned will not contain performances by the Artist of more than two (2) Musical Compositions, in whole or in part; and

(ii) not more than one-half (?) of any version of the Picture may consist of featured musical performances (defined below) by the Artist or anyone else.

(b) "Featured musical performance", in this paragraph, means: any visual performance of a Musical Composition; and any background performance of a Musical Composition which is intended as a focus of audience attention, whether or not the visual matter is related dramatically to the lyrics or concept of the Musical Composition.

This clause not only deals with feature films, but also with commercials. The company is protecting itself from being excluded from revenue streams.

14.04 You may perform as a background musician ("sideman") accompanying a featured artist for the purpose of making Phonograph Records for others, provided:

(a) You have then fulfilled all of your material obligations under this Agreement, and the engagement does not interfere with the continuing prompt performance of your material obligations to Company.

(b)

(i) You will not render a solo or "step-out" performance; and

(ii) The musical style of the recording will not be so substantially similar to the characteristic musical style of Recordings made by you for Company so as to be likely to cause confusion with such Recordings.

(c) You will not record any material which you have then recorded for Company, and will not agree to be restricted from recording the same material for Company.

(d) You will not accept the sideman engagement unless the Person for whom the recordings are being made agrees in writing, for Company's benefit, that:

(i) Your name may be used in a courtesy credit to Company on the Album liners used for such Records, in the same position as the credits accorded to other sidemen and in type identical in size, prominence and all other respects; and

(ii) Except as expressly provided in section 15.03(d)(i) above, neither your name (or any similar name), nor any picture, portrait or likeness of you will be used in connection with such Recordings, including, without limitation, on the front covers of Album containers, on sleeves or labels used for Singles, or in videos, advertising, publicity or any other for of promotion or exploitation, without Company's express written consent, which Company may withhold in its unrestricted discretion.

(e) Before you accept the sideman engagement you will notify Company of the name of the Person for whom the recordings are being made and the record Company which will have the right to distribute Records. Your notice will be addressed to Company's Executive Vice President, Business Affairs.

The purpose of this clause is to prevent the artist from being a featured artist on a record that is not his or her own. However, it also prevents the artist from acting as a sideman or a producer and should be negotiated out of the contract.

15. [THERE IS NO ARTICLE 15]

16. UNIQUE SERVICES.

16.01   You expressly acknowledge that your and the Artist's services hereunder are of a special, unique, intellectual, and extraordinary character which gives them peculiar value, and that in the event of a breach by you or the Artist of any term hereof, Company will be caused irreparable injury which cannot adequately be compensated by money damages. Accordingly, Company shall be entitled to injunctive relief, in addition to any other rights or remedies, which Company may have, to enforce the terms of this Agreement.

In this clause, insert the word "seek," before "injunctive relief ..."

16.02 You acknowledge that your failure to timely complete your Delivery obligation will jeopardize Company's investment in the Artist in that it may adversely affect Artist's career and appearance in the public eye and will have an adverse impact upon Company's ability to properly market and promote records embodying Artist's performances and to build Artist's career. You further acknowledge that Company relies upon timely Delivery in order to establish its release schedule and marketing and promotional policies; that failure to timely Deliver adversely affects Company's ability to support its overhead costs, promotional costs and other expenditures necessary to properly record, promote and market phonograph records; and that such failure to timely Deliver will cause Company substantial damages in an amount not readily susceptible of computation.

Insert word "may" adversely affect the company's ability.........

17. CERTAIN REMEDIES.

17.01 If you do not fulfill any portion of your Recording Commitment within thirty (30) days after the time prescribed in paragraph 3.02, Company will have the following options:

(a) to suspend Company's obligations to make payments to you under this Agreement until you have cured the default;

(b) to terminate the term of this Agreement at any time, whether or not you have commenced curing the default before such termination occurs; and

(c) to require you to repay to Company the amount, not then recouped, of any Advance previously paid to you by Company and not specifically attributable under Article 8 to an Album which has actually been fully Delivered. You will not be required to repay any such Advance to the extent to which you furnish Company with documentation satisfactory to Company establishing that you have actually used the Advance to make payments, to parties not affiliated with you or Artist and in which neither you nor the Artist has any interest, for recording costs incurred in connection with the Album concerned before Company's demand for payment. ("recording costs", in the preceding sentence, means items which would constitute Recording Costs if paid or incurred by Company.)

Company may exercise each of those options by sending you the appropriate notice. If Company terminates the term under clause 17.01(b) all parties will be deemed to have fulfilled all of their obligations under this agreement except those obligations which survive the end of the term (such as indemnification obligations, re-recording restrictions, and your obligations under clause 17.01(c)). No exercise of an option under this paragraph will limit Company's rights to recover damages by reason of your default, its rights to exercise any other option under this paragraph, or any of its other rights.

17.02 If because of: act of God; inevitable accident; fire; lockout, strike or other labor dispute; riot or civil commotion; act of public enemy; enactment, rule, order or act of any government or governmental instrumentality (whether federal, state, local or foreign);

failure of technical facilities; illness or incapacity of any performer or producer; or other cause of a similar or different nature not reasonably within Company's control; Company is materially hampered in the recording, manufacture, distribution or sale of records, then, without limiting Company's rights, Company shall have the option by giving you notice to suspend the running of the then-current Contract Period for the duration of any such contingency plus such additional time as is necessary so that Company shall have no less than thirty (30) days after the cessation of such contingency in which to exercise its option, if any, to extend the term of this agreement for the next following Option Period.

17.03   If Company refuses, without cause, to permit you to fulfill your minimum Recording Commitment for any Contract Period, (irrespective of whether or not you have commenced recording the particular Album for such Recording Commitment), other than as a result of an event or contingency referred to in paragraph 17.01 above, Company shall have no obligations or liabilities to you in connection therewith unless you shall notify Company of your desire to fulfill your minimum Recording Commitment for that Contract Period and within thirty (30) days after Company's receipt of that notice Company shall fail to advise you in writing that Company shall permit you to fulfill your minimum Recording Commitment for that Contract Period. If Company shall fail to so advise you in writing that Company shall permit you to fulfill your minimum Recording Commitment for that Contract Period, the Term shall expire as of the end of that thirty (30) day period and Company shall have no obligations or liabilities to you whatsoever in connection with Company's failure to permit you to fulfill your Recording Commitment for that Contract Period. Company shall, however, pay you promptly after the expiration of that thirty (30) day period, as an advance recoupable from royalties hereunder, with respect to your Recording Commitment for the Initial Period, the sum of Twenty Thousand ($20,000) Dollars, less any Advances or other monies already paid to you in connection with such Recording Commitment; and with respect to the First and any subsequent Option Period, an amount equal to the difference between the applicable Recording Fund minimum set forth in paragraph 8.02(a) for the Album then remaining unrecorded of your Recording Commitment for the Contract Period during which such termination occurs less one hundred (100%) percent of the Recording Costs for the last Committed Album recorded by you hereunder, less any Advances or other monies already paid to you in connection with such Recording Commitment; provided, however, in no event shall Company be obligated to so pay to you more than an amount equal to one-third (1/3) of the Recording Fund minimum for the Album then remaining unrecorded of your Recording Commitment for the Contract Period during which such termination occurs.

All negotiable if not struck entirely.

18. PRODUCER AND OTHER ROYALTIES.

18.01   You shall be solely responsible for and shall pay all royalties and other Compensation which may be payable to any producers of the Masters or to any others rendering services in connection with the recording of the Masters.

18.02   Notwithstanding the foregoing, Company may (but shall not be obligated to) enter into an agreement with any producer (or other royalty participant) of the Masters which provides for the payment by Company, rather than you, of royalties or other compensation payable to that producer. In that event (or in the event Company pays any such party pursuant to a letter of direction) Company may deduct any amounts payable by Company to that producer or director from any royalties or other sums payable by Company hereunder or under any other agreement between you and Company or Company's affiliates. Furthermore, for the purposes of the recoupment of any Advances or charges under this Agreement, the royalty rates contained in Article 9 with respect to those Masters shall be deemed reduced by the amount of the applicable royalty rates with respect to Masters which are contained in Company's agreement with any producer (or such party). Any Advances payable by Company to a producer (or such party) which are not recouped by Company from royalties payable to that producer may be recouped by Company from any royalties or other sums payable by Company hereunder or under any other agreement between you and Company or Company's affiliates.

This is an "all in deal."

19. DEFINITIONS.

19.01   The term "Advance" shall mean prepayment of royalties. Company may recoup Advances from royalties to be paid to you or on your behalf pursuant to this Agreement. Except as otherwise set forth herein, Advances shall be non-refundable.

19.02   The term "Album" shall mean an audio only long-playing Phonograph Record which is not an EP, Single, or Long-Play Single, and where the context requires, Master Recordings sufficient to constitute a long-playing audio only Phonograph Record.

19.03   The term "Audiovisual Record" shall mean a Record embodying an Audiovisual Recording. Without limiting the generality of the foregoing, any CD-ROM Record or other interactive audiovisual Record which is not intended primarily for audio playback shall be deemed to be an Audiovisual Record hereunder. For purposes of the preceding sentence, so-called "enhanced CDs" and CD-Plus Records are intended primarily for audio playback.

19.04   The term "Audiovisual Recording" shall mean every form of Master Recording embodying visual images.

19.05   The term "Container Charge" shall mean the applicable percentage, specified as follows, of the Gross Royalty Base applicable to the particular Record concerned: twelve and one-half (12 ?%) percent for Singles packaged in color or other special printed sleeves, and for Albums, EPs, and Long-Playing Singles in disc form packaged in Company's standard singlefold jackets without any special elements (such as, but not limited to, plastic, cardboard, or printed inner sleeves, inserts, or attachments); seventeen (17%) percent thereof for all other Albums, EPs or Long-Playing Singles in disc form, and for all other sound-only Phonograph Records in disc form; and twenty (20%) percent thereof for Audiovisual Records, all Phonograph Records in tape form, such as reel-to-reel tapes, cartridges, cassettes (whether audio or video) and for all other recorded devices, but twenty-five (25%) percent for compact disc Records and all New Media Records.

The container charge for the standard configuration is 25% here and the artist should try to negotiate.

19.06   The term "Contract Period" shall mean the Initial Period or any Option Period of the Term (as they may be suspended or extended).

19.07   The term "Controlled Composition" shall mean a Musical Composition or other Selection, written or composed by you, the Artist, any producer of the Masters, or any other persons engaged by you in connection with the production of Masters, in whole or in part, alone or in collaboration with others, or which is owned or controlled, in whole or in part, directly or indirectly, by you, the Artist or any person firm or corporation in which you or the Artist have a direct or indirect interest.

19.08   The terms "Conventional Phonograph Record", "Conventional discs and tapes" and "Conventional Album" shall refer to discs or tapes of the quality used for the majority of units of a particular Phonograph Record released. If, at any particular time, Company has ceased to regularly manufacture plain, black "vinyl" disc records and only manufactures tapes, compact discs and/or "premium vinyl" (e.g., so-called "half-speed mastered") discs, then the terms "Conventional discs" or "Conventional Album in disc form", and the like, shall refer to conventional tapes.

19.09   The term "Delivery" or "delivery to Company" (or "Delivery to Company") or words of similar connotation used in connection with Master Recordings or Masters shall mean delivery to a person designated by Company at such location or locations designated by Company of fully-mixed, leadered, sequenced, equalized and unequalized master tapes in proper form for the production of the parts necessary to manufacture phonograph records therefrom, which Masters have been approved by Company as commercially and technically satisfactory for the manufacture and sale of Phonograph Records, and delivery to a person designated by Company at such location or locations designated by Company of all consents, approvals, copy information, credits, mechanical licenses and other material and documents (including those described in paragraph 4.03(b) above) required by Company to release Phonograph Records embodying those Master Recordings or Masters and to manufacture album covers or other packaging therefor. Company may (but shall not be obligated to) send you written notice of the date which Company deems to be the applicable date of Delivery to Company of any Master Recordings made hereunder. If you dispute the date of such notice, you shall give notice in writing to Company within ten (10) business days of Company's notice to you. Your failure to so notify Company shall be deemed your acceptance of the date contained in Company's notice. The sending of Company's notice shall be without prejudice to Company's rights and remedies hereunder if Company later discovers that such delivery has not been fully and completely made. Company's election to make a payment to you which was to have been made upon Delivery of Master Recordings or to release a Record derived from such Master Recording shall not be deemed to be its acknowledgement that such "Delivery" was properly made and Company shall not be deemed to have waived either its right to require such complete and proper performance thereafter or its remedies for your failure to perform in accordance therewith.

19.10   The term "EP" shall mean an audio only Phonograph Record embodying no fewer than five (5) different Musical Compositions and no more than seven (7) different Musical Compositions.

19.11   The term "Long-Play Single" shall mean an audio only Phonograph Record embodying no more than four (4) different Musical Compositions.

19.12   The term "Master Recording" shall mean every form of recording, whether now known or unknown, embodying sound, or sound accompanied by visual images.

19.13   The term "Masters" shall mean Master Recordings embodying the performances of the Artist recorded hereunder.

19.14

(a) The term "Mid-Priced Record" shall mean a Phonograph Record which bears a Gross Royalty Base at least twenty (20%) percent lower, but not more than thirty-five (35%) percent lower than the Gross Royalty Base applicable to Company's then-current highest prevailing "top-line" record of comparable repertoire and in the same configuration (e.g., Album, Multiple Record Set, Long Play Single, tape cassette, compact disc, etc.) released by Company or Company's licensees in the territory concerned.

(b) The term "Budget Record" shall mean a Phonograph Record which bears a Gross Royalty Base greater than thirty-five (35%) percent lower than the Gross Royalty Base applicable to Company's then-current highest prevailing "top line" record of comparable repertoire and in the same configuration (e.g., Album, Multiple Record Set, Long Play Single, tape cassette, compact disc, etc.) released by Company or Company's licensees in the territory concerned.

19.15   The term "Multiple Album" shall mean an Album which contains two (2) or more units of a particular configuration of Record, which is sold as a single unit.

19.16   The terms "Musical Composition" and "Composition" shall mean a single musical composition and, for the purposes of computing mechanical royalties hereunder, shall include medleys and spoken word pieces. Different versions of a Composition embodied on the same Phonograph Record will be considered one (1) Composition (and one(1) Selection) for all purposes hereunder.

19.17   The term "Net Receipts" shall mean an amount equal to the gross monies received by Company in the United States from a person, firm or corporation from the exploitation by that person, firm or corporation of rights in Audiovisual Recordings (including any monies received by Company for the use of Audiovisual Recordings in

Audiovisual Records) less thirty (30%) percent of those gross monies as a distribution fee, and less all costs paid or incurred by Company in connection with the exploitation of those rights and the collection of those monies.

19.18   The term "Net Royalty" or "Net Flat Fee" shall mean the gross royalty or gross flat fee received by Company in the United States from a person, firm or corporation from the exploitation by that person, firm or corporation of rights in Masters (other than Audiovisual Recordings), less all costs paid or incurred by Company in connection with the exploitation of those rights and the collection of those monies, and less all royalties or other sums payable by Company to any person, firm or corporation in connection with the exploitation of those rights, except for royalties or other sums payable to producers of those Masters, which shall be borne solely by you.

19.19   The term "Net Sales" shall mean gross sales to wholesale and retail customers, less returns, credits and reserves against anticipated returns and credits.

19.20   The term "through Normal Retail Channels" shall refer to sales of Phonograph Records hereunder other than as described in paragraphs 9.03, 9.04, 9.05 (other than subsection (b) thereof), 9.06, 9.07 and 9.08 above;

19.21   The terms "Phonograph Record" and "Record" shall mean every form of reproduction, transmission or communication of Master Recordings, whether now known or unknown, embodying sound alone, or sound accompanied by visual images, distributed, transmitted or communicated primarily for home use, school use, jukebox use, and use in means of transportation, including, without limitation, discs of any speed or size, reel-to-reel tapes, cartridges, cassettes, or other pre-recorded tapes.

19.22   The term "New Media Records" shall mean Records in the following configurations: mini-discs, digital compact cassettes, digital audio tapes, laser discs, digital compact discs capable of bearing visual images (including, without limitation, CD-Plus and CD-ROM) and other Records embodying, employing or otherwise utilizing any non-analog technology, whether such Records are interactive (i.e. the user is able to access, select or manipulate the materials therein) or non-interactive, and whether now known or hereafter devised, but specifically excluding audio-only compact discs.

19.23   The term "Royalty Base Price" shall mean the amount specified below ("Gross Royalty Base") applicable to the Records concerned, less all excise, purchase, value added, or similar taxes (included in the Royalty Base Price) and less the applicable Container Charge:

(a) With respect to Records (other than Audiovisual Records) sold for distribution in the United States, the "Gross Royalty Base" shall be the suggested retail list price ("SRLP") for such Record; or if there is no SRLP, the lowest wholesale price payable by the largest category of Company's (or its distributor's) customers in the normal course of business with respect to such Records sold for distribution during the applicable semi-annual accounting period, multiplied by an "up-lift" of one hundred thirty (130%) percent.

(b) With respect to Records sold for distribution outside of the United States, the

"Gross Royalty Base" shall be the same royalty base price on which Company is accounted to by its licensee in the country concerned provided that Company is accounted to based on the SRLP of such Records in the country concerned, or a substitute for an actual or hypothetical retail price ("Retail-Related Price"). If Company is accounted to based on a royalty base price other than a Retail-Related Price, the "Gross Royalty Base" for such Records shall be the published price to dealers ("ppd") in the country concerned for such Records, multiplied by an "up-lift" of one hundred twenty-six (126%) percent.

(c) With respect to Audiovisual Records, "Gross Royalty Base" shall mean Company's (or its distributor's) published wholesale price as of the commencement of the accounting period concerned.

19.24   The term "Selection" shall mean a Musical Composition, poem, dramatic work, comedy routine, or other verbal expression.

19.25   The term "Single" shall mean an audio-only seven (7") inch disc Phonograph Record or its tape or other equivalent, embodying no more than two (2) Compositions.

19.26   The term "Territory" shall mean the universe.

19.27   The term "other agreement between you and Company or Company's affiliates" and like words shall mean any other agreement between you, Artist or any entity furnishing Artist's services and Company or Company's affiliates which relates to recordings embodying Artist's performances.

19.28   The term "Person" "person" or "Party" shall mean any individual, corporation, partnership, association or other organized group of persons or the legal successors or representatives of the foregoing.

19.29   Notwithstanding paragraphs 19.02, 19.10, 19.11 and 19.25 above, if a particular record is marketed and priced by Company or its Licensees as a particular configuration of record (e.g., Single, Long-Play Single, EP, etc.), then, for royalty purposes only, such record shall be deemed to be such form of configuration.

20. INDEMNITY.

20.01   You hereby indemnify, save, and hold Company harmless from any and all damages, liabilities, costs, losses and expenses (including legal costs and reasonable attorneys' fees) arising out of or connected with any claim, demand or action which is inconsistent with any of the warranties, representations, covenants or agreements made by you in this Agreement, which has resulted in a final judgment or has been settled with your written consent (it being understood that your consent shall be deemed given to any settlement not in excess of Five Thousand ($5,000) Dollars). Notwithstanding the foregoing, if you withhold consent to any settlement which Company is willing to make, the foregoing indemnity shall apply and Company may settle such claim in its sole discretion unless you promptly assume all costs of defending against such claim, demand or action including, without limitation, court costs, reasonable attorneys' fees, and direct expenses theretofore incurred by Company in connection with said claim, demand or action; provided that in the event you assume said costs, Company shall nonetheless have the right to settle such claim, demand or action in its sole discretion without your consent, provided that, in such event, the foregoing indemnification shall not apply with respect thereto. You shall reimburse Company, on demand, for any payment made by Company at any time with respect to any damage, liability, cost, loss or expense to which the foregoing indemnity applies. Pending the determination of any claim, demand or action, Company may, at its election, withhold payment of any monies otherwise payable to you hereunder in an amount which does not exceed your potential liability to Company pursuant to this paragraph; provided, however, that if you shall deliver to Company an indemnity or surety bond, in a form and with a Company acceptable to Company, which in respect of such claim, demand or action shall cover the amount of such claim, demand or action and Company's estimated attorneys' fees and legal costs in connection therewith, then Company shall not withhold payment of monies otherwise payable to you hereunder in respect of such claim, demand or action; and provided further that Company shall liquidate any such withheld amounts if within twelve (12) months no lawsuit has been commenced and active settlement discussions are not then taking place. You may participate in the defense of any claim referred to in this paragraph 20 through counsel of your selection at your own expense, but Company will have the right at all times, in its sole discretion, to retain or resume control of the conduct of the defense of such claim.

21. ASSIGNMENT.

21.01

(a) Company shall have the right, at its election, to assign any of Company's rights hereunder, in whole or in part, to any subsidiary, affiliated, controlling or other related Company, and to any Person, firm or corporation owning or acquiring a substantial portion of Company's stock or assets, and any rights so assigned may also be assigned by the assignee. Company shall also have the right to assign any of its rights hereunder to any of its licensees in order to effectuate the purposes hereof. You shall not have the right to assign any of your rights hereunder.

It may be hard to take but non-negotiable.

(b) Notwithstanding the foregoing, you may assign your rights under this Agreement to a corporation, all of whose capital stock is owned solely by you, subject to the following conditions:

(i) The assignee will be subject to Company's approval in Company's sole discretion;

(ii) The assignment will not be effective until you have delivered to Company an instrument satisfactory to Company in Company's sole discretion effecting the assignment and the assignee's assumption of your obligations, and Company has executed that instrument to evidence Company's approval of it;

(iii) No such assignment will relieve you of your obligations under this Agreement; and

(iv) If such an assignment takes place, any further transfer of the rights assigned will be subject to the same conditions.

22. NOTICES.

22.01　All notices to be given to you hereunder and all statements and payments to be sent to you hereunder shall be addressed to you at the address set forth on page 1 hereof or at such other address as you shall designate in writing from time to time. All notices to be given to Company hereunder shall be addressed to Company to the attention of the Executive Vice President of Business Affairs at the address set forth on page 1 hereof or at such other address as Company shall designate in writing from time to time. All notices shall be in writing and shall either be served by personal delivery, mail, or telegraph, all charges prepaid. Except as otherwise provided herein, notices shall be deemed given when personally delivered, mailed, or delivered to a telegraph office, all charges prepaid, except that notices of change of address shall be effective only after actual receipt. A copy of all notices to Company shall be sent to {Name}, {Address}.

Insert in 22.01 that a courtesy copy of all notices by sent directly to the artist's attorney.

23. MISCELLANEOUS.

23.01

(a) This Agreement sets forth your and Company's entire understanding relating to its subject matter and all prior and contemporaneous understandings relating to the same have been merged herein. No modification, amendment, waiver, termination or discharge of this Agreement or any of its terms shall be binding upon Company unless confirmed by a document signed by a duly authorized officer of Company. No waiver by you or Company of any term of this Agreement or of any default hereunder shall affect your or Company's respective rights thereafter to enforce that term or to exercise any right or remedy in the event of any other default, whether or not similar.

(b) If any part of this Agreement is determined to be void, invalid, inoperative or unenforceable by a court of competent jurisdiction or by any other legally constituted body having jurisdiction to make such determination, such decision shall not affect any other provisions hereof, and the remainder of this Agreement shall be effective as though such void, invalid, inoperative or unenforceable provision had not been contained herein. If the payments provided by this Agreement shall exceed the amount permitted by any present or future law or governmental order or regulation, such stated payments shall be reduced while such limitation is in effect to the amount which is so permitted; and the payment of such amount shall be deemed to constitute full performance by Company of its obligations to you and Artist hereunder with respect to compensation during the term when such limitation is in effect.

23.02

(a) Company shall not be deemed to be in breach of any of Company's obligations hereunder unless and until you shall have given Company specific written notice by certified or registered mail, return receipt requested, describing in detail the breach and Company shall have failed to cure that breach within thirty (30) days after Company's receipt of that written notice or, if the breach cannot be cured within said thirty (30) day period, if Company does not commence to cure such breach within said thirty (30) day period and continue to so cure with reasonable diligence.

(b) Except with respect to: (i) your obligation to timely Deliver any Album hereunder, (ii) your warranties hereunder, (iii) where a specific cure provision is provided herein, (iv) breaches incapable of being cured, or (v) an application for injunctive relief, the failure by you to perform any of your obligations hereunder shall not be deemed a breach of this Agreement unless Company gives you written notice of such failure to perform and such failure is not corrected within thirty (30) days from the date you receive such notice.

23.03   Company's payment obligations under this Agreement are conditioned upon your full and faithful performance of the terms hereof.

23.04   Wherever your approval or consent is required hereunder, that approval or consent shall not be unreasonably withheld. Company may require you to formally give or withhold approval or consent by giving you notice of Company's request that you do so and by furnishing you with the information or material in respect of which the approval or consent is sought. You shall give Company written notice of your approval or disapproval or of your consent or non-consent within five (5) days after Company's notice is sent and, in the event of your disapproval or non-consent, your notice shall contain the specific reasons therefor. Your failure to give Company notice as aforesaid shall be deemed to be consent or approval, as the case may be, with respect to the matter submitted. In the event the word "you" includes members of a group, then, at Company's election, any member of the group shall have the right to give approval or consent on behalf of the entire group.

23.05   Nothing herein contained shall constitute a partnership, joint venture or other agency relationship between you and Company. Except as otherwise expressly provided herein, you and the Artist are performing your obligations hereunder as independent contractors. Neither party hereto shall hold itself out contrary to the terms of this paragraph, and neither you nor Company shall become liable for any representation, act or omission of the other contrary to the provisions hereof. You do not have the right to execute any agreement or incur any obligation for which Company may be liable or otherwise bound.

23.06   This Agreement shall not be deemed to give any right or remedy to any third party whatsoever unless that right or remedy is specifically granted by Company in writing to that third party.

23.07   The provisions of any applicable collective bargaining agreement between Company and any labor union or guild which are required by the terms of that agreement to be included in this Agreement shall be deemed incorporated herein as if those provisions were expressly set forth in this Agreement.

23.08   Except as otherwise expressly provided herein, all rights and remedies herein or otherwise shall be cumulative and none of them shall be in limitation of any other right or remedy.

23.09 **THIS AGREEMENT HAS BEEN ENTERED INTO IN THE STATE OF NEW YORK, AND ITS VALIDITY, CONSTRUCTION, INTERPRETATION AND LEGAL EFFECT SHALL BE GOVERNED BY THE LAWS OF THE STATE OF NEW YORK APPLICABLE TO CONTRACTS ENTERED INTO AND PERFORMED ENTIRELY WITHIN THE STATE OF NEW YORK. ALL CLAIMS, DISPUTES OR DISAGREEMENTS WHICH MAY ARISE OUT OF THE INTERPRETATION, PERFORMANCE OR BREACH OF THIS AGREEMENT SHALL BE SUBMITTED EXCLUSIVELY TO THE JURISDICTION OF THE STATE COURTS OF THE STATE OF NEW YORK OR THE FEDERAL DISTRICT COURTS LOCATED IN NEW YORK CITY; PROVIDED, HOWEVER, IF COMPANY IS SUED OR JOINED IN ANY OTHER COURT OR FORUM (INCLUDING AN ARBITRATION PROCEEDING) IN RESPECT OF ANY MATTER WHICH MAY GIVE RISE TO A CLAIM BY COMPANY HEREUNDER, YOU AND ARTIST CONSENT TO THE JURISDICTION OF SUCH COURT OR FORUM OVER ANY SUCH CLAIM WHICH MAY BE ASSERTED BY COMPANY. ANY PROCESS IN ANY ACTION OR PROCEEDING COMMENCED IN THE COURTS OF THE STATE OF NEW YORK ARISING OUT OF ANY SUCH CLAIM, DISPUTE OR DISAGREEMENT, MAY AMONG OTHER METHODS, BE SERVED UPON YOU BY DELIVERING OR MAILING THE SAME, VIA CERTIFIED MAIL, ADDRESSED TO YOU AT THE ADDRESS GIVEN IN THIS AGREEMENT OR SUCH OTHER ADDRESS AS YOU MAY FROM TIME TO TIME DESIGNATE BY NOTICE IN CONFORMITY WITH ARTICLE 22 HEREIN.**

23.10   This Agreement shall not become effective until signed by you and countersigned by a duly authorized officer of Company.

23.11

(a) The paragraph headings herein are solely for the purpose of convenience and shall be disregarded completely in the interpretation of this Agreement or any of its terms.

(b) No deletion, addition, revision, change or other alteration in drafts of this Agreement prepared prior to the execution of this Agreement shall be used for the purpose of construction or interpretation of any term, provision or language of this Agreement.

23.12   Company may at any time during the Term obtain, at Company's cost, insurance on the lives of one (1) or more members of the Artist. Company or its designees shall be the sole beneficiary of that insurance and neither you, nor any member of the Artist, nor any person, firm or corporation claiming rights through or from you or the Artist shall have any rights in that insurance. You shall cause those members of the Artist as Company may designate to submit to such physical examinations and to complete and deliver such forms as Company may reasonably require and otherwise to cooperate with Company fully for the purpose of enabling Company to secure that insurance.

23.13   From time to time at Company's request, you shall cause Artist to appear for photography, artwork and similar sessions under the direction of Company or Company's duly authorized agent, appear for interviews with such representatives of newspapers, magazines and other publications, and of publicity and public relations firms as

Company may arrange, and confer and consult with Company regarding Artist's performances hereunder and other matters which may concern the parties hereto. Artist shall also, if requested by Company, be available for personal appearances (including performances) on radio, television, record stores and elsewhere, and to record taped interviews, spot announcements, trailers and electrical transcriptions, all for the purpose of advertising, promoting, publicizing and exploiting records released or to be released hereunder and for other general public relations and promotional purposes related to the record business of Company or Company's subsidiary and related companies. Neither you nor Artist shall be entitled to any compensation from Company for such services, other than minimum union scale to Artist if such payment is required by applicable agreements.

23.14 Intentionally deleted.

23.15 You acknowledge that there exists no formal or informal fiduciary relationship between you and Company and that there exists no special relationship of trust and confidence between you and Company independent of the contractual rights, duties and obligations set forth in this Agreement, and that the future course of dealing between you and Company shall neither explicitly nor implicitly indicate such a relationship or the undertaking of any such extra-contractual duties or obligations by Company.

23.16 If Artist's voice should be or become materially and permanently impaired or if Artist should otherwise become physically or mentally disabled in performing, recording and/or personal appearances and/or if Artist should cease to pursue a career as an entertainer, Company may elect to terminate this agreement, by notice to you at any time during the period in which such contingency arose or continues and thereby be relieved of any liability for the executory provisions of this agreement.

24. GROUP ARTIST.

24.01.

(a) You warrant, represent and agree that, for so long as this agreement shall be in effect, Artist will perform together as a group for Company. If any individual comprising Artist refuses, neglects or fails to perform together with the other individuals comprising Artist in fulfillment of the obligations agreed to be performed under this agreement or leaves the group, you shall give Company prompt written notice thereof. (The term "leaving member" shall hereinafter be used to define each individual who leaves the group or no longer performs with the group, or each member of the group if the group disbands.) Company shall have the right, to be exercised by written notice to you within ninety (90) days following its receipt of your notice:

To continue with the services of any such leaving member pursuant to paragraph 24.04 below;

To terminate the Term of this agreement with respect to the remaining members of Artist whether or not Company has exercised its right to continue with the services of a leaving member;

To treat all the members of Artist as leaving members, and have the right to exercise its rights with respect to each in accordance with this Article 24.

(b) In the event that Company fails to send notice of its exercise of rights pursuant to paragraph 24.01(a) above, the Term of this agreement shall be deemed terminated with respect to such leaving member.

(c) If at any time Company believes or has knowledge that a member of Artist is or may be a leaving member, then Company shall have the right (but not the obligation) to exercise Company's rights in accordance with this Article 24. If Company sends a notice to you pursuant to this paragraph 24.01(c), you shall have the right, within fifteen (15) days following the date of such notice, to furnish Company with affirmative documentation that the member of Artist shall continue to fulfill such member's obligations under this agreement and remain a member of Artist. Such documentation shall be satisfactory to Company in its sole discretion and shall include, without limitation, a signed notification from the member that such member shall continue as a member of Artist. Notwithstanding anything to the contrary expressed or implied in this paragraph 24.01(c), Company's action or inaction with respect to Company's belief or knowledge that a member of Artist may be, or may become, a leaving member shall not act as a waiver of any of Company's duties, obligations, representations or warranties under this Agreement, including, but not limited to, those obligations under paragraph 24.01(a), or as a waiver of any of Company's rights or remedies under this Agreement.

Negotiate longer than fifteen days.

A leaving member, whether or not his engagement is terminated hereunder, may not perform for others for the purpose of recording any selection as to which the applicable restrictive period specified in paragraph 14.02 of this agreement has not expired.

A leaving member shall not, without Company's consent, use the professional name of the group in any commercial or artistic endeavor; the said professional name shall remain your property and the property of and those members of the group who continue to perform their obligations hereunder and whose engagements are not terminated; and, the person, if any, engaged to replace the individual whose engagement is terminated shall be mutually agreed upon by you and Company, and each such person added to Artist, as a replacement or otherwise, shall become bound by the terms and conditions of this agreement and shall execute a letter to Company in the form attached here as Exhibit A as a condition precedent to being so added. Changes in the individuals comprising Artist shall be made by mutual agreement between you and Company.

24.04   In addition to the rights provided in the preceding paragraphs, Company shall have, and you hereby grant to Company, an irrevocable option for the individual and exclusive services of each leaving member as follows: Said option, with respect to such individual, may be exercised by Company giving you notice in writing within ninety (90) days after Company receives your notice provided for in paragraph 24.01(a) above. In the event of Company's exercise of such option, you and such leaving member shall be deemed to have entered into an agreement with Company with respect to such individual's exclusive recording services upon all the terms and conditions of this agreement except that: (i) The Minimum Recording Obligation in the Initial Period shall be two (2) Sides, with a so-called "overcall" option, at Company's election, for sufficient additional Master Recordings to constitute up to one (1) Album, with an additional number (the "Number") of options granted to Company to extend the term of such agreement for consecutive option periods for one (1) Album each, each of which options shall be exercised within nine (9) months after delivery to Company of the Minimum Recording Obligation for the immediately preceding contract period of such leaving member's agreement. The Number shall be equal to the remaining number of Albums embodying performances of Artist which you would be obligated to deliver hereunder if Company exercised each of its options, but in no event shall the Number be less than four (4); (ii) the provisions contained in paragraph 8.02 shall not be applicable, but Company shall pay all Recording Costs for Master Recordings to be recorded by such individual up to the amount of the budget approved by Company therefor; (iii) Company's royalty obligation to you in respect of Recordings by such individual shall be the payment to you of the royalties computed as set forth in this agreement but at only three quarters (3/4) the rates set forth herein; (iv) Company shall be entitled to combine such leaving member's account with Artist's account hereunder; and (v) Recordings by such individual shall not be applied in diminution of your Minimum Recording Obligation as set forth in this agreement.

Remember with all recording contracts an artist signs the contract as an individual and as a group member. The company will require the complete control over who is in the group, who leaves, and who will be allowed to continue to be a recording musician. Clause twenty-four requires the member to continue his/her career with the company. Some of this is negotiable.

IN WITNESS WHEREOF, the parties hereto have this day signed in the spaces provided below.

{COMPANY}

By:_____
An Authorized Signatory

ACCEPTED AND AGREED:

_____
{ARTIST}

By:_____
An Authorized Signatory

EXHIBIT "A"

{COMPANY}

{ADDRESS}

As of {DATE}

Gentlemen:

Pursuant to an exclusive recording contract (the "Recording Contract") between _____ ("Grantor") and me, Grantor is entitled to my exclusive services as a recording artist and is the sole owner of the entire worldwide right, title and interest in and to the results and proceeds of my services as a recording artist under the Recording Contract, including, without limitation, master recordings embodying my performances and the phonograph records derived therefrom. I have been advised that Grantor is entering into a written agreement with you (the "Agreement"), pursuant to which Grantor is agreeing to furnish my services as a recording artist exclusively to you and pursuant to which you shall be the sole owner of the entire worldwide right, title and interest in and to the results and proceeds of my services as a recording artist.

In consideration of your entering into the Agreement, and as a further inducement for you to do so, it being to my benefit as a recording artist that you enter into the Agreement, I hereby represent and agree as follows:

1.

(a) I have read the Agreement in its entirety and fully understand the Agreement and all of the terms thereof were explained to me before signing this document.

(b) Grantor has the right, insofar as I am concerned, to enter into the Agreement and to assume all of the obligations, warranties and undertakings to you on the part of Grantor contained therein, and Grantor shall continue to have those rights during the term of the Agreement and thereafter until all of those obligations, warranties and undertakings shall have been fully performed and discharged.

(c) I shall fully and to the best of my abilities perform and discharge all of the obligations, warranties and undertakings contained in the Agreement insofar as the same are required of me and to the extent Grantor has undertaken to cause the performance and discharge by me of those obligations and undertakings.

2.   If during the term of the Agreement or any extensions or renewals thereof, Grantor shall, for any reason, cease to be entitled to my services as a recording artist or the results and proceeds thereof in accordance with the terms thereof or Grantor shall, for any reason, fail or refuse to furnish my services as a recording artist or the results and proceeds thereof exclusively to you as and when required under the Agreement or

Grantor shall commit any action or omission proscribed in the Agreement, I shall, at your written request, for the remaining balance of the term of the Agreement upon the terms contained therein, be deemed substituted for Grantor as a party to the Agreement as of the date of your notice to me. Without limitation of the foregoing, in the event I am substituted in place of Grantor as a party to the Agreement, I shall render all services and perform all acts as shall give to you the same rights, privileges and benefits to which you are entitled under the Agreement as if Grantor had continued to be entitled to my services as a recording artist and had continued to furnish my services as a recording artist and the results and proceeds thereof exclusively to you as and when required under the Agreement, and such rights, privileges and benefits shall be enforceable in your behalf against me.

3.   You and any person, firm or corporation designated by you shall have the perpetual, worldwide right to use and to permit others to use my name (both legal and professional, and whether presently or hereafter used by me), likeness, other identification and biographical material concerning me, for purposes of trade and advertising. You shall have the further right to refer to me during the term of the Agreement as your exclusive recording artist, and I shall in all my activities in the entertainment field use reasonable efforts to be billed and advertised during the term of the Agreement as your exclusive recording artist. The rights granted to you pursuant to this paragraph with respect to my name, likeness, other identification and biographical material concerning me shall be exclusive during the term of the Agreement and nonexclusive thereafter. Accordingly, but without limiting the generality of the foregoing, I shall not authorize or permit any person, firm or corporation other than you to use during the term of the Agreement my legal or professional name or my likeness in connection with the advertising or sale of phonograph records (including, without limitation, audiovisual records.)

4.   During the term of the Agreement, I shall not enter into any agreement or make any commitment which would interfere with my performance of my obligations under the Agreement, and I shall not perform or render services in connection with the recording of master recordings for any person, firm or corporation other than you. After the expiration or termination of the term of the Agreement, I shall not prior to the later of the following dates perform for any person, firm or corporation other than you, for the purpose of making recordings of phonograph records, any selection which had been recorded under the Agreement or under any other agreement between Grantor or me and you or your affiliates: (a) the date five (5) years subsequent to the date on which that selection shall have been last delivered to you in a master recording recorded under the Agreement; or (b) the date three (3) years subsequent to the expiration or termination of the term of the Agreement.

5.   No termination of the Agreement shall diminish my liability or obligation hereunder without your written consent.

6.   You may, in your name, institute any action or proceeding against me individually or collectively, at your election, to enforce your rights under the Agreement, under this guarantee or under the Recording Contract.

7.   I expressly acknowledge that my services hereunder and under the Agreement are of a special, unique, intellectual and extraordinary character which gives them peculiar value, and that if I breach any term hereof or of the Agreement, you will be caused irreparable injury which cannot adequately be compensated by money damages. Accordingly, you shall be entitled to injunctive relief, in addition to any other rights or remedies which you may have, to enforce the terms hereof or of the Agreement.

8.   Except as otherwise provided in Articles 15 and 24 of the Agreement and paragraph 9 below, I shall look solely to Grantor for any and all royalties, recording fees or other monies payable to me in respect of the recording of all recordings under the Recording Contract and under the Agreement and in respect of your manufacture, distribution, sale or other use or recordings recorded under the Agreement and all phonograph records and other reproductions derived therefrom, all throughout the world.

9.   I warrant and represent that, pursuant to the Recording Contract, each individual signatory hereto is guaranteed to receive from Grantor during each consecutive twelve (12) month period of the term of the Agreement ("Term Year") compensation of no less than the Designated Dollar Amount (as that term is defined in paragraph 24.03 of the Agreement) solely in respect of such signatory's services as a recording artist under the Recording Contract. If, for any reason, Grantor shall fail to pay to any signatory at least the Designated Dollar Amount during any Term Year, you shall pay to such signatory an amount which, when added to the amounts, if any, so paid by Grantor to such signatory during the Term Year, shall equal the Designated Dollar Amount. I agree that you shall have the right to demand that Grantor pay to you an amount equal to any amounts so paid by you pursuant to this paragraph, and you may, without limiting your other rights and remedies, deduct that amount from any monies payable by you under the Agreement or under any other agreement between Grantor or me and you or your affiliates. No later than thirty (30) days prior to the end of each Term Year, I shall advise you in writing of whether of not Grantor shall have paid to each signatory at least the Designated Dollar Amount during that Term Year. If in any Term Year the aggregate amount of the compensation paid by Grantor or you to any signatory exceeds the Designated Dollar Amount, such excess compensation shall apply to reduce the Designated Dollar Amount for any subsequent Term Years. I acknowledge that the provisions of this paragraph relating to the guaranteed payment to me of at least the Designated Dollared Amount during each Term Year and the corresponding provisions of the Agreement are intended to be construed and implemented is such a manner so as to comply with the provisions of Section 526 of the Code of Civil Procedure of the State of California and Section 3423 of The Civil Code of the State of California, concerning the availability of injunctive relief to prevent the breach of a contract in writing for the rendition or furnishing of personal services (although nothing contained in this paragraph 9 or elsewhere herein shall be deemed to make this agreement subject to the aforesaid statutory provisions).

10.   I, on behalf of myself and on behalf of any publisher or other person or entity which has or may have any interest in or to any Controlled Composition (as defined in the Agreement) hereby license to you mechanical reproduction rights with respect to each Controlled Composition upon the terms and at the mechanical royalty rates applicable to Controlled Compositions licensed to you by Grantor as set forth in Article 11 of the Agreement.

11.   If there is more than one (1) individual signatory to this agreement, our obligations hereunder and under the Agreement are joint and several, and your rights hereunder and under the Agreement apply with respect to each of us individually and collectively.

12.   THIS AGREEMENT HAS BEEN ENTERED INTO THE STATE OF NEW YORK, AND ITS VALIDITY, CONSTRUCTION, INTERPRETATION AND LEGAL EFFECT SHALL BE GOVERNED BY THE LAWS OF THE STATE OF NEW YORK APPLICABLE TO CONTRACTS ENTERED INTO AND PERFORMED ENTIRELY WITHIN THE STATE OF NEW YORK. ALL CLAIMS, DISPUTES OR DISAGREEMENTS WHICH MAY ARISE OUT OF THE INTERPRETATION, PERFORMANCE OR BREACH OF THIS AGREEMENT SHALL BE SUBMITTED EXCLUSIVELY TO THE JURISDICTION OF THE STATE COURTS OF THE STATE OF NEW YORK OR THE FEDERAL DISTRICT COURTS LOCATED IN NEW YORK CITY; PROVIDED, HOWEVER, IF YOU ARE SUED OR JOINED IN ANY OTHER COURT OR FORUM (INCLUDING AN ARBITRATION PROCEEDING) IN RESPECT OF ANY MATTER WHICH MAY GIVE RISE TO A CLAIM BY YOU HEREUNDER, I CONSENT TO THE JURISDICTION OF SUCH COURT OR FORUM OVER ANY SUCH CLAIM WHICH MAY BE ASSERTED BY YOU. ANY PROCESS IN ANY ACTION OR PROCEEDING COMMENCED IN THE COURTS OF THE STATE OF NEW YORK ARISING OUT OF ANY SUCH CLAIM, DISPUTE OR DISAGREEMENT, MAY AMONG OTHER METHODS, BE SERVED UPON ME BY DELIVERING OR MAILING THE SAME, VIA CERTIFIED MAIL.

Very truly yours,

SSN: _____   SSN:_____

Birth Date:_____   Birth Date:_____

SSN:_____   SSN:_____

Birth Date:_____   Birth Date:_____

SSN:_____   SSN:_____

Birth Date:_____   Birth Date:_____

SUMMARY

1. A successful artist-record company relationship is one of the most important business arrangements needed for success.

2. The record contract is one of the most important and complicated agreements in the industry.

3. An artist should not be expected to understand every clause of the contract.

4. A competent music attorney must negotiate the record contract for the artist.

5. Every item in a record contract should be considered negotiable, especially royalty rates.

6. Most new artists must settle for a contract less favorable to them than an established superstar.

7. In negotiations, a good rule-of-thumb to follow is, "if you don't ask for it, you won't get it."

PROJECTS

1. Team up and perform mock negotiations.

2. Find out if any bands you know have record contracts (even with small independent labels):

   a. ask the band if they understood the terms when they signed

   b. find out what they don't and do like about the contract

   c. ask them what they would like to renegotiate if they were given the chance

   d. ask to see the contract and compare the terms with the example in this chapter

   e. renegotiate the contract for them explaining what you would insert or strike

3. Research other agreements and compare their terms to the example in this chapter.

CHAPTER EIGHT
Care and Feeding of the Creative

Brown's "Confusional Model of Creativity"

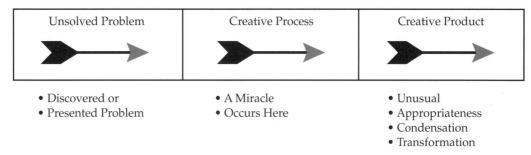

Unsolved Problem	Creative Process	Creative Product
• Discovered or • Presented Problem	• A Miracle • Occurs Here	• Unusual • Appropriateness • Condensation • Transformation

(Brown, Robert. "Confusional Model of Creativity". from *Handbook of Creativity*. Edited by Glover, Ronning, & Reynolds. Plenum Press, New York. 1989. pg. 30)

By the end of this chapter you should be able to:

1. Discuss the characteristics of the creative process.

2. List the traits of the creative person and the creative product.

3. Discuss the factors that accompany age change that bring about a reduction in creativity.

4. Describe some methods to evaluate creativity.

5. Discuss the art and craft of songwriting.

6. List the characteristics of a potentially successful song.

7. Discuss how songwriters make money.

8. When given a songwriter/publisher agreement, discuss the important clauses.

9. Discuss the publisher's role in song exploitation.

10. List the six basic song uses that are revenue producing.

11. List the RIAA criteria for Gold and Platinum Video Awards.

12. Describe the first music videos and how they were presented.

13. Discuss the nonlinear concept of story evolution.

14. When given a recording contract, discuss the important issues of the video production clauses.

15. Discuss the differences among the live vs. audio vs. video media.

16. Discuss the role industry management should play in guiding creative talent.

THE CREATIVE PROCESS

Creativity itself is a quicksilver thing: an intangible, subjectively evaluated property,
often purchased in commercial circles by the slightest whim or fancy."

(Buxton, Edward. Creative People At Work.
Executive Communications, Inc. N.Y. 1975 pg ix.)

How does it happen? Why do some people have it and others don't? What is the mystique about it? Can you learn to be creative? What's the big deal anyway?

The truth is that the people involved with the creative aspects of this industry are the highest paid. And one of the reasons they are the highest paid is because of the mystique that surrounds the creative process. Non-creative people find it magical that someone can be creative, a feat that is so superhuman that many will pay any price to be a part of the process.

Our creative thought is the function of the right hemisphere of the brain. The further to the "right" someone feels comfortable existing in, the more creative (but not necessarily useful), their output is. Accountants and scientists make daily use of the brain's left hemisphere. Because society has made laws and rules to govern its people, one must make use of the left side of the brain in order to survive. Supposedly, the more "centered" you are, the easier it is to cope with life's daily activities and the happier you are. Many creative people, (those referred to as "right sided"), are uncomfortable making business decisions. They find it tedious and boring to constantly use the left side of their brain. Besides, it's not as much fun. (This may be why so many entertainment attorneys are frustrated producers, songwriters, and musicians.)

This chapter explores the creativity as it pertains to this industry. It is divided into two sections, the creative process and the creative product. The areas investigated include: the creative personality; measuring creativity, guiding the creative talent, followed by a detailed description of the industry's creative products.

Creative Traits

JACKSON AND MESSICK: FOUR CHARACTERISTICS OF CREATIVITY

Traits of the Person		Traits of the Product		
Intellectual Traits	Personal Traits	Product Properties	Standards	Reflective Reaction
1. Tolerance of Incongrutiy	Original	Unusualness	Norms	Surprise
2. Analysis and Intuition	Sensitive	Appropriateness	Context	Satisfaction
3. Open-mindedness	Flexible	Transformation	Constraint	Stimulation
4. Reflection & Spontaneity	Poetic	Condensation	Summary Power	Savoring

Figure 8.1 John S. Dacey. Fundamentals of Creative Thinking. Lexington Books. Lexington, MA. 1989 pg. 7.

Figure 8.1, Jackson and Messick's "Four Characteristics of Creativity" illustrates the attributes of creative people and their products. It is divided into two areas: "Traits of the Creative Person" and "Traits of the Creative Product." Intellectual traits of the creative person include being fearless of the unknown; being intuitive, open-minded, and spontaneous. Other personal traits of the creative personality include originality, sensitivity, and flexibility.

Accordingly, properties of the creative product are its unusualness, appropriateness, newness, and compactness. Jackson and Messick also say that our reaction to a truly creative product is one of surprise, satisfaction, and stimulation.1

In the music business, truly creative people are few in numbers. But many artists are truly creative, sensitive, fearless, and willing to take risks. And in order for their products sell, they must satisfy a need.

Then what does the creative process entail? Well, not only is it different for different people, but it is different for the same individual at different times. And there is never a guarantee that the result will be creative. In fact, the literature explains methods to help the creative process occur, but fails to agree on the contents of the process itself. Management must always be conscious of creating an environments that allows for the artist's own creative process to occur. (Further discussion appears later in this chapter).

The Creative Personality

"The creative person is commonly regarded as being filled with new ideas and projects; he views life from surprising perspectives, formulates problems contrary to what he has been told by parents and teachers, turns traditional and seemingly self-evident conceptions topsy-turvy, and wants to retest the validity of accepted truths."[2]

When creative people are described in the music business, such phrases as self-centered and ego driven are used. "According to psychologists, the general view is that creative people have a stronger, more pronounced sense of self. Call it ego, pride of authorship, or a larger-than-normal need for praise and approval."[3] One only needs to watch the annual telecast of the Grammy Awards presentation to agree.

Researchers have found the following characteristics (in one or more studies) differentiate highly creative persons from less creative ones. Obviously with a list so long, one or several of these traits can be found in every entertainment artist. So the characteristics noted in **Bold** are frequently attributed to creative people in the music business.

1. **Accepts disorder**
2. **Adventurous**
3. **Strong affection**
4. Altruistic
5. Awareness of others
6. Always baffled by something
7. **Attracted to disorder**
8. **Attracted to mysterious**
9. Attempts difficult jobs
10. **Bashful outwardly**
11. Constructive in criticism
12. Courageous
13. Deep and conscientious conventions
14. Defies conventions of courtesy
15. **Defies conventions of health**
16. Desires to excel
17. Determination
18. Differentiated value-hierarchy
19. Discontented
20. Disturbs organization
21. Dominant
22. **Emotional**
23. **Emotionally sensitive**
24. Energetic
25. A fault-finder
26. **Doesn't fear being thought as different**
27. **Feels whole parade is out of step**
28. Full of curiosity
29. Appears haughty and self-satisfied at times
30. **Likes solitude**
31. Independence in judgment
32. Independent in thinking
33. **Individualistic**
34. Intuitive
35. Industrious
36. Introversive
37. **Keeps unusual hours**
38. **Lack business ability**
39. Makes mistakes
40. Never bored
41. Nonconforming
42. Not hostile or negativistic
43. Not popular
44. **Oddities of habit**
45. Persistent
46. Becomes preoccupied with problem
47. Preference for complex ideas
48. Questioning
49. **Radical**
50. Receptive to external stimuli
51. Receptive to ideas of others
52. **Regresses occasionally**
53. Rejection of suppression as a mechanism of impulse control
54. Rejection of repression
55. Reserved
56. Resolute
57. Self-assertive
58. Self-aware
59. Self-starter
60. Self-confident
61. Self-sufficient
62. Sense of destiny
63. **Sense of humor**
64. Sensitive to beauty
65. Shuns power
66. Sincere
67. Not interested in small details
68. Speculative
69. Spirited in disagreement
70. Strives for distant goals
71. **Stubborn**
72. **Temperamental**
73. **Tenacious**
74. **Tender emotions**
75. Timid
76. Thorough
77. Unconcerned about power
78. Somewhat uncultured, primitive
79. Unsophisticated, naive
80. Unwilling to accept anything on mere say-so
81. Visionary
82. **Versatile**
83. **Willing to take risks**
84. **Somewhat withdrawn**

Figure 8.2. Paul E. Torrance. Guiding Creative Talent. *Prentice-Hall Inc. Englewood Cliffs, NJ, 1962. Pg. 66-67.*

Also, creative people think of themselves as special. Therefore, when there is a lack of recognition outside of their own community of peers, it leads many to frustration. People often say that creative people are very difficult to work with, and some creative people feel they are prisoners of the whims of their audience. Emotions run on high in this business and managers must deal with each artist accordingly.

Once You Have It, Do You Have It Forever

"Creativity is a cognitive, attitudinal, personal trait that every person has to some degree (unless in a coma or of very low intelligence)."[4]

The peripherals of music industry are filled with people who were "one hit wonders". Why can't the successes be easily repeated? Obviously there is no one answer. However there have been studies concerning, among other things, age and creative productivity. Lehman (1953) found that the greatest contributions to their field were made by musicians between the ages of thirty and forty. Lehman (1956) also pointed out that not age itself, but the factors that accompany **age change** bring about reduction in creative production.[5] Some of the general factors he found are listed in Figure 8.3.

1. A decline in physical vigor energy, and resistance to fatigue occur before the age of forty.

2. Sensory capacity and motor precision decline with age.

3. Serious illness and bodily infirmities have more negative effects on older than younger persons.

4. Creativity curves may be related to glandular changes.

5. Marital difficulties and sexual problems increase with age and may have a negative effect on creativity.

6. Indifference toward creativity may develop more frequently among older people because of the death of a loved one.

7. Older persons are more likely to be preoccupied with the practical demands of life.

8. Success, promotion, increased prestige, and responsibility may lead to less favorable conditions for concentrated work.

9. Having achieved these goals, those that desire prestige and recognition, rather than the creation of something new, strive less for achievement.

10. Easily won and early fame may lead to contentment with what has been done before accomplishing what could be the most creative work.

11. Non-recognition and destructive criticism may lead to apathy of older workers.

12. Negative transfer, resulting in inflexibility, may be more of a handicap among older workers.

13. Older workers may become less motivated because of these factors.

14. Younger people may be better educated and lived in more stimulating environments.

15. Psychoses, which occur more frequently in later life, may have clouded what was previously a brilliant mind.

16. Alcohol, narcotics, and such may have sapped an individual's productive power.

Figure 8.3. Paul E. Torrance. Guiding Creative Talent. *Prentice-Hall Inc. Englewood Cliffs, NJ, 1962. Pg. 101-102.*

So can you have it forever? Individuals are individuals and a general rule doesn't exist. However, as a word of caution, throughout history there have been few successful revolutionists over age forty.

Can It Be Taught?

"I think that talented, creative people are going to be successful anyway. I don't think a training program has anything to do with it."[6]

Unfortunately in areas that do not require a great deal of technique or prerequisite skills, the above quote is usually true. The craft of any creative endeavor (such as songwriting) can be learned, but learning the craft does not necessarily make someone successful. What can be taught is how to recognize creative uses of a craft, and exercises can be designed to practice those uses. However, this is refining the craft not the art. Composers study the Mozart Symphonies to learn the mechanics of composing in the classical style and to acknowledge the genius in Mozart's artistic use of the tools. Students then imitate the Mozart classical style to explore his techniques. With practice they improve, and the techniques of the style are learned. The craft is refined. Although there are rules that govern the use of certain notes, the artistry lies in the choice of notes. The notes are chosen from what the composer hears, and what is heard is an individual's choice. And that is where the creativity lies!

Evaluating Creativity

Can creativity be measured without measuring the creative product? How is the evaluation criterion derived? Are there critical factors? Who is qualified to do the measuring?

The literature does not agree on a method for evaluating creativity. Although most would agree that a quantitative measure alone, such as record sales, would do an injustice to a large amount of quality work, but should a quantitative statistic play a role in the decision.

One method of measurement might be to identify creative people who are innovators by the number of representatives they spawn. For example, if someone decides to drive a car in reverse looking over his or her shoulder instead of in forward and no one chooses to pick up on the idea (the innovation) and drive like that (as a representative of the innovation), the original person who started driving in reverse would not be considered an innovator, but probably considered crazy! However, if several people liked the idea and started to drive in reverse, and then millions of people followed, the innovator would be considered a genius. If the driving fad lasted two weeks and then someone began driving sideways, driving backwards would be considered part of the evolution of modern driving and a creative step in reaching the current state of driving practices. Because millions became users or representatives of the innovation, the innovator would be recognized as highly creative. Therefore, using this logic, record sales as a quantitative measure, can be a valid part of the test for measuring creativity.

As a second example, if a composer composed a composition (an innovation) and no one performed it, it would not be considered a good work. However, if it received hundreds of performances (as representations) it would be.

A final definition of creativity, this one by Morris I. Stein reads, "Creativity is a process that results in a novel work that is accepted as useful, tenable, or satisfying by a significant group of people at some point in time."7 Stein is including a quantitative measure, by employing the acceptance by a significant group of people, ie: record buyers or listeners as the evidence of creativity.

THE CREATIVE PRODUCT
Songwriting

"At the dawn of the century Chas K. Harris published a little red book of rules and secrets called How To Write A Popular Song. *To his readers he advised: Look at newspapers for your story line. Acquaint yourself with the style in vogue. Avoid slang. Know the copyright laws."8*

Is it an art or a craft? Most debates settle with the compromise, "well it's both." This seems to be true as songwriting methods teach the mechanics of the craft but do not guarantee artistic or commercial acceptance. Some songs, such as Paul McCartney's "Yesterday" have great lyrics and a great melody, and others are successful because they fit the style that's in at the time (remember the big hit of the late 1970's "Shake Your Booty"). Concerning the craft, Harris gave very good advice. Most of what he said is still useful today.

In the Music Business Handbook, Baskerville suggests that if a song exhibits the following characteristics, it has very strong potential for making it in the marketplace:

1. is memorable; it sticks in the mind. This is accomplished particularly by use of a "hook"

2. has immediate appeal

3. uses some kind of special imagery

4. is well-crafted

5. everything lyrical and musical holds to a central theme

6. has an element of mystery[9]

Songwriting "how to" texts agree with Baskerville. There is a method to learning the craft, but creating hits cannot be guaranteed. Baskerville adds that the transformation of an artistic achievement into a commercial success may occur if the following takes place:

1. The song gets an appealing initial performance.

2. The record company promotes strong airplay.

3. The song and the record suit the taste of the current market.

4. The record is effectively distributed and is made readily available nationally.[10]

These events fall beyond the scope of the creative process, and are the personal manager's responsibility to see that they occur.

Making Money At It

The key to receiving revenue from the efforts of songwriting is through the use of the song. In the business this is referred to as "exploiting the copyright" and is the main function of the song's publisher. Revenue producing uses include:

1. recording sales (all configurations) through the issuing of mechanical licenses which generate mechanical royalties.

2. jukebox play

3. sheet music sales

4. special use licenses (i.e.. use in advertising jingles)

5. synchronization license (using the music in conjunction with visuals)

6. home taping tax (fee levied on digital audio tape recorders and blank tape)

7. broadcast performances (including network and local TV and radio, public and college broadcasts, cable and satellite, internet)

8. non-broadcast performances (including concert and club performances, and other uses such as "Muzak", airline, and health club play)

9. dramatic performances, also known as "Grand" rights performances, which make use of live play acting.

Because revenue collection for the songwriter relies so heavily on the function of the song's publisher, the Songwriters Guild of America publishes a **Popular Songwriter Contract**. This songwriter/publisher agreement includes basic descriptions of all the revenue producing areas that are handled by the publisher for the songwriter. Although some major publishers feel that the contract is weighted in favor of the songwriter, and therefore insist on their own contracts, it is a good resource to use as a guide and an outline when beginning negotiations on one's own deal. Pay particular attention to all parts of clauses numbered **4**, **6**, **9**, and **18**, and the instructions included in parenthesis. Since the terms of the contract are based on the strength of the songwriter's track record, the percentages noted in each sub clause vary greatly. What follows is a reprint of those specific clauses with comments and advice. However, like all agreements **should not** be signed without legal representation.

4.   In consideration of this contract, the Publisher agrees to pay the Writer as follows:

(a) $.....as an advance against royalties, receipt of which is hereby acknowledged, which sum shall remain the property of the Writer and shall be deductible only form payments hereafter becoming due the Writer under their contract.

*In 4a, the advance money conditions are stated. The money is advanced free and clear, and will be paid back to the publisher **before** any royalties are distributed. This contract does not include a clause forbidding "cross-collateralization", which means that monies advanced against one song under the guise of this contract may be collected against the royalties on another song. As a songwriter, although you may not be in favor of this, it is a standard clause in the industry, and unproven songwriters must accept it.*

(b) In respect of regular piano copies sold and paid for in he United States and Canada, the following royalties per copy:...% (in no case, however, less than 10%) of the wholesale selling price of the first 200,00 copies or less; plus ...% (in no case less than 12%) of the wholesale selling price of copies in excess of 200,00 and not exceeding 500,00; plus ...% (in no case, however, less than 15%) of wholesale selling price of copies in excess of 500,000.

*This is a sliding scale of percentages that should increase the songwriter's participation in revenues as the print sales increase. Here it is based on the wholesale selling price, and the percentages should be **twice** as large as if based on the selling price at retail.*

(c) ...% (in no case, however, less than 50%) of all net sums received by the Publisher in respect of regular piano copies, orchestrations, band arrangements, octavos, quartets, arrangements for combination of voices and/or instruments, and/or copies of the composition sold in any country other than the United States and Canada, provided, however, that if the Publisher should sell such copies through, or cause them to be sold by, a subsidiary or affiliate which is actually doing business in a foreign country, then in respect of such sales, the Publisher shall pay to the Writer not less than 5% of the market retail selling price in respect of each such copy sold and paid for.

*This clause deals with the publishing of arrangements of the work outside of the U.S. and Canada. If the publisher signing the agreement publishes the work, the writer is entitled to at least 50% of the **net** sums received. However, if the publisher sells or licenses the copies through an affiliate or subsidiary in the foreign country, the writer will receive not less than 5% of the market retail selling price for each copy sold and **paid for**. Make note of the inclusion of the phrase "paid for". With foreign publications it is sometimes very difficult to receive payment, and furthermore there is a time lapse between the sale and delivery of funds. Also, this clause does not specify if the payment will be made in U.S. or foreign currency. Many foreign companies hold funds collected until the currency exchange rate favors them, and there could be a different rate on the day the check is written than on the day of the sale.*

(d) In respect of each copy sold and paid for in the United States and Canada, or for export from the United States, of orchestrations, band arrangements, octavos, quartets, arrangements for combinations of voices and/or instruments, and/or other copies of the composition (other than regular piano copies) the following royalties on the wholesale selling price (after trade discounts, if any):

...% (in no case however, less than 10%) on the first 200,000 copies or less; plus

...% (in no case, less than 12%) of all copies in excess of 200,00 and not exceeding 500,000; plus ...% (in no case, however, less than 15%) on all copies in excess of 500,000.

This clause pertains to orchestrations and other arrangements printed and sold in the U.S. and Canada, or printed and exported.

(e)

(i) If the composition, or any part thereof, is included in any song book, folio or similar publication issued by the Publisher containing at least four, but not more than twenty-five musical compositions, the royalty to be paid by the Publisher to the Writer shall be an amount determined by dividing 10% of the Wholesale selling price (after trade Discounts, if any) of the copies sold, among the total number of the Publisher's copyrighted musical compositions included in such publication. If such publication contains more than twenty-five musical compositions, the said 10% shall be increased by an additional 1/2% for each additional musical composition.

(ii) If, pursuant to a license granted by the Publisher to a licensee not controlled by or affiliated with it, the composition, or any part thereof, is included in any song book, folio or similar publication, containing at least four musical compositions, the royalty to be paid by the Publisher to the Writer shall be that proportion of 50% of the gross amount received by it from the licensee, as the number of uses of the composition under the license and during the license period, bears to the total number of uses of the Publisher's copyrighted musical compositions under the license and during the license period.

(iii) In computing the number of the Publisher's copyrighted musical compositions under subdivisions (i) and (ii) hereof, there shall be excluded musical compositions in the public domain and arrangements thereof and those with respect to which the Publisher does not currently publish and offer for sale regular piano copies.

(iv) Royalties on publications containing less than four musical compositions shall be payable at regular piano copy rates.

This clause deals with songbooks and folios that are published by the publisher and/or licensed by the publisher. It is a given, that the writer wants the printed editions of the song published, however, there is no mention as to if the songs are going to be coupled with other writer's works. The songwriter may insist that the material in all folios published is exclusively his/hers. Also make note that all percentages and numbers are negotiable.

(f) As to "professional material" not sold or resold, no royalty shall be payable. Free copies of the lyrics of the composition shall not be distributed except under the following conditions: (i) with the Writer's written consent; or (ii) when printed without music in limited numbers for charitable, religious or governmental purposes, or for similar public purposes, if no profit is derived, directly or indirectly; or (iii) when authorized for printing in a book, magazine or periodical, where provided that any such use shall bear the Writer's name and the proper copyright notice; or (iv) when distributed solely for the purpose of exploiting the composition, provided, that such exploitation is restricted to the distribution of limited numbers of such copies for the purpose of influencing the sale of the composition, that the distribution is independent of the sale of any other musical compositions, services, goods, wares or merchandise, and that no profit is made, directly or indirectly, in connection therewith.

In this clause free copies and other professional uses are explained. The writer has the power to limit such uses, especially regarding religious and governmental purposes.

(g) ...% (in no case, however, less than 50%) of:All gross receipts of the Publisher in respect of any licenses (including statutory royalties) authorizing the manufacture of parts of instruments serving to mechanically reproduce the composition, or to use the composition in synchronization with sound motion pictures, or to reproduce it upon electrical transcription for broadcasting purposes, and of any and all gross receipts of the Publisher from any other source or right now known or which may hereafter come into existence, except as provided in paragraph 2.

All other rights are discussed here. And although 50% is the standard split, the importance of all of these revenue-producing areas probably merits more detailed descriptions.

(h) If the Publisher administers licenses authorizing the manufacture of parts of instruments serving to mechanically reproduce said composition, or the use of said composition in synchronization or in timed relation with sound motion pictures or its reproduction upon electrical transcriptions, or any of them, through an agent, trustee or other administrator acting for a substantial part of the industry and not under the exclusive control of the Publisher (hereafter sometimes referred to as licensing agent), the Publisher, in determining his receipts, shall be entitled to deduct from gross license fees paid by the Licensees, a sum equal to the charges paid by the Publisher to said licensing agent, provided, however, that in respect to synchronization or timed relation with sound motion pictures, said deduction shall in no event exceed $150 or 10% of said gross license fee, whichever is less; in connection with the manufacture of parts of instruments serving to mechanically reproduce said composition, said deductions shall not exceed 5% of said gross license fee; and in connection with electrical transcriptions, said deduction shall not exceed 10% of said gross license fee.

Here the Publisher administers licenses for the material through a licensing agent, any and all fees for the services performed by the Publisher will be shared by the writer.

(i) The Publisher agrees that the use of the composition will not be included in any bulk or block license heretofore or hereafter granted, and that it will not grant any bulk or block license to include the same, without the written consent of the Writer in each instance, except (i) that the Publisher may grant such license with respect to electrical transcription for broadcasting purposes, A bulk or block license shall be deemed to mean any license or agreement, domestic or foreign, whereby rights are granted in respect of two or more musical compositions.

This is a particularly long clause (only partially reprinted here) that describes what a block license is. The Writer must give his/her consent before the Publisher is allowed to license two or more compositions together. It also includes exclusions, however, they are of standard practice.

(j) Except to the extent that the Publisher and Writer have heretofore of may hereafter assign to or vest in the small performing rights licensing organization with which Writer and Publisher are affiliated, the said rights or the right to grant licenses therefore, it is agreed that no licenses shall be granted without the written consent, in each instance, of the Writer for the use of the composition by means of television, or by any means, or for any purposes not commercially established, of for which licenses were not granted by the Publisher on musical compositions prior to June 1, 1937.

The Writer must give consent for any television or new delivery system use, such as internet streaming or downloading.

(k) The Publisher shall not, without the written consent of the Writer in each case, give or grant any right or license (i) to use the title of the composition, or (ii) for the exclusive use of the composition in any form or for any purpose, or for any period of time, or for any territory, other than its customary arrangements with foreign publishers, or (iii) to give a dramatic representation of the composition or to dramatize the plot or story thereof, or (iv) for a vocal rendition of the composition in synchronization with sound motion pictures, or (v) for any synchronization use thereof, of (vi) for the use of the composition or a quotation or excerpt therefrom in any article, book, periodical, advertisement or other similar publication. If, however, the Publisher shall give to the Writer written notice by certified mail, return receipt requested, or telegram, specifying the right or license to be given or granted, the name of the licensee and the terms and conditions thereof, including the price of other compensation to be received therefore, then, unless the Writer (or any one or more of them) shall, within five business days after the delivery of such notice to the address of the Writer herein designated, object thereto, the Publisher may grant such right or license accordance with the said notice without first obtaining the consent of the Writer. Such notice shall be deemed sufficient if sent to the writer at the address or addresses hereinafter designated or at the address or addresses last furnished to the Publisher in writing by the Writer.

This clause protects the writer against any unwanted licensing of his/her material.

(l)   Any portion of the receipts which may become due to the Writer from license fees (in excess of offsets), whether received directly from the licensee or from any licensing agent of the Publisher, shall, if not paid immediately on the receipt thereof by the Publisher, belong to the Writer and shall be held in trust for the Writer until payment is made; the ownership of said trust fund by the Writer shall not be questioned whether the monies are physically segregated or not.

(m) The Publisher agrees that it will not issue any license as a result of which it will receive any financial benefit in which the Writer does not participate.

On all regular piano copies, orchestrations, band or other arrangements, octavos, quartets, commercial sound recordings and other reproductions of the composition or parts thereof, in whatever form and however produced, Publisher shall include or cause to be included, in addition to the copyright notice, the name of the Writer, and Publisher shall include a similar requirement in every license or authorization issued by it with respect to the composition.

6.   (a) The Publisher shall

(i)   within ..... months from the date of this contract (the "initial period"), cause a commercial sound recording of the composition to be made and released in the customary form and through the customary commercial channels. If at the end of such initial period a sound recording has not been made and released, as above provided, then, subject to the provisions of the next subdivision, this contract shall terminate.

A new writer should negotiate for the shortest number of months that is agreeable, however, it is customary to give the publisher 12 to 18 months to secure a deal. The clause does not state which record labels would be acceptable, and there is a major difference between a release on Sony Records and one on "Pointless." A compromise might include "a commercial recording distributed by one of the five major record distributors, or a RIAA member label."

(ii)   If, prior to the expiration of the initial period, Publisher pays the Writer the sum of $....(which shall not be charged against or recoupable out of any advances, royalties or other monies theretofore paid, then due, or which thereafter may become due the Writer from the Publisher pursuant to this contract or otherwise), Publisher shall have an additional .... months (the "additional period") commencing with the end of the initial period, within which to cause such commercial sound recording to be made and released as provided in subdivision (i) above. If at the end of the additional period a commercial sound recording has not been made and released, as above provided, then this contract shall terminate.

Here there are two figures to be negotiated. The sum allows the publisher to buy some additional time to secure a deal. This clause is included in case the publisher is working on a record deal and it's beyond his/her control to close when s/he would like. The writer should not give the publisher more than six additional months, and should receive a sum s/he feels comfortable with.

(iii) Upon termination pursuant to this Paragraph 6(a), all rights of any and every nature in and to the composition and in and to any and all copyrights secured thereon in the United States and throughout the world shall automatically re-vest in and become the property of the Writer and shall be reassigned to him by the Publisher. The Writer shall not be obligated to return or pay to the Publisher any advance or indebtedness as a condition of such reassignment; the said reassignment shall be in accordance with and subject to the provisions of Paragraph 8 hereof, and, in addition, the Publisher shall pay to the Writer all gross sums which it has theretofore or may thereafter receive in respect of the composition.

This is a clause that the Publisher will have difficulty signing as stated. S/he will want to participate in future revenues that may be generated due to agreements that s/he may have initiated but did not complete. Sometimes there is a compromise (a sunset clause) that suggests that if any revenue is generated during the first ...months immediately following the termination date, the Publisher will receive ...% of the sums.

(b) The Publisher shall furnish, or cause to be furnished, to the Writer six copies of the commercial sound recording referred to in Paragraph 6(a).

Remember that all numbers are negotiable.

(c) The Publisher shall

(i) within 30 days after the initial release of a commercial sound recording of the composition, make, publish and offer for sale regular piano copies of the composition in the form and through the channels customarily employed by it for that purpose;

(ii) within 30 days after execution of this contract make a piano arrangement or lead sheet for he composition and furnish six copies thereof to the Writer.

In the event neither subdivision (i) nor (ii) of this subparagraph (c) is selected, the provisions of subdivision (ii) shall be automatically deemed to have been selected by the parties.

Since sheets are no longer manufactured for every song recorded, (ii) would be sufficient.

9. If the Publisher desires to exercise a right in and to the composition now known or which may hereafter become known, but for which no specific provision has been made herein, the Publisher shall give written notice to the Writer thereof. Negotiations respecting all the terms and conditions of any such disposition shall thereupon be entered into between the Publisher and the Writer and no such right shall be exercised until specific agreement has been made.

18.   Except to the extent herein otherwise expressly provided, the Publisher shall not sell, transfer, assign, convey, encumber or otherwise dispose of the compositions or the copyright or copyrights secured thereon without the prior written consent of the Writer. The Writer has been induces to enter into this contract in reliance upon the value to him of the personal service and ability of the Publisher in the exploitation of the composition, and by reason thereof it is the intention of the parties and the essence of the relationship between them that the rights herein granted to the Publisher shall remain with the Publisher and that the same shall not pass to any other person, including, without limitations, successors to or receivers or trustees of the property of the Publisher, either by act or deed of the Publisher or by operation of law, and in the event of the voluntary or involuntary bankruptcy of the Publisher, this contract shall terminate, provided, however, that the composition may be included by the Publisher in a bona fide voluntary sale of its music business or its entire catalog of musical compositions, or in a merger or consolidation of the Publisher with another corporation, in which event the Publisher shall immediately give written notice thereof to the Writer; and provided further that the composition and the copyright therein may be assigned by the Publisher to a subsidiary or affiliated company generally engaged in the music publishing business. If the Publisher is an individual, the composition may pass to a legatee or distributee as part of the inheritance of the Publisher's music business and entire catalog of musical compositions. Any such transfer or assignment shall, however, be conditioned upon the execution and delivery by the transferee or assignee to the Writer of an agreement to be bound by and to perform all of the terms and conditions of this contract to be performed on the part of the Publisher.

This clause does not allow the publisher to sell or trade any of the writer's songs without prior written consent of the writer. It protects the writer from being part of a package deal that the publisher may want to execute to obtain the rights to a song or catalog. However, if the publisher is sold to another music publisher in the business, then the writer cannot stop his/her material from being assigned, provided that the contract between the writer and the new publisher contains all of the terms included in this contract.

Publishing

Record companies have taken over many of the responsibilities of the early music publishers, narrowing their role in exploiting the copyright. In fact, today virtually all record companies own publishing firms, and try to secure the rights to their artist's songs. So the main function of the independent music publisher is to generate "covers" of their clients catalog. This may include the following:

1. covering the song for other markets by having a different artist record the song

2. completing several arrangements of the work ie: big band, piano arrangements, etc.

3. licensing the song for use in advertising, promotional commercials, or e commerce

4. licensing the song for print editions

5. permitting the song to be used with time-related visuals (synchronization)

6. sub-publishing the work for foreign income.

The consequence of these avenues of exploitation is the generation of income. The more ways a song is used, the better the chances that it will generate income. And a publisher's strength is in the success of his/her catalog.

Over the past decade, the size of the catalog has been of major concern. In the 1980's, bigger was better. Many catalogs were sold for what seemed like huge amounts of money. This was due to several reasons: Some companies were experiencing cash flow problems and needed revenue quickly; it was more cost effective to purchase an entire catalog than it was to purchase one or two hits; and lastly, with the development of new and different "delivery systems", it was advantageous to own the song rather than secure a license for one use. If you own the song, it is your option to license it or use it anyway you see fit. The strength is in the catalog!

There is a joke in the business, the idea of it is that Paul McCartney and Michael Jackson own all the songs that were ever written! It's true that they both own large catalogs (Yoko Ono and Paul joined together to purchase the remaining Beatle songs that Paul didn't already own, but were out bid by Michael), however, they own them not only for their respective egos, but because one of the surest safest investment in the music business is owning a song catalog.

Sources of Income

Publishers (and songwriters) receive income from six basic song uses or licenses. They are:

1. mechanical licensing

2. performance licensing

3. synchronization licensing

4. print licensing

5. foreign licensing

6. special use licensing

1. **Mechanical Licensing**   As a songwriter, if someone wants to manufacture (mechanically reproduce) a sound recording of your song, s/he must obtain a mechanical license from your publisher. In 1909, the statutory rate was $.02 per song and it cost $.03 to mail a letter. The current price for the license (the statutory rate) is $.08 per song or $.0155 per minute, whichever is greater, on every record manufactured and sold, and it now costs over eleven times as great to mail a letter! (Obviously the rate has not kept up with inflation or the U.S. Postal Service rates,

and has been quite a deal for the record companies.} The rate*, now in effect, was set and adjusted according to the Consumer Price Index by the now disbanded U.S. Copyright Tribunal, whose responsibilities have been taken over by the U.S. Copyright Office. If 500,000 copies of the recording are sold, the mechanical license generates $40,000 (500,000 X $.08), which is split between the songwriter and the publisher. Once the initial recording is released, if anyone is willing to pay the current statutory rate, the song's owner must issue the license. Since the rate is set by law, many feel that it discriminates against successful songwriters. For example, is a song written by Paul McCartney worth the same amount as one written by John Doe? Many feel that the licensing rate should be free to be negotiated on the open market. And in a way it is, through the use of the negotiated license. If the copyright holder agrees, the manufacturer (record company), may pay a rate lower than the statutory rate. This negotiated mechanical license is used throughout the industry, especially on initial recordings and when the artist is more famous than the songwriter. The record company may want to pay only $.02 on every recording manufactured and sold and may negotiate that rate with the song owner (publisher). Therefore on 500,000 copies sold, it would cost the company only $10,000 (500,000 X $.02) instead of $40,000.

In the U.S., most publishers issue mechanical licenses through one of the mechanical rights organizations. The largest is the Harry Fox Agency, who charges a fee (circa 3.5%) for its services. The services include the issuing of licenses, collecting royalties, and auditing record companies as well.

The statutory compulsory license rate will increase as follows:
2004: $.085 per song or $.0165 cents per minute
2006 and later $.091 per song or $.0175 cents per minute

2. **Performance Licensing** Another right the copyright owner is granted by law is the right to perform the copyrighted material in public. This includes the actual live performance of the work or the performance of a mechanical reproduction of the work. Consequently, the user of the work must obtain a license to broadcast a performance or have a live performance occur in his/her venue. Broadcast stations, internet broadcasts, wire services, auditoriums, arenas, and clubs throughout the world, all obtain various types of performance licenses. Because the issuing of these licenses would be an enormous task for individual copyright owners, performing rights organizations act as clearinghouses for their respective clients.

In the U.S. there are three performing rights organizations (PRO's): ASCAP (American Society of Authors, Composers, and Publishers), BMI (Broadcast Music Incorporated), and SESAC (Society of European Stage Authors and Composers). ASCAP and BMI are the largest and not for profit. A composer must exclusively belong to one of the three, however, a publisher may belong to all three. Their responsibilities include granting licenses, collecting royalties, and distributing the income to their clients.

The structure of the organizations include a broadcast licensing area, and a general licensing area. The broadcast license revenues are determined by a survey or logging procedure, where different broadcast performances are given a value (or a weight). A sophisticated formula determines how much revenue is produced by each performance.

The general licensing area issues licenses to venues. The fee for the license is determined by the capacity of the venue and various other factors. The revenue collected is distributed for the most part by the number of logged or surveyed **broadcast performances, rather than public performances**. Therefore, songs that are performed a great deal live but have ceased (or never were) to be heard from broadcasts, lose out because they are disproportionately accounted for. The performing rights organizations are beginning to survey actual performances in the largest venues in the country, however, a system for accounting for every live performance in America has not been established.

The PRO's distribute the income (after expenses) individually to the writers and the publishers (usually on a 50/50% share basis). Performance license royalties are the only license royalties that are not funneled through the publisher to be split and distributed to the writer.

A performance right for webcasting a recorded performance has now been established. The right not only includes the songwriter and publisher but the performer as well. This is the only performance license granted in this country that includes the performer.

3. **Synchronization Licensing** Anytime music is combined with visual motion it becomes what is known as "time related" and requires a "synch license." These uses include music in motion pictures (theatrical releases or made for TV movies), and music videos. The producer of the work must obtain the license form the publisher. Obviously, revenue from synch licenses can be very substantial. These revenues are collected by the publisher who in turn splits them (usually 50/50) with the writer.

4. **Print Licensing** Before the recording industry took over, music publishers printed sheet music of the songs that they owned. This is what it meant to publish! Today, only a few music publishers are in the print manufacturing business. Most license the rights to another company and receive a percentage of the revenue on the sheet music sold. They, in turn, pay the writer a small percent of what is received. Sheets or folios are not printed for every song recorded, and for new artists, they are not printed until it is determined that the record has "some legs." However, big hits can produce substantial folio revenue.

5. **Foreign Licensing** Foreign income is derive from licensing and subpublishing throughout the world. The percentage of revenues realized from each license is substantively lower than revenue from similar domestic uses. Exchange rates, tariffs, and distribution costs play a major role in how much income is generated. Some songwriters are counseled to retain their foreign rights and issue their own licenses. Although this sounds great, it may prove to be disastrous because the hardest

aspect of foreign licensing is receiving the revenues (getting paid), and an individual songwriter may not have the resources a publisher may have to track down money due to them.

6. **Special Use Licensing** These licenses include using the music in advertising jingles, greeting cards, and other merchandise. Sponsors who want music in their commercial notify their advertising agency that may produce the music in-house, or rely on the services of a music supplier. The commercials may run in a national television campaign or a 15 second local radio spot. The use of the music may vary from using the original recording of the song followed by a voice over, as a background "bed" under a voice over, or the use of the music with lyrics selling the product sung to the original melody. Therefore the special use release of the song usually a form of a synch license as well.

The chart that follows sums up the normal income distribution between the publisher and the songwriter. These figures can be only be used as a guide, either for one song contracts or long term agreements.

INCOME

License	Split
Mechanical	Publisher collects 100% and pays affiliated composer 50%
Performance	PRO pays composer and publisher individual shares directly
Synchronization	Publisher collects and pays affiliated composer 50%
Print	Publisher collects 100% and pays composer small royalty at approximately $.10 per printed edition sold
Foreign	When received from foreign or subpublisher, 50% of income is paid to composer
Special Use	Publisher collects 100% and pays affiliated composer 50%

Performing

Only in the last 25 years has the technology been available to perform in the arenas and stadiums that are so common practice today. There is a great picture of the Beatles performing their now famous Shea Stadium Concert. The two baselines of the baseball diamond are lined with five foot sound columns, with six or seven speakers in each. That was the sound reinforcement system for the fifty thousand fans seated (and screaming) in the stands!

There was also less emphasis placed on the performance as another retailing opportunity for the artist. It was looked upon as another way of enhancing record sales, instead of a large revenue generating experience. Today a worldwide concert tour takes years to complete and produces millions for top artists in ticket and merchandising sales revenues. Today, artists are totally aware of the potential and power of the live performance, and approach the live show creatively, to bring the consumer the most unforgettable experience possible. **CONCERTS DON'T SELL,**

EVENTS SELLOUT! (A more in-depth discussion of a show appears in Chapter Nine.)

Video

How important is it? Should we spend the money? I don't know how to act anyway? Are we sure that they sell recordings? Is everyone still releasing videos?

The video impact on the business is obvious. The Recording Industry Association of America (RIAA) has established the quotas for Gold and Platinum video awards. Figure 8.4 lists the number of units needed to be sold for video singles, long forms, and matchbox sets to be certified as gold, platinum, and multi-platinum sellers.

GOLD & PLATINUM AWARDS CERTIFICATION LEVELS

	Gold	Platinum	Multi-Platinum
Video Single	25,000 units: max. running time of 15 minutes: two songs per title	50,000 units: max. running time of 15 minutes: two songs per title	100,000 units: max. running time of 15 minutes: two songs per title
Video Long Form	50,000 units	100,000 units	200,000 units
Video Multi-Box	50,000 units	100,000 units	200,000 units

Figure 8.4 Gold and Platinum Awards Certification Levels (Audio and Video). Statistical Overview 1991. Inside the Record Industry. RIAA, Washington DC p. 16.

Although they represent only one-twentieth of the amounts needed for audio recording certifications, it should be noted that the configuration (or some form of video configuration) is still in its infancy stage.

Also, the sale of music videos has not come close to what has been expected. In the early 1980's, it was thought that consumers would no longer purchase audio recordings. Their sales would be replaced by videos of entire albums that would be watched as well as listened to. That has not yet become a reality. Consumers seem to still want the freedom to do what they want when they want to, and use music in a variety of ways. Therefore, personal listening has continued to rise and the purchasing of entire video albums has yet to blossom. Also must be noted is the inferior quality of the VHS format. As the digital perfection of the Cd listening experience became the standard, the inferior quality of the VHS became more obvious. The DVD format will take care of any quality issue.

Promotional videos have become an industry staple. MTV recognized this in the mid 1980's and offered to pay major record companies for the exclusive right to exhibit new releases. The radio industry was astonished that MTV would be willing to pay for a service that radio stations have always received for free. However, MTV gambled that the way to stifle competition from other video presenters was to gain exclusivity to new releases and was willing to pay for that access. It proved to be a brilliant decision as MTV is now THE worldwide video presenter.

The forerunners to the modern videos were called "**soundies**". They surfaced in the 1940's, and "were an ambitious attempt to merge the jukebox concept with three-minute filmclips."[11] They were made by the Mills Novelty Company in Chicago who in 1941, also began manufacturing Panorams. The Panorams were the hardware (viewing and listening machines) that were used to play the soundies. The screens were the size of two pieces of letterhead stationery, and selections were changed twice a month. Because racism prevailed, two separate catalogs were issued and distributed along color lines. Customers paid a dime to see a clip, almost entirely made of close-up shots with crude lip syncing. Because reels became outdated in a matter of days, the idea suffered from a built-in obsolescence.[12]

The early modern videos were basically concert footage (either live or staged) of the group performing. During the early 1980's the concept video appeared. In some related loose form, the story told in the lyrics was acted out by members of the group. The concept was usually a nonlinear approach, where certain scenes and symbols would appear and reappear without any simple storytelling logic.

The nonlinear concept was new, exciting, and fresh to television. Up until that point, TV shows used a linear approach. For example, in a detective show, a crime would be committed and then solved. A situation comedy would set up a dilemma (situation), and then act out the solution. Soap operas would do the same thing, only they would add a few twists and turns to unravel the story over time.

The first network show to use the nonlinear approach over any length of time was NBC's Miami Vice. The fashion statements were perfect for the 1980's video viewing age group, and the quasi nonlinear concept with rock stars making guest appearances, gave the show a long run.

The concept music video is commonplace today. Video producers and directors must consciously develop concepts that compliment the artist's image. If it is so unbelievable that it's down right silly, it could spell trouble for the artist. Even video king, Michael Jackson was criticized for (and quickly pulled) the smashing of the cars scenes from the Dangerous album's initial video.

Record companies realize the promotional importance of videos and the possibility that their sales or licensing may become strong revenue producers. Therefore, what was once a few paragraphs of a recording contract, now encompasses several pages. Below are key video clauses and commentary from a recent recording contract. Use it as guide. **Do not** negotiate video rights without consulting an entertainment attorney.

Video Clauses

1.

(a) In addition to ARTIST's recordings and PRODUCTIONS, production and delivery commitments as set forth in Paragraph # of this Agreement, PRODUCTIONS and ARTIST shall comply with requests, if any, made by COMPANY in connection with the production of Pictures. In this connection, PRODUCTIONS shall cause ARTIST to appear on dates and at places requested by COMPANY for the filming, taping or other fixation of audiovisual recordings. PRODUCTIONS and ARTIST shall perform services with respect thereto as COMPANY deems desirable in a timely and first-class manner. PRODUCTIONS and ARTIST acknowledge that the production of Pictures involves matters of judgment with respect to art and taste, which judgment shall mutually exercised by COMPANY and PRODUCTIONS in good faith, it being understood that if agreement cannot be reached, COMPANY's decisions with respect thereto shall be final.

In this contract, the artist's works are being produced by a company called PRODUCTIONS, and the COMPANY is requiring the artist to appear for "pictures" when asked. It also states that the record company will have the final word on the release of the audiovisual work, even though it plans on discussing the matter with the artist in good faith.

(b)

(i) Each picture produced during the Term of this Agreement shall be owned by **COMPANY** (including the worldwide copyrights therein and thereto and all extensions and renewals thereof) to the same extent as COMPANY's rights in master recordings made under this Agreement.

(ii) COMPANY will have the unlimited right to manufacture Videoshows of the Picture and to rent, sell, distribute, transfer, sublicense of otherwise deal in such Videoshows under any trademarks, tradenames and labels; to exploit the Picture by any means now or hereafter known or developed; or to refrain from any such exploitation, throughout the world.

(c)

(i) Following COMPANY's receipt of invoices therefor, COMPANY agrees to pay all costs actually incurred in the production of Pictures made at COMPANY's request hereunder, provided such costs have been previously approved by COMPANY in writing. In this connection, prior to commencing production of any Picture, PRODUCTIONS shall submit to COMPANY, in writing, a detailed budget for each Picture. Said budget shall include the following information: (i) the musical compositions and other material to be embodied thereon (ii) the general concept therefor and (iii) the producer, director, and any other key personnel therefor. Following PRODUCTIONS' receipt of COMPANY's approval of said budget, PRODUCTIONS' shall commence production if the Picture. All costs incurred in excess of the applicable approved budget shall be PRODUCTIONS' sole responsibility and PRODUCTIONS agrees to pay any such excess costs on

PRODUCTIONS' behalf, PRODUCTIONS shall, upon demand, reimburses COMPANY for such excess costs and/or COMPANY may deduct such excess costs from any and all monies due to PRODUCTIONS pursuant to this or any other agreement between the parties hereto. All sums paid by COMPANY in connection with each Picture shall be an advance against and recoupable by COMPANY out of all royalties becoming payable to PRODUCTIONS pursuant to this or any other agreement, provided that COMPANY shall not recoup more than fifty (50%) percent of such sums from royalties becoming payable to PRODUCTIONS pursuant to Paragraph # of this Agreement.

These clauses specify ownership and how production costs will be paid. It also addresses COMPANY'S right to cross-collateralize up to 50% of sum stated in an earlier paragraph. Remember that almost all percentages are negotiable.

(ii) Each of the following sums, if any, paid by COMPANY in connection with each Picture shall be an advance against and recoupable by COMPANY out of all royalties becoming payable to PRODUCTIONS pursuant to this or any other agreement, provided that COMPANY shall not recoup more than fifty (50%) percent of such sums from royalties becoming payable to PRODUCTIONS pursuant to Paragraph # of this Agreement:

Fifty percent is the standard sum.

(A) All expenses incurred by COMPANY in connection with the preparation and production of the Picture and the conversion of the Picture to Video Masters that are made to serve as prototypes for the duplication of the Videoshows of the Picture;

(B) All of COMPANY'S direct out-of-pocket costs (such as for rights, artists (including ARTIST), other personnel, facilities, materials, services, and the use of equipment) in connection with all steps in the production of the Picture and the process leading to and including the production of such Video Masters (including, but not limited to, packaging costs and the costs of making and delivering duplicate copies of such Video Masters); and (COMPANY) If in connection therewith COMPANY furnishes any of its own facilities, materials, services or equipment for which COMPANY has a standard rate, the amount of such standard rate or if there is no standard rate, the market value for the services or thing furnished.

(iii) All sums that COMPANY in its sole discretion deems necessary or advisable to pay in connection with the production of Pictures and the exploitation of COMPANY'S right therein in order to clear rights or to make any contractual payments that are or may become due on the part of COMPANY, to PRODUCTIONS, ARTIST or any other person, form or corporation by virtue of the exploitation of COMPANY'S rights therein, in order to avoid, satisfy or make unnecessary any claims or demands by any person, firm or corporation claiming the right to payment therefor, including, but not limited to, any payment to an actual or alleged copyright owner, patent owner, union, union-related trust fund, pension plan or other entity, and any payment for an actual or alleged rerun fee, residual, royalty, license fee or otherwise shall constitute advances against and recoupable out of all royalties becoming payable to PRODUCTIONS pursuant to this or any other agreement between the parties hereto. No payment pursuant to this subparagraph shall constitute a waiver of any of PRODUCTIONS' express or implied warranties and representations.

(d) Conditioned upon PRODUCTIONS' and ARTIST'S full and faithful performance of all of the terms and conditions of this Agreement, COMPANY shall pay PRODUCTIONS the following royalties with respect to Pictures:

(i) In respect of COMPANY'S commercial exploitation, if any, of Video shows solely embodying Pictures subject hereto which are sold through normal retailer channels for the "home video market" (as such term is commonly understood in the music and video industry):

(A)

(1) With respect to Album Video shows sold through normal retailer channels in the United States, full priced as initially released, a royalty rate at the rate equal to applicable Basic U.S. Album Rate;

The rate should be negotiated, and the basic album rate should not be accepted.

(2) The royalty rate set forth in the last paragraph is hereinafter sometimes referred to as the "Basic U.S. Home Video Rate".

(B)

(1) With respect to Album Video shows sold through normal retailer channels outside the United States, full priced as initially released, the royalty rate shall be the applicable Basic Foreign Album Rate;

(2) The royalty rate set forth in the last paragraph is hereinafter sometimes referred to as the "Basic Foreign Home Video Rate".

As a reminder, all rates are negotiable.

(C) Except as otherwise set forth in this Agreement, the applicable Basic U.S. Home Video Rate and the applicable Basic Foreign Home Video Rate shall be calculated, computed, determined, prorated, reduced, adjusted (but not escalated) and paid in the same manner and at the same times (e.g., configurations other than Albums, "free goods", reserves, percentages of sales, price, number of units for which royalties are payable, calculated, computed, determined, prorated, reduced, adjusted (but not escalated) pursuant to Paragraph # of this Agreement

(ii)

(A) The applicable Basic U.S. Home Video Rate and applicable Basic Foreign Home Video Rate shall be applied against COMPANY's wholesale price, as hereinafter defined (less COMPANY's container deductions, distribution fees, excise taxes, duties and other applicable taxes) for Videoshows sold which are paid for and not returned. The term "wholesale price" as used in this Paragraph # shall mean that amount which COMPANY received from COMPANY's distributor(s), whether or not affiliated with COMPANY, for each such Videoshow. In computing sales, COMPANY shall have the right to deduct all so-called "free goods" and all returns made at any time and for any reason. COMPANY may maintain reasonable reserves against returns. Videoshows distributed in the United States by any of COMPANY's affiliated branch wholesalers shall be deemed sold for the purposes of this Agreement only if sold by any such affiliated branch wholesaler to one of its independent third party customers.

Here the company is attempting to define what is meant by wholesale price, free goods, and returns. It also is attempting to maintain "reasonable" reserves against returns. These reserves should not be greater than the reserves held against the audio recording returns.

(B) COMPANY's container deductions in respect of Videoshows shall be a sum equal to: (i) twenty (20%) percent of the wholesale price of the applicable Videoshow for Videoshows in COMPANY's standard packaging for one cassette, disc, cartridge or other unit, and (ii) thirty (30%) percent of the whole-sale price of the applicable Videoshow for Videoshow in packaging for more than one cassette, disc, cartridge or other unit, or packaging with special materials, components, inserts or elements, or in any form of package, container or box other than COMPANY's standard packaging for one cassette, disc, cartridge or other unit.

Wow! These percentages are high.

(iii) With respect to sales and uses of Pictures hereunder other than Videoshow sold through normal retailer channels for the home video market, COMPANY shall pay PRODUCTIONS royalties equal to fifty (50%) percent of COMPANY's Video Net Receipts with respect to COMPANY's exploitation of Pictures subject to this Agreement, unless otherwise elsewhere provided to the contrary in this Agreement Monies earned and received by COMPANY form any licensee (rather than monies earned and received by the licensee) in respect of exploitation from Pictures shall be included in the conjunction of Video Net Receipts.

(iv) No royalties shall be payable to PRODUCTIONS hereunder in respect of Videoshows comprising so-called "video magazines", sampler or other promotional formats, or in respect of Pictures or Videoshows used or distributed for promotional purposes, whether or not COMPANY receives payment therefor.

(v) The royalties provided in subparagraphs (d) (i) and (iii) include any royalty obligations COMPANY may have to any other person, firm or corporation who supplied services or rights used in connection with pictures, including, without limitation, producers, directors, extras, and music publisher, and any such royalties shall be deducted form the video royalties otherwise payable to PRODUCTIONS.

(vi) With respect to records embodying Pictures made hereunder together with other material, royalties payable to PRODUCTIONS shall be computed by multiplying the royalties otherwise applicable by a fraction, the numerator of which is the amount of playing time in any such record of Pictures made hereunder and the denominator of which is the total playing time of all material in any such record.

(vii) As to Pictures embodying performances of ARTIST together with the performances of another artist or artists, the royalties otherwise payable hereunder shall be prorated by multiplying such royalties by a fraction, the numerator of which is one and the denominator of which is the total number of artists whose performances are embodies on such Pictures. COMPANY shall not require ARTIST to so perform with other artists without PRODUCTIONS' consent, however, if ARTIST does perform with other artists, such performance shall constitute consent.

The formula stated in vi and vii is okay for a short form video where the artist is the star of the picture. However, in a long form video, if the artist is the biggest star on the video and his/her performance does not constitute the majority of the playing time, then this formula would have to be negotiated.

(e) COMPANY shall have the right to use and allow others to use each Picture for advertising and promotional purposes with no payment to PRODUCTIONS or ARTIST.

(f)

(i) During the Term of this Agreement, no person, firm or corporation other than COMPANY will be authorized to make, sell, broadcast or otherwise exploit audiovisual materials unless: (A) PRODUCTIONS first notifies COMPANY of all of the material terms and conditions of the proposed agreement pursuant to which the audiovisual materials is to be made, sold, broadcast or otherwise exploited, including, but no limited to, the titles of the compositions covered by the proposed agreement, the format to be used, the manner of exploitation proposed and the identities of all proposed parties to the agreement, and (B) PRODUCTIONS offers to enter into an agreement with COMPANY containing the same terms and conditions described in such notice and otherwise in the same form as this Agreement. If COMPANY does not accept PRODUCTIONS' offer within sixty (60) days after COMPANY's receipt of same, PRODUCTIONS may then enter into that proposed agreement with the same parties mentioned in such notice, subject to subparagraph (f) (ii) hereof and provided that such agreement is consummated with those parties within thirty (30) days after the end of that sixty (60) day period upon the same financial terms land condition set forth in PRODUCTIONS' notice and latter thirty (30) day period, no party except COMPANY will be authorized to make, sell, broadcast or otherwise exploit such audiovisual materials unless PRODUCTIONS first offers to enter into an agreement with COMPANY as provided in the first sentence of this subparagraph . . . .

(ii) If COMPANY does not accept an offer made to it pursuant to this subparagraph (f), such nonacceptance shall not be considered a waiver of any of COMPANY's rights pursuant this Agreement. Such rights include, without limitation, the right to prevent PRODUCTIONS from exploiting audiovisual material featuring ARTIST in the form of Videoshows, and the right to prevent PRODUCTIONS from authorizing any use of masters owned by or exclusively licensed to COMPANY unless COMPANY so agree. PRODUCTIONS shall not act in contravention of such rights.

COMPANY is exercising a right to first refusal by asking for notice and a time period to respond. It also is stating that it is not given up any of its rights to masters.

(g) Not withstanding anything to the contrary contained in subparagraph (f), ARTIST shall have the right to perform as an actor in motion pictures or other visual media, the contents of which are dramatic and substantially non-musical.

(h) In all other respects (e.g., the times for accounting to be rendered, and warranties . . . .

Media Check! Live vs. Audio vs. Video

It is often said that artists that land a recording deal and don't make it, fail because of one of two reasons: poor management (read this book) or a lack of understanding of the differences between live performance and recorded performance. So many artists have said "we don't know what happened man, we sounded so great on stage, but the excitement was not captured on our record." Demo recordings of many great young bands do not sound as good as the band does in a club. On the other hand, occasionally, bands that sell a whole bunch of records, are disappointments when seen in concert. One of the reasons is that young bands that play in clubs night after night become really proficient at playing in the live medium. And some bands with record deals make records that are produced by producers who understand the medium of recording make great records, however, when they play in front of 10,000 people for the first time, they don't sound so hot because they have yet to master the arena performance medium.

Some things that work great on stage for a live performance can not be captured in the audio (recorded) medium. However, on the record, something different takes the place of the stage happening to generate excitement. For example, listen to a Rolling Stone's record, the excitement that is generated by Mick Jagger prancing across the stage making faces at the audience, is somehow compensated for in the studio medium to develop that excitement. Secondly, The Stones are not intimidated by the physical characteristics of the recording studio. They do not let the isolation of the studio hinder their performance. To capture their sound they layer tracks, double themselves, and use every studio trick ever invented (I'm certain that they invented quite a few themselves). The record is produced with the clear understanding that it must generate the excitement of the visual effects of their show without being scene. The producer understands the recording medium and its uniqueness.

Over the last ten years, a third, yet different medium has become important. Artists must have an understanding of what is successful in the video medium. Television and computer screens (video) wash colors and make one appear to be heavier than s/he really is. The illusion of movement can be created by moving the camera or background scenery. Lyrics and solos can be lip-synced to allow for exaggerated acting. Producers and directors make videos work. Again, it is the understanding of the uniqueness of the medium that is important.

As a manager, it is suggested that if an artist has not had experience in the recorded medium, the making of an entire album master (rather than a demo) should be discouraged. More often than not, a great deal of expense is incurred, and the end result of the ego trip is a record that does not capture the live excitement of the band's club performances. The same must be said for the budget video. Leave it the pros. In the end money will be saved.

Guiding The Creative Talent

What is the manager's role in guiding an artist? On page 63 in *Guiding Creative Talent*, Paul Torrance lists both general and specific goals in guiding creative talent. He lists the general goals as:

1. encouraging of a healthy kind of individuality

2. developing of conditions which will permit creativeness

3. regressing in the service of the ego and

4. counteracting pressures of regression to the average.

In order to achieve the general goals, he suggest obtaining the following specific goals as essential:

1. reward diverse contributions

2. help creative persons recognize the value of their own talents

3. avoid exploitation

4. accept limitations creatively

5. develop minimum skills

6. make use of opportunities

7. develop values and purposes

8. hold to purposes

9. avoid the equation of divergent with mental illness or delinquency

10. reduce overemphasis or misplace emphasis on sex roles

11. help them learn how to be less obnoxious

12. reduce isolation and

13. help them learn how to cope with anxieties, fears, hardships, and failures.[13]

And who said management wasn't fun!

SUMMARY

1. The creative process is a function of the right hemisphere of the brain.

2. The creative process is different for different people and different for the same individual at different times.

3. Traits of the creative individual include being intuitive, open-minded, spontaneous, sensitive, flexible, and original.

4. Traits of the creative product include: unusualness, appropriateness, newness, and compactness.

5. Unless in a coma, everyone has some degree of creativity.

6. Research has found that the greatest contributions to their field were made by musicians between thirty and forty years old.

7. Factors that accompany age change bring about a reduction in creativity.

8. Creativity cannot be taught, but creative uses of a craft can.

9. Creativity can be evaluated by some quantitative measure.

10. Songwriting is both an art and a craft.

11. Songs that have a potential of being successful have certain characteristics.

12. Money is made from songwriting by exploiting the copyright.

13. The Songwriter's Guild of America publishes a Popular Songwriter's Contract that contains clauses describing all revenue producing areas.

14. The music publisher's role of exploiting the song's copyright includes many functions.

15. Publishers receive income form six basic song uses.

16. The publisher and songwriter usually split income on an equal basis.

17. The RIAA now lists criteria for Gold and Platinum Video Awards.

18. The first videos were called soundies and were viewed on panorams.

19. Many modern music videos use the nonlinear concept of story evolution.

20. Record company video clauses have grown larger and more complex.

21. Many artists with record contracts are not successful because they do not understand the differences between the live vs. audio and now video media.

22. Management must play a role in guiding creative talent.

PROJECTS

1. Think of someone you know who you feel is very creative. List his/her personality characteristics.

2. Analyze why a song is successful. List the characteristics that make it successful.

3. Discuss whether songwriting is an art or a craft.

4. Compile a songwriter/publisher agreement that is fair for both parties.

5. Discuss the nonlinear approach of story evolution in a current music video.

6. List the different characteristics of live vs. audio vs. video performance.

7. Discuss the role of management in the nurturing of creative talent.

NOTES

John S. Dacey. Fundamentals of Creative Thinking. Lexington Books. Lexington, MA. 1989, pg. 7-8.

Gudmund J. Smith & Ingegerd M. Carlsson. The Creative Process. International Universities Press, Inc. Madison, CT. 1990. pg. 1.

Edward Buxton. Creative People at Work. *Executive Communications, Inc.* New York, 1975. pg. x.

Op. Cit., *Fundamentals of Creative Thinking.* pg. 5.

E. Paul Torrance. Guiding Creative Talent. Prentice Hall, Inc., Englewood Cliffs, NJ, 1962. pg. 100.

Op. Cit., Creative People at Work. Interview with Marvin Honig of Dole, Dane, Bernback Agency. pg. 17.

Morris I. Stein. Stimulating Creativity Vol 2. Academic Press Inc., New York, 1973, pg. vii.

Ian Whitcomb. After The Ball. Penguin Books Inc. Baltimore, MD. 1972. pg. 3.

David Baskerville, Music Business Handbook. Sherwood Publishing, Los Angeles, 1990. pg. 28-29.

Ibid. pg. 29.

R. Serge Denisoff, assisted by William Schurk. Tarnished Gold. Transaction Books, New Brunswick, NJ. 1986. pg. 330.

Ibid. pg. 331.

Op. Cit., Guiding Creative Talent. pg. 63.

CHAPTER NINE
Touring

"I've made seven albums and two babies in the last five years, but it's not the same as touring.
There's something so positive about it . . . Not that you're adulated,
but that you feel euphorically encouraged and completely whole."
Tina Weymouth, formerly of Talking Heads . . . Rolling Stone Magazine: *RS 491*

By the end of this chapter you should be able to:

1. Discuss the five basic tour objectives
2. Draw a timeline, listing the approximate deadlines for specific tour-related procedures
3. Discuss the most productive routing for most tours
4. Discuss the procedure for securing a concert performance
5. Discuss the various concert performance fee structures
6. Discuss the basic budget lines for an artist's tour
7. Discuss the various categories of a concert contract rider
8. Discuss tour publicity
9. Discuss all aspects of staging and production
10. Discuss how to evaluate a tour's objectives
11. Discuss the manager's role before, during, and after the tour.

ITS HISTORY

Touring has always played a role in musicians' lives. From the eleventh to the end of the thirteenth centuries, many poet-musicians traveled the southern regions of France, singing lyric poetry. In America, during the nineteenth century, minstrel shows with singers, musicians and variety acts combed the south daily. Around 1900, vaudeville entertainers visited the newly developed industrial urban centers, playing one- nighters. In the early 1920's, jazz musicians traveled from New Orleans, up the Mississippi toward Chicago, performing in every city along the way.

The big bands of the 1930's and early 1940's really solidified the idea of musicians being "married" to the road. Stories about the effects of travel on a musician's physical and emotional well being from this era are numerous. Although the players have changed and our transportation systems have improved, the road is still an essential part of a musician's life.

Rock musicians and rock bands have taken on the role of the big bands of 1930's and 40's. Each metropolitan area and region of the country had its own favorite big bands in those days. They included the nationally famous bands of the era. . . The Benny Goodman Band, The Glen Miller Orchestra, The Duke Ellington Orchestra, and others. Today, local and regional rock bands hope to gather a following of fans who are as loyal and who will allow them to perform their own material. Eventually they hope this will lead to a recording contract with a nationally distributed record company.

The live performance has been and continues to be a form of artist-to-consumer retailing. When someone purchases a ticket to see an artist perform, he or she is the consumer. The concert promoter is the retailer. The music is the product. And the live performance is a way of selling the artist's product. For this reason, performance, and touring remain very necessary aspects of an artist's career.

Fortunately, for most modern musicians, "the road" no longer means an old bus, cheap hotels, junk food, and beer joints. Most musicians have a strong desire to experience the rewards that an immediate response from an audience provides. As a manager, you'll need to know why, when, and where to tour. Some guidelines follow. A timeline is included, showing, when certain aspects of tour preparation should be completed. Take note of the objectives you will want to accomplish during the tour. Finally, you will be given some pointers on how to evaluate the tour's success. In this example, the artist on tour holds a recording contract with a major label and performs in arena venues of approximately 10,000 seats or more.

TOUR OBJECTIVES

Why tour at all? It's very expensive, and it consumes a great deal of time and energy from the artist and the manager. A successful tour can meet useful objectives. Several of these are:

ONE: To increase the artist's visibility in a given market.

Obviously, the artist's presence in a market increases the likelihood that the concertgoer will buy his or her record. In turn, the concertgoer will introduce the music to other people who might also buy the record. A concert provides the opportunity for an audience to see the artist perform in person, and to identify with him or her. While videos capture some aspects of an artist's personality, this "cool" medium does not have the same impact as the artist's physical presence. A video cannot really capture Bruce Springsteen's charisma!

TWO: To increase the number of industry workers on the artist's team and win their loyalty.

When an artist arrives in a city for a concert performance, he or she should spend the time wisely. The artist should make contact with the record company's local representatives (which generally include the promotion and sales representatives), radio stations and other media personnel, the local record retail community, and anyone else who might prove useful in furthering his or her career. These meetings, although sometimes tiresome and repetitious to the artist, pay off "down the road." These individuals appreciate the opportunity to meet the person behind the music.

THREE: To make the artist's performance "an event" on a performance by performance basis.

Unless an artist is well-known enough to receive immediate national media exposure via "Entertainment Tonight," "The Today Show," or other news and information programs, a ground swell effect must be created on a market-by-market basis. The objective is to develop a ripple effect that will extend to additional markets. Creating a media event pays off! They almost always sell out; most ordinary performances or concerts do not. Contests, give-aways, tie-ins with local sponsors, will help to distinguish your artist's concert as special. The same promotional "gimmicks" maybe used throughout the tour. But they must be tailored to every individual stop so they seem fresh and exciting.

FOUR: To provide an opportunity for the artist to perform in a major market when the record is reaching its "stride."

Many releases usually reach their "stride" about twelve weeks after they are released. At that point, some haven't peaked yet, but have had time to gather enough momentum so that they begin to sell themselves. By this time, the ripple effect should have reached enough people, given an artist has the opportunity to perform in a major market and make a profit. (A performance should not be scheduled in a major market if enough tickets won't be sold to make any money!) According to the 2000 Rand McNally Commercial Atlas and Marketing Guide, over forty percent of the American population live in the twenty major markets. Selling product in these markets is critical to an artist's success.

FIVE: To make a profit.

An artist may derive a tremendous amount of creative fulfillment from performing. And you may get personal satisfaction from managing. But the bottom line is the artist is a business.

Below is a brief summary of an article that appeared in *Rolling Stone Magazine* on November 28, 1996. It ran just after the group, Pearl Jam, made a goal line stance for its fans and challenged the monopoly that Ticketmaster has on the entertainment industry. The band was upset with the high service charges that Ticketmaster was demanding for tickets to its shows. It estimates that the band might have given up over $30 million. Too bad other headliners didn't join the band in its pursuit.

"If Pearl Jam simply plugged into the established summertime concert system both this year and last - playing approximately 40 shows each summer at mostly Ticketmaster-controlled amphitheaters - they could have earned $20 million from ticket sales. The band could have raked in an additional $5 million from merchandising and $6 million from corporate sponsorships.

Assuming that Pearl Jam had sold out 20,000 seat capacity venues at $23 a ticket, generating $460,000 in revenues each night the band would have taken home $330,000 from each of the 40 performances, or $13.2 million each summer. After deducting for eight-week production costs ($800,000), an agent's 6 percent commission ($792,000), and a manager's 15 percent commission ($1.7 million), that would have left Pearl Jam with $9.9 million each year, reported at year's end by *Performance Magazine*. The Rolling Stones' "Bridges to Babylon" was the top-grossing tour of 1997, taking in $90 million, and continuing to hold its top-grossing record from its 1989 and '94 tours. U2 grossed $78 million, followed by Metallica, with $37 million. Overall, the top 50 touring acts took in $781 million.[2] As reported in several places in this text, the prospects look even brighter for the current tours.

PREPARING FOR THE TOUR

WHEN AND WHERE TO START

Deciding where to begin a tour depends upon a number of factors. The tour should begin far from media attention and industry visibility. This insulation gives the artist a chance to iron out unforeseen problems before moving into a major market. Problems may occur in the actual stage/performance, the technical production preparation, or the performance publicity. Any media attention at this point might focus negatives, and could damage the tour.

One rule of thumb is to begin a tour approximately eight weeks after the release of the record. By this time, the album's first single should be getting airplay, and album should be coming into its "stride." The artist should play the secondary and tertiary markets (metro areas numbers 16-30 in Figure 9.1) for three or four weeks, and then perform in the major target markets about twelve weeks after the release (see Figure 9.2).

ROUTING

In which secondary market should the tour begin? In which secondary market will the artist draw a large enough audience to show a profit? Where is a good place to

1996 RAND MCNALLY METRO AREAS
RANKED BY POPULATION

RMA	POP. EST
1.New York, NY-NJ-CT	18,105,300
2.Los Angeles	12,393,700
3.Chicago, ILL-IN-WI	8,177,900
4.San Francisco	5,769,100
5.Phil, PA-NJ-DE-MD	5,620,400
6 Boston, MA-NH	4,469,000
7.Detroit, MI-CAN	4,409,400
8.Wash, DC-MD-VA	4,041,100
9.Dallas	4,026,800
10.Miami	3,765,400
11.Houston	3,734,000
12.Atlanta	3,072,300
13.Seattle	2,817,500
14.Minneapolis, MN-WI	2,486,100
15.Phoenix	2,475,100
16.St. Louis, MO-IL	2,368,400
17.San Diego, CA- MEX	2,353,100
18.Cleveland	2,160,100
19.Baltimore	2,099,400
20.Pittsburgh	2,047,500
21.Denver	1,841,500
22.Cinc, OH-KY-IN	1,609,700
23.Portland, OR-WA 24	1,586,000
24.Kansas City, MO-KS	1,465,900
25.Milwaukee	1,426,300
26.Riverside, CA	1,413,900
27.Sacramento	1,301,000
28.San Antonio	1,283,000
29.Indianapolis	1,251,400
30.New Orleans	1,168,000

Source: 1997 Rand McNally Commercial Atlas & Marketing Guide, *Pg.126.*
Figure 9.1

try out the material and warm up the show? Should the tour begin in the east or someplace in the Midwest?

The key to a successful tour is flexibility. As manager, you must be willing to add additional dates and reroute the artist at any time. The tentative routing of the tour should begin several months prior to its start (see Figure 9.2). It makes good business sense to begin somewhat close to the artist's home. People and equipment will only need to travel a short distance. If the artist lives in Atlanta, why cart the equipment across the country to begin in Boise, Idaho? Sketch out where (in which major market) you would like to be when you anticipate the record hitting its stride. Use the weekend nights as cornerstones for the routing and build the rest of the tour around these dates. It's feasible to play markets that are starved for entertainment on weekday nights; however, it is great if the dates in major markets are booked for weekends. Of course, if the artist is very popular, it doesn't matter if the concert is

Tour Plan Timeline

January	April		July
Management & Agent Begin Tour Plan	Record rehearsed	Secure service of travel agent	Major markets performed
	Holds on venues	Dates Confirmed	
	Opening act chosen	Tunes chosen to be performed	
	Scale model of production made	Rehearsal begins	
	Tour announcement to medio	Tour manager hired	
		Tour begins	

Figure 9.2

on a weekday or a weekend. However, if the venue attracts audiences from great distances, people needing to go to work the next day might affect attendance at a weekday concert. If the artist has toured before, use the results of previous tours to rationalize why a certain routing should be successful.

Some variables may decrease the size of the anticipated audience. First, be aware of the other "traffic" in the market (traffic refers to concerts by competing artists). If an artist that draws the same audience that your artist does has performed in the market within two weeks prior to your artist's show, it may seriously hurt ticket sales. This is especially true if your artist's audience has a limited disposable income, or the market's population cannot with stand a too heavy concert schedule.

Second, be aware of the economic conditions of the market. A depressed economy may seriously decrease the expected number of ticket sales in a geographic area; no matter how much publicity you have. An example of this would be the effect the price of oil has on Houston, Texas.

PROCEDURE

The process of securing a concert performance involves the artist's manager, the booking agent, and the concert promoter. The following is a typical sequence of events:

STEP 1: The manager and agent arrive at a fee the artist is seeking for his or her performance.

This price is based on the tour's budget, and the artist's worth in the marketplace. The price may be represented in three different forms:

1. A flat guarantee

2. A guarantee vs. a percentage (whichever is greater) after verified expenses

3. A guarantee plus a percentage after verified expenses

4. A percentage after verified expenses

1. A flat guarantee

Today, even though a headlining artist usually does not perform solely for a guaranteed price, it is still an option. A flat guarantee is most often the price offered to an opening act. For example, **"The artist will perform one 45 minute set for $2500 flat guarantee."**

2. A guarantee vs. a percentage

Many headlining artists require a concert promoter to guarantee them a sum of money to perform, and will also want to share in the profits from the number of tickets sold. This option assures them a sum of money in case ticket sales don't meet their expectations. For example, **"The artist will perform for $60,000 guarantee vs. 85% of the Gross Box Office Receipts after verified expenses, whichever is greater."** In this case, if the gross potential from the ticket receipts after taxes is $400,000, and the promoter has incurred expenses of $220,000 (the artist's guarantee may or may not be included in these calculations), the remainder would be $180,000. The artist would receive 85% of the remainder or $153,000. The concert promoter would receive the rest — $27,000.

$400,000 GP
-$220,000 Expenses
$180,000 Remaining
$180,000
      x .85
$153,000 Artist receives

$ 27,000 Promoter receives

3. A guarantee plus a percentage after verified expense

Headlining artists may require a concert promoter to guarantee them a sum of money to perform, and will also want to share in the profits from the number of tickets sold (see Figure 9.4). This option assures them a sum of money plus an over-ride. For example, **"The artist will perform for $60,000 guarantee plus 85% of the Gross Box Office Receipts after verified expenses, including 15% promoter's fee."** In this case, if the gross potential from the ticket receipts after taxes is $400,000, and the promoter has incurred expenses of $280,000 (the artist's guarantee is included in these calculations), the remainder would be $120,000. The artist would receive 85% of the remainder or $102,000 (plus $60,000). The concert promoter would receive the rest — $18,000.

> $400,000 GP
> -$220,000 Expenses
> -$60,000 artist guarantee
> $120,000
>   x .85
> $102,000 + $60,000 Artist receives
>
> $ 18,000 Promoter receives

4. A percentage after verified expenses

On occasion, headlining artists may not require a concert promoter to guarantee a performance fee, but demand a higher percentage of the net receipts (after verified expenses). These are artists who are in demand at show time because of a long awaited release of an album or are just simply hot. The contract would read **"90% of the Gross Box Office Receipts after verified expenses (including taxes, if required)."** In this case, if the gross potential from the ticket sales after taxes is $400,000, and the promoter has incurred expense of $220,000, the remaining $180,000 would be split $162,000 for the artist and $18,000 for the concert promoter.

> $400,000 Gross Potential
> -$220,000 Expenses
> $180,000
>
>
> $180,000
>   x .90
> $162,000 Artist Receives
>
> $ 18,000 Promoter Receives

This method gives the artist a greater percentage of the profit and may be demanded by management when a sellout is almost assured.

Some headliners may demand a graduated scale of the compensation agreed upon (with or without a guarantee). As an example, this clause might read:

"85% of the Gross Box Office Receipts up to 80% capacity,

87.5% of the Gross Box Office Receipts from 81-90% capacity,

90% of the Gross Box Office Receipts from 91% capacity and over.

All Percentages are after verified expenses."

So if we use these percentages in our example, we still have a Gross Potential of $400,000 and expenses of $220,000. However, if the show is not a sellout, the actual ticket sales will not reach the gross potential, but the expenses will remain the same. (In fact, expenses usually rise because additional advertising is needed that was not originally budgeted, and thus becomes an added expense.) So at 80% capacity, the revenue from ticket sales is only $320,000. $320,000 - $220,000 expenses leaves only $100,000. The artist would receive only $85,000 and the promoter $15,000. (The artist would probably never perform for the promoter again!)

At 80% capacity:

$320,000 Gross
$220,000 expenses
$100,000 net

$100,000
x .85
$ 85,000 Artist receives

$ 15,000 Promoter receives

At 90% capacity:

$360,000 Gross
$220,000 expenses
$140,000 net

$140,000
x .875
$122,500 Artist receives

$ 17,500 Promoter receives

At sellout, the split would be the same as our first example in this section. The artist would receive $162,000 and the promoter $18,000.

In both circumstances, when there is a sellout (in numbers two and three), the promoter expects to receive to receive around 5% of the concert's gross after all expenses, including the artist's share. As stated in an article about Pace Concerts, one of the largest promoters in the country: "Pace Concerts expects to net 4 percent to 7 percent of a concert's gross after accounting for expenses and settling with the band."[3]

STEP 2: The agent solicits concert promoters in each region of the country, or calls venues in each region to inquire about available dates.

The booking agent calls each concert promoter with the artist's price requirement and other details to determine if the promoter will buy or "pass" on the act's package. Even at this early stage, some negotiations occur concerning the selling price of tickets, and the scaling of the house (how many seats at what price). In fact, some managers insist that every item is thoroughly discussed. However, now the promoter must decide if he or she can deliver a sellout show.

In 1998, the concert business drastically changed. Robert Sillerman created SFX (for "S"illerman and his middle initials "F" and "X") Entertainment. One of the objectives of the company was to control the production of live concert performances throughout the world by owning the concert promotion business and the venues. Today, it owns or manages over 135 concert venues worldwide, and is present in 31 of the top 50 U.S. markets. It also owns an online ticket-sales site. Currently, CC/SFX tours include: Backstreet Boys, U2, and Billy Joel & Elton John.

In 2000, Clear Channel Communications bought SFX in an all stock deal. The company was founded in 1972 and owns over 1000 radio stations, domestic and foreign, in 47 or the 50 largest U.S. cities; 500,000 billboards; and 20 TV stations.[4] The strategic plan and business model for the conglomerate is obvious. After all, why pay others when you can pay yourself!

Although there are promoters still doing business as either SFX affiliates or independents, a manager may now be offered an SFX tour or a string of dates in SFX venues instead of a traditional region by region tour.

STEP 3: Traditionally, the promoter or agent puts a tentative hold on a venue for a specific date (or dates).

Professional and college sports, circuses, ice shows, auto shows, trade shows, etc. are held in arenas. So they are booked very heavily across the country. At times, very few dates that allow sufficient time for concert setup and breakdown are available to the promoter. So tentative holds on specific dates should be placed as early as possible.

STEP 4: Dates are confirmed with weekend nights as cornerstones.

As the manager accepts the offers to perform, the dates are confirmed with each venue. Using the weekend nights as the basis for building the rest of the tour, the routing begins to take shape. As this occurs, the manager and agent make decisions as to how many miles they want the artist and the entourage to travel between performances in each region. Obviously, the number of miles between performances will differ in the west as compared to the northeast. After this decision has been made, the rest of the performance dates are accepted to complete the tour itinerary.

The confirming of the dates indicates that a decision has been made as to the selling price of the admission tickets. The concert promoter in each region must negotiate an admission price that matches the economic conditions of his/her region, and still meets all expenses, including a profit for him/herself. According to John Scher, a former concert promoter and part-owner of Metropolitan Entertainment, and then head of Polygram Diversified Entertainment, the factors entering into the decision concerning how much to charge include: the artist guarantee and the cost of media advertising space and time.5 Both have risen significantly in recent years, and the concert business has suffered. Scher goes on to say that the ticket price a consumer will pay is rarely established by the promoter or the artist; but by the ticket scalper.

"... for hot attractions people are willing to pay very large sums of money for the best tickets. A high ticket price minimizes the difference between what these tickets are ultimately being sold for by scalpers and what the box office is getting for them."6

Then why aren't ticket prices for super attractions higher in general? Richard Thayer, an economist at Cornell says that "those with businesses cannot afford the "perception of unfairness." He argues, "if you gouge skiers at Christmas, they won't come back in March."7 Consequently, because the concert promoter's business is at risk, the ticket price is extremely important.

Recently, concert ticket surcharges have caused ill feelings. Ticket surcharges include add-ons such as parking, ticket service charges, and facility fees. Generally, these fees are non-negotiable and the artist does not share in the revenue. "If they're putting $3-$5 on as a facility charge, what do we pay rent for?" asks Doc McGhee, manager of Kiss. "If you're talking 20,000 people in a shed, that's $100,000 the artist is not participating in. If you want to charge more rent, then do it. Don't call it something else."8 Consequently, if a ticket is advertised at $50 and is really much higher, the artist looks insensitive but isn't participating in the extra revenue.

The author recently bought two tickets for a show online.

Total Face Value	$ 75.00
Facility Charge	$ 4.00
Subtotal	$ 79.00
Convenience Charge	$ 18.10
Order Proc. Fee	$ 3.55
TOTAL CHARGE	$ 100.65

BUDGET

A manager can never be too conservative in estimating a tour budget! If an artist is "going out" for a guarantee against a percentage, the tour budget should be based roughly on the guarantee with only a small percentage of potential additional earnings being anticipated.

TRAVEL AND ACCOMMODATIONS

Secure the services of a competent, reliable travel agent for booking hotel rooms, public transportation, and local car rentals. An agent's services do not cost anything, and an efficient one allows the manager to concentrate on the tour's other pressing issues. Trailer trucks and a band bus (provided the artist has agreed to this mode of travel) are usually leased separately from a leasing firm and are not the travel agent's responsibility.

CHOOSING AN OPENING ACT

All consumers respond to value for their money. When they purchase their tickets, many concertgoers are aware of who is the opening act. Therefore a hot opening act should increase ticket sales. If the agent, record company, or promoter hasn't forced an opening act on the show, a smart manager should look for an opening act that has had a level of success that will have name recognition with the audience. An opening act should have an image that complements the headliner. An act that has already toured should have a small base of ticket buyers already established. However, nothing guarantees that the opening act will help fill the seats. A manager must rely on his or her own intuition plus any hard data concerning the prospective opening act's performing ability.

Once the manager chooses the act, he or she must "buy" the act before some other act's manager does. The term "buying an act" means that the headliner's manager offers the act a series of performance dates for a flat guaranteed price per show. In return, most often, the opening act uses the headliner's sound system and lights. In special cases, the offer to the opening act is negotiated to include a guarantee and a bonus based on the number of tickets sold per concert. However, this occurs only when the opening act's career has such momentum that it is in a position to demand it, or the competition for the opening act's participation amongst several other headlining acts requires it.

THE CONTRACT

In an article titled "What's Behind Soaring Ticket Prices" (*Billboard*, 15 May 1999) it was estimated that the breakdown of revenue cuts from tickets sales is distributed as follows:

Venue:	38%
Artist:	34%
Ticketmaster:	10%
Facility Fee:	8%
Opening Act:	7%
Taxes:	3%

These percentages seem to be in line with the examples given. In figure 9.4 the artist is receiving about 40% and in figure 9.5 the venue rent is approximately 35%.

The agreement that is normally issued for a live engagement is a form of the American Federation of Musicians' live engagement contract. Because the AF of M licenses booking agents, the union logo appears on the booking agency's letterhead and/or contract form. The contract is a standard agreement that contains the name and place of the engagement, the name of the artist, the date and time of the performance, how much and how the artist will be compensated for the appearance, and other important information. The signatures that appear on the contract are the buyer of the show, usually the concert promoter, the artist (or representative of the artist), and the booking agent's; however the booking agent's role is only as a conduit or middleman.

The buyer or concert promoter is not recognized as an employer of the musicians, but rather a **purchaser**. As a purchaser, s/he is not libel for any damages or accidents that the musicians (and crew) might encounter, and has very little responsibility concerning the personal welfare of any of the performers. If the concert promoter was considered an employer, then the musicians performing would be subject to workman's compensation insurance, and all other employee benefits bound by law. As the contract reads, the musician is considered an **independent contractor** and is responsible for declaring the net revenue of the proceeds on his/her income tax form.

Figures 9.4 and 9.5 are actual engagement contracts issued by a booking agency to the headlining act. The name of the artist and the date of the event have been omitted, however, the other information is as it appeared on the original document. Figure 9.4's gross potential is considerably less than 9.5's.

(HEREIN CALLED "FEDERATION")

CONTRACT

(Form T-2)

FOR TRAVELING ENGAGEMENTS ONLY

Whenever The Term "The Local Union" is Used in This Contract, It Shall Mean The Local Union Of The Federation With Jurisdiction Over The Territory In Which The Engagement Covered By This Contract is To be Performed.

THIS CONTRACT for the personal services of musicians on the engagement described below is made this 24 day of February, 1999, between the undersigned purchaser of music (herein called 'Purchaser') and the undersigned musician or musicians.

1. Name and Address of Place of Engagement:

Flynn Theatre
153 Main St.
Burlington, VT 05401
Ph: Fax

Name of Artist:

2. Show Details:

Monday,   ...20__. Doors: 7:OOpm, ...:7:30pm, Capacity: 1,381,Ticket Scaling & Deductions: ,
Reserved:329 @ $32.00, Reserved 2:1,152 @ $23.50 Comp/Kill:-50 @ $32.00, Comp/Kill 2:-50 @ $23.50, Gross Potential:
$34,825.00.

3. Merchandising: 3a. On Sale:

80/20 Sells Artist

4. Compensation Agreed:

$12,500 GUARANTEE + 85% OF THE GROSS BOX OFFICE RECEIPTS AFTER VERIFIED EXPENSES AND 15% PROMOTER
PROFIT. PURCHASER TO PROVIDE AND PAY FOR SOUND AND LIGHTS PER ARTIST'S SPECIFICATIONS.
ARTIST TO RECEIVE 100% HEADLINE BILLING. SHOW TO BE AN EVENING WITH (NO SUPPORT).

5. Purchaser Will Make Payments As Follows:

50% ($6,250) DUE UPON ON SALE VIA CERTIFIED CHECK, MONEY ORDER OR BANK WIRE.

WIRE INFO:

6. No performance on the engagement shall be recorded, reproduced or transmitted from the place of performance, in any manner or by any means whatsoever, in the absence of a specific written agreement with the Federation relating to and permitting such recording, reproduction or transmission.

7. It is expressly understood by the Purchaser and the musicians who are parties to this contract that neither the Federation no the Local Union are parties to this contract in any capacity except as expressly provided in 6 above and, therefore, that neither the Federation nor the Local Union shall be liable for the performance or breach of any provision hereof.

8. A representative of the Local Union, or the Federation, shall have access to the place of engagement covered by this contract for purposes of communicating with the musician(s) performing the engagement and the Purchaser.

9. The agreement of the musicians to perform is subject to proven detention by sickness, accidents, riots, strikes, epidemics, acts of God, or any other legitimate conditions beyond their control.

10. Attached addenda and Artist's Rider are made part of this contract herein

IN WITNESS HEREOF, The parties hereto have hereunto set their names and seals on the day and year above written.

PURCHASER: ARTIST:

_____   _____

Figure 9.4

Artist:			Show Dates:		Monday,	99

Deal Type: Gross Split Point w/Promoter Profit

Venue: Flynn Theatre **Promoter:** –
Address: 153 Main St. **Address:**
Burlington, VT 05401

Ticket Scale	# Seats	Price	Gross
Reserved	329	$32.00	$10,528.00
Reserved	2115	$23.50	$27,072.00
Comp/Kill	-50	$32.00	($1,600.00)
Comp/Kill 2	-50	$23.50	($1,175.00)
TOTAL GROSS	1381		$34,825.00

Talent and Production Costs

	$12,500.00
Total Talent Costs	$12,500.00

Fixed Expenses

Advertising	$4,000.00	Rent	$2,450.00
ASCAP	$150.00	Runners	$100.00
Facility Services	$350.00	Security	$100.00
Hospitality	$1,500.00	Site Coordinator	$350.00
Local Production	$2,500.00	Spotlights	$262.50
Miscellaneous	$250.00	Stagehands	$2,500.00
Phones	$100.00	Towels	$50.00
Piano Tuner	$500.00	Ushers/Tix Takers	$200.00
Total Fixed Expenses			**$15,362.50**

Variable Expenses	Rate	Sellout	Guarantee	Ceiling	Total
BMI	0.30%	$104.48			$104.48
Insurance	1.78%	$619.89			$619.89
Total Variable Expenses					**$724.36**

Summary

Total Projected Show Costs	$15,362.50
Variable Cost at Sellout	$724.36
Talent and Production	$12,500.00
Breakeven Dollars & Tickets	$28,586.86
Concert Gross(less taxes)	$34,825.00
Less Promoter Profit	$4,288.03
Less Costs at Sellout	$28,586.86
Sharing Gross (Net Receipts)	$1,950.11

Earnings Potential

Artists Percentage	$1,657.59	85%	$14,157.59
Promoter Percentage	$292.52	15%	$4,580.55

Expenses must be documented on the night of the engagement and approved by the Artist's representative. Any expenses not documented shall be the Purchaser's sole responsibility. Producer requires notarized affidavits from all sources with whom commercials are placed including, but not limited to, radio stations, television stations, and print media, to be presented at settlement. If the Purchaser has other or greater expenses than those indicated above, the break figure shall not be affected. If however, the bonafide aggregate paid bills relating to any of the above listed costs shall total less than stated above, the break figure will be reduced accordingly.

Purchaser/Local Manager **Artist**

Figure 9.4

Line 2 expresses the show details, including, date of the performance, and also includes the time the doors will open, the time the headliner will go on, and the capacity of the house. It also states the prices of the tickets, excluding any service charge, the scaling of the house, the types of tickets (general admission or reserve), the number of complimentary tickets at each price level, and the gross potential for a sellout.

Line 3 is the merchandising arrangement, in this case the artist will sell the merchandise and receive 80% of sales. 3a list the date the tickets will go on sale.

Line 4 contains the terms of how the compensation will occur. For this performance, the headliner is receiving **a guarantee of $12,500 plus 85% of the gross box office receipts after verified expenses and 15% promoter profit**. The percentage is based on the amount of tickets the promoter sells. A sellout will reap the artist and the promoter considerably more money than less than a sellout, as discussed earlier in this chapter. The list of verifiable fixed expenses and variable expenses appears towards the end of the contract and has been agreed upon by the buyer and the artists' representatives. This deal is called a "gross split point w/promoter profit." If the concert is a sellout, the revenue moves the deal into the "splits" and at a sellout, the earning's potential are calculated as presented at the end of the contract. The artist gross potential is $12500. + $1657.59 (85% of override) = $14,157.59

Line 5 states how the payment will be made. Artists usually demand about 50% of guarantee upon the signing of the contract. Should the promoter really screw up, this amount is non-refundable . It also locks in the performance date. Without a considerable amount of money upfront, the artist might be asked to perform somewhere else and have to decline the offer believing that s/he is already booked for a performance that may never happen.

Line 6 states that the performance may not be recorded or transmitted with a specific agreement allowing such to occur. The A F of M has insisted on this language since commercial recordings began.

The second page of the contract itemizes the deal. This should be studied. It reinforces the fact that the artist spends his/her own money on (85% of) the show's expenses.

AMERICAN FEDERATION OF MUSICIANS OF THE UNITED STATES AND CANADA
(THERIN CALLED FEDERATION)

CONTRACT
(FORM T-2)

FOR TRAVELING ENGAGEMENTS ONLY

Whenever The Term "The Local Union" Is Used For This Contract It Shall Mean The Local Union Of The Federation With Jurisdiction Over The Territory In Which The Engagement Covered By This Contract Is To Be Performed.

THIS CONTRACT for the personal services of musicians on the engagement described below is made this 20 day of October 1997 between the undersigned purchaser of music (herein called Purchaser) and the undersigned musician or musicians.

1. **Name and Address of Engagement:** _____
   Name of Artist:_____

   Number of Musicians: 4   Number of Vocalists: 1

2. **Date(s) of Engagement, Daily or weekly schedule and daily clock hours:**
   Wednesday   1997 Doors: 6:30 PM   Opening Act: 7:30PM   Opening Act: 8:00PM
   Headliner: 9:15 PM   Capacity: 14,612 Ticket Scaling: 8,087 @ $65.00 6,525 @ $35.00
   Gross Potential: $754,030 00 . There is an additional $2 00 Facility Fee to patrons at the box office
   TicketMaster patrons are subject to Ticket Master service fees. On Sale Date:

3. **Type of Engagement**: Concert   3a. Merchandising Deal: 60/40 Venue Sells

4. **Compensation Agreed:** $300,000   All Inclusive Guarantee vs. 85% of the gross box office receipts after verified expense whichever is greater. (Headliner to receive $187,500 Guarantee plus a $15,000 Production Fee. Opening Act to receive $97 500 Guarantee. Headliner to pay any overages due Opening Act.)

5. **Purchaser Will Make Payments As Follows:** 50% ($93,750)   Due upon on sale via certified check money order or bank wire. Balance Due immediately prior to performance via, cash certified check or money order.

6. No performance on the engagement shall be recorded, reproduced, or transmitted from the place of performance in any manner or by any means whatsoever in the absence of a specific written agreement with the Federation relating to and permitting such recording reproduction or transmission.

7. It is expressly understood by the Purchaser and the musicians who are parties to this contract that neither the Federation no the Local Union are parties to this contract in any capacity except as expressly provided in & above and, therefore, that neither the Federation nor the Local Union shall be liable for the performance or breach of any provision hereof.

8. A representative of the Local Union, or the Federation, shall have access to the place of engagement covered by the contract for purposes of communicating with the musicians performing the engagement and the Purchaser.

9. The agreement of the musicians to perform is subject to proven detention by sickness, accidents, riots, strikes, epidemics, acts of God, or any other legitimate conditions beyond their control.

10. Attached addenda and Artist's Rider are made part of this contract herein.

IN WITNESS WHEREOF, The parties hereto have hereunto set their names and seals on the day and year above written.

PURCHASER: _____   ARTIST: _____

Figure 9.5

FIXED EXPENSES

/97 WEDNESDAY

CAPACITY: < 14,612>
POTENTIAL: $754,030.0

TOTAL: $615,275.00
New York, NY 10001

Expense Categories	Ind.	Budget Amount	Notes
FLAT RENT/ BLDG EXP.	F	16,000.00	INCL. SPOTLIGHTS, PHONE/LINES
ADVERTISING	F	70,000.00	CLEANING, MEDICAL, POLICE, FIRE
ASCAP/BMI	F	925.00	SECURITY, STAGEHANDS, USHERS,
CATERING	F	7,000.00	TIX TAKERS & BOX OFFICE
ADDT'L PHONE LINES	F	600.00	$300 PER LINE
INSURANCE	F	9,000.00	$321 + $0.57 PER HEAD
PRODUCTION MANAGER	F	750.00	
RUNNERS (3)	F	450.00	
SECURITY	F	1,200.00	
TOWELS	F	200.00	
FURNITURE RENTAL	F	1,200.00	
CREDIT CARD CHARGES	F	1,200.00	
MISCELLANEOUS	F	750.00	
TRANSPORTATION	F	2,500.00	
* *INTENTIONALLY OMITTED*	F	2,500.00	
ARTISTS GUARANTEE	F	300,000.00	
		$615,275.00	

Expenses must be documented on the night of the engagement and approved by Artist's representative. Any expenses not documented shall be the Purchasers sole responsibility. Producer requires notarized affidavits from all sources with whom commercials are placed including, but not limited to, radio stations, television stations, and print media, to be presented at settlement. If the Purchaser has other or greater expenses than those indicated above, the break figure shall not be affected. However the bona fide aggregate paid bills relating to any of the above listed costs shall total less than breakeven stated above, the break Figure will be reduced accordingly.

ACCEPTED and AGREED TO:

PURCHASER:_____ ARTIST:_____

Figure 9.5

Line 2 expresses the date of the performance, and also includes the time the doors will open, the time any support act will begin, the time the headliner will go on, and the capacity of the house. It also states the price of the ticket, excluding any service charge, the type of ticket (general admission or reserve), the gross potential for a sellout (including taxes), and the date tickets will go on sale.

Line 3 includes the type of engagement and 3a the merchandising arrangement. 3a may list the company that will handle the merchandising, or the percentage arrangement, ie. 60/40 if the venue concessionaires are to be involved with the physically selling the merchandise.

Line 4 contains the terms of how the compensation will occur. For this performance, the headliner is receiving **a guarantee vs. 85% of the gross box office receipts after verified expenses whichever is greater**. The percentage is based on the amount of tickets the promoter sells. A sellout will reap the artist and the promoter considerably more money than less than a sellout, as discussed earlier in this chapter. The list of verifiable or fixed expenses appears at the end of the contract as an addendum and has been agreed upon by the buyer and the artists' representatives. If the concert revenue moves the deal into the splits, the artists' guarantee of $300,000 does not enter the calculation of expenses, because they stand to earn a considerably larger amount of money. This example is rare, as the opening act is performing for a very high guarantee and will take part in the splits.

Line 5 states how the payment will be made. Artists usually demand about 50% upon the signing of the contract. Should the promoter really screw up, this amount is non-refundable . It also locks in the performance date. Without a considerable amount of money upfront, the artist might be asked to perform somewhere else and have to decline the offer believing that s/he is already booked for a performance that may never happen.

Line 6 states that the performance may not be recorded or transmitted with a specific agreement allowing such to occur. The A F of M has insisted on this language since commercial recordings began.

THE CONCERT CONTRACT RIDER

The most important reason for the existence of a contract rider is to inform the promoter of the artist's expectations and requirements, and to protect the artist against any unforeseen difficulties. Is there a way to react to a problem legally? Is there some language in the written agreement that will allow the artist to cancel the performance? Do we really need twelve cases of French wine in the dressing room after every show?

Of course, there are other reasons for attaching a rider to a contract. Some artists want to feel as at home on the road as they possibly can, and they expect the concert promoter to see that they do. Others carry a spectacular visual production and massive sound systems that have extraordinary technical needs. Specific requirements for this sophisticated equipment should be listed in the rider.

Most concert riders include the following categories. Some artists require more details on some categories than others. For the concert promoter, the technical requirements are most important since they will insure the promoter's preparedness with everything from electrical power to the number of stagehands needed.

Rider Categories

The following are the usual categories found in a concert rider..

1. Billing and Advertising

Headlining artist require "100% sole star billing" in all advertising and publicity for the show. This means that nothing else connected with the performance will be larger than the artist's name.

2. Cameras/VCRs/Recorders

Cameras or recorders of any type are not permitted by the artist (with the exception of the press) unless specific arrangements have been made.

3. Financial Considerations (including ticket sales, merchandising requirements and insurance)

Specifics concerning the guest list and other box office requirements are listed. Concert gate receipts and expenses not detailed in the actual contract are also listed. The purchasers obligations as to the sale of concert merchandise, and the artist's rights are also specified. On some tours, the official concert merchandise is sold by the venue's concessionaires, and on others, the artist has personal vendors.

The purchaser (concert promoter) must provide for full public liability insurance coverage to protect against any accidents during the load in, operation, and load out of the equipment. The purchaser must also carry insurance that excludes any of the artist's entourage from any claims that may arise due to the personal injury of an audience member.

4. Backstage Accommodations, Catering, and Security

Although this section of the rider makes for the most humorous reading, the essential aspects of these three areas cannot be ignored.

Specifics concerning backstage accommodations are not only important to the artist, but also the crew and management. Some "legs" of tours last six to eight months. The road becomes home! Hassle free comfort is important in maintaining one's sanity and concentration.

The same is true for the catering requirements. Everyone in the crew must eat a nourishing, balanced, diet. Energy levels must be maintained and fatigue must be kept at a minimum. Dietary requirements such as beefless meals, or special diets due to medical needs must be honored.

Limited access, security, and safety are the responsibility of the purchaser. It is here that details are specified.

5. Crew Arrangements

Accommodations and catering requirements must be specified for the crew as well. Meals must be served at the times specified and other essentials, such as showers and restrooms must be available. Space for truck and bus parking must be reserved as well as information concerning medical emergency facilities.

6. Productions and Technical Requirements

As previously stated, this is the most important aspect of the concert rider. Specific electrical requirements, and the purchaser's responsibility for hiring the carpenters, electricians, spotlight operators, stagehands, riggers (climbing and ground), truck loaders, and forklift operators are listed. Remember, the actual success of the artist's presentation relies heavily on the total compliance with this section of the rider.

Amusement Business, Billboard, and Rolling Stone magazines include articles on the elaborate production requirements of tours. Convoys of tractor trailer trucks and banks of computers are normal parts of all headling acts today.

7. Cancellation and Force Majeure

Usually the artist states that if any member of the act or production staff becomes ill (or incapacitated), the artist maintains the right to cancel and not be obligated to reschedule the show. The force majeure clause also includes other events beyond the control of the artist, such as civil unrest or Acts of God.

8. Legal Remedies

In case of any breech of the contract by the purchaser or any damages, this section specifies the legal remedies available.

Originally, concert riders were initiated because promoters agreed to supply certain production requirements and then didn't. For example, the artist would request a stage with dimensions of 64'x 48'x 8' high. The promoter would say "no problem" and then deliver a stage that was only 4' high! However, today this is the exception. Delinquent or unprofessional concert promoters do not stay in business.

Cutting extraneous expenses can be critical to the profitability of a tour. As mentioned earlier, most headlining artists perform for a percentage of the profits. While the artist receives a percentage of every $20 ticket sold, it is also true that the artist looses a percentage for every $20 spent on expenses!

RECORD COMPANY SUPPORT

In some instances, record companies contribute tour support money to new artists recently signed to the label. This is sometimes negotiated into the artist's contract and then administered by the artist development department. However, for an established artist, record companies offer financial support very reluctantly. They support their artists in terms of promotion and merchandising in each market where the artist performs. But money is another story.

Record companies want to determine the fan support for the artist in each market. They want to keep track of how the record is selling in the performance market and they'll want to do whatever is needed to increase sales.

Record companies may also want the act to perform in markets where the record isn't selling. Since the artist's agent would like to sell as many concert tickets as possible, s/he want the artist to perform where the record is doing well. The manager must resolve this dilemma.

CHOOSING MATERIAL FOR THE PERFORMANCE

Another question facing the artist and the manager is what to perform on the tour. The audience wants to hear songs that are familiar. The artist may be tired of performing hits that are often years old and wants to perform new material. How many songs should be included from the new album? How many songs should be repeated from the last tour? When should the hits be performed? Should any cover material, such as rock classics, be included?

When deciding what to perform, one rule of thumb is to choose material that works well in the live setting. Songs that rely on sound production techniques may not "come off" on stage as well as on the recording. Simpler tunes may work best. A good rule is to give the audience as much familiar material as possible and save the biggest hit for the encore. The old show business adage still holds true: "Leave them wanting more!"

TOUR REHEARSAL

Each artist sets his or her own rehearsal schedule for the tour. The schedule is based on how long it's been since the band has played together or how many new players will be on the tour. Most bands rehearse for only a few weeks as a group before the tour begins. The material to be performed should be chosen before rehearsals begin.

Before the start of the tour, it's useful to hold the final tour dress rehearsals in the opening arena. An artist's manager will book the arena for a few days to a week before the beginning of the tour, and rehearse the music and production. These dress rehearsals benefit the production crew. However, they also give the artist an opportunity to rehearse different stage moves and choreography.

PRODUCTION PREPARATION

As a tour headliner, the artist is responsible for the concert staging. Stage production design should be completed as far in advance of opening night as possible to allow for competitive bidding for the actual construction of the stage and rigging. The manager and the tour production manager should estimate the production budget and then meet with a designer for the actual design. A drawing to scale or an actual scale model should be completed at least two months before the beginning of the tour. Unless the artist knows exactly what he or she wants, or has had some experience in stage design, the artist won't view the model until this point.

The production development budget for a headlining act can be in the millions depending on the design. Artists generally own the stage production rather than lease and, most often, use it for only one tour.

TRANSPORTATION

The vehicles used to transport tour equipment are usually leased. If a highway breakdown occurs, the leasing company is responsible for transporting the equipment to the arena. It is important to work with reputable leasing companies that offer commercial leasing agreements.

TOUR PUBLICITY

The tour should be announced to the media no earlier than two months before the opening date (see Chapter Four). There are mixed opinions as to the importance of any announcement that doesn't publicize a specific date. However, most managers do release a press announcement with details about the entire tour. The release is then disseminated to various publications throughout the country. If the artist retains the services of a publicist, then the publicist uses his or her influence to get the information published. Posters and other tour paraphernalia which uses the artist's name and likeness is usually licensed to a merchandising company. This will be covered in the next chapter.

ENTOURAGE

The number of people that travel with the artist varies. They include: musicians, support crew, and guests. The concert rider contains the list of entourage members that travel with the band and the crew members that are hired locally for each specific site. On the 1997 U2 Zoo TV Tour. The traveling crew numbered 180 people, transported in 12 buses, and a 40 passenger chartered jet, plus an addition 200 locally hired laborers.

ROAD CREW

A road crew consists of sound people, lighting people, stage construction people, drivers, etc. The production manager usually hires the crew for the entire tour. A simple rule is "Don't pay people until you need them!"

TOUR MANAGER

The tour manager (road manager) is responsible for the logistics of transporting the artist during the tour and for the daily activities of the entire tour entourage. S/he must be organized, articulate, and able to make decisions under stress. The tour manager sometimes acts as the tour "accountant." His or her responsibilities include "settling" the show with the promoter by receiving payment for each performance, as well as handling the weekly petty cash needs. The tour manager usually begins receiving a salary two weeks before the tour begins. During these two weeks s/he begins advancing the initial concert dates with the promoters, and reviewing the transportation and hotel arrangements. S/he also meets with the manager and accountant to determine what bookkeeping and other duties will be expected.

SECURITY

Artists either contract their own security personnel for the entire tour or rely on the security personnel contracted by each concert promoter for each performance.

INSURANCE

The entire tour must be covered by the various forms liability insurance (refer back to the budget section). Sometimes artists also purchase performance cancellation insurance. This means that if a performance is cancelled for any reason, the artist receives a percentage of his or he fee. Performance cancellation insurance premiums are very expensive. The manager usually budgets the fee into the artist's performance price. Promoters carry weather insurance for outdoor events. Lloyds of London writes this type of protection.

DURING THE TOUR

Manager's Responsibilities

As a manager, you must carry on the daily activities of the management office, and handle the maintenance and execution of all unforeseen emergencies! Since every tour date is a major financial transaction involving thousands, if not millions of dollars, it's your responsibility to see that every date is as successful as possible.

Typically, there are ten to twenty performances on sale simultaneously, and maybe five or six different concert promoters presenting the shows. You should telephone every promoter daily. You should also arrange for and monitor 90% of all details for each show. You must keep track of the artist on the road, as well as promotional materials, ticket sales, radio spots, and any media coverage for each performance. This requires good organizational skills. Managers use computers to organize their jobs or create working forms for specific tasks. Forms are designed to help keep track of all the promotional materials, press interviews, and concert production details.

A calendar should also be kept for each performance date of the tour. The calendar information should include the artist's itinerary and the daily advertising schedule. The calendar will remind you when every radio spot on every station will be aired, and when the other pieces in the advertising mix are scheduled.

Artist Fatigue

Fatigue can lead to sloppy performances. That's why it's important to schedule periodic days off for the artist and make certain they remain days "off" rather than just days without a performance. The artist should not give interviews or attend rehearsals on these days (unless it is absolutely necessary). And, it's also important to keep all tour problems away from the artist. The tour manager should solve problems. Lastly, a proper diet and rest are essential to the artist's health. An artist who is in good shape will be in a better frame of mind with a positive attitude.

SETTLING WITH THE PROMOTER

The artist representative (usually the tour manager) and the concert promoter make the financial settlement for the date on the night of the performance. When the box office has tallied the evening's receipts, the financial transaction takes place. Most often it occurs after the first few songs of the headliner's set. The promoter submits his or her expenses incurred in producing the performance, and the figures are totaled per the written contract. If the expenses appear to be in excess if what was anticipated, they are negotiated. However, artists work with the same concert promoters for many dates and a mutual respect is reached. Figure 9.6 is a show **settlement form**. You may plug in the amounts from the contract in Figure 9.4 to see how

Show:_____ Date:_____

SETTLEMENT STATEMENT

Total Tickets Sold   Plus Comps   Total Attendance

I: Night of Show Settlement

Artist Reconciliation

Net Gross	_____
Less Exp.	_____
Less Other	_____
To be split	_____
% to Artist	_____
Due Artist	_____
vs. Guar.	_____

Due Artist	_____
Less Dep.	_____
Subtotal	_____
Less Other	_____
Check to Art.	_____

Fee to Artist	_____ _____% Gross
Plus Prod.	_____
Total Artist	_____

Promoter Reconciliation

To be split	_____
% to Prom.	_____
Due Prom.	_____ _____% Gross

II. Final Settlement

Due Artist	_____
Due Promoter	_____

Comments:_____
_____

Figure 9.6

the settlement would be calculated. From time to time, a mathematical error may occur. To avoid this, is important for the tour manager/accountant to check and recheck all figures. A 2% error on a $240,000 performance fee is $4800. The same error could cost the artist $96,000 if it was multiplied over 20 shows!

AFTER THE TOUR

After the tour ends and everyone has rested, the entire experience should be evaluated to see which of the objectives have been met. The obvious question is: Did the tour make money and how much? However, the other tour objectives are important as well. Did the artist increase his or her visibility in a given market? Have any new industry personnel been added to the artist's support system? Have any left? Why? On a market-by-market basis, did any concert reach the status of being recognized as an event? Did the artist perform in the major markets while the record was peaking? Does the artist consider the tour successful? Do you? What was learned from the total experience?

SUMMARY

1. The main objectives for any tour are: to increase the artist's visibility in a given market; to increase the number of industry players on an artist's team and win their loyalty; to make the artist's performance an "event" on a performance-by-performance basis; to provide an opportunity to perform in a major market when the record is reaching its stride; and to make a profit.

2. A tour should begin in a secondary market close to the artist's home.

3. The booking agent and manager should work closely to arrive at all the specifications for the tour.

4. The procedure for booking a tour entails: the manager and agent arrive at a price the artist is seeking for the performance; the agent solicits concert promoters in each region to inquire about bookings; the promoter or agent puts a tentative hold on a venue for a specific date; and dates are confirmed.

5. Tour budgets should be based on conservative estimates.

6. An opening act should be chosen on its ability to generate ticket sales.

7. A concert rider should protect the artist against any unforeseen difficulties. The categories should include: billing and artist approval; recording; financial considerations; backstage accommodations and catering; crew arrangements; cancellation; and legal considerations.

8. Material for concert performance should be familiar to the audience and should work well in a live setting.

9. Production preparation should include the actual staging specifications.

10. The entire tour should be announced to the press no earlier than two months in advance.

11. During the tour, the manager must monitor 90% of all details for each show on a daily basis.

12. After the tour, the experience should be evaluated.

PROJECTS

1. Cost out a three-day regional tour, including a budget (with real cost figures) for expenses.

2. Draw up a production budget, including a sound system, lights, and staging.

3. Formulate a fair and meaningful concert rider, including the categories listed in this chapter.

4. Write a press release announcing an artist's tour.

5. Role play the job of a concert promoter; negotiate a contract for a performance, and submit a realistic list of expenses using the Gross Split Point Deal method.....do the math!

Notes

Eric Boehlert. "Road Woes: What It Costs." Rolling Stone. November 28, 1996. Pg. 53.

Neil Strauss. "Stones Tour Ranks No. 1." New York Times. December 18, 1997. Pg. E7

Rick Mitchell. "The Music Mogul" Houston Chronicle. March 19, 1995. Pg. 8.

Jerry Mosemak, "Entertainment clout builds." USA Today. March 1, 2000. Pg. 1B.

John Scher. "Why are Ticket Prices so High?" Musician Magazine. January, 1994. Pg. 12.

Ibid.

Peter Passell. "If scalpers can get so much, why aren't tickets costlier?" Economic Scene. New York Times. 23 December 1993. Pg. D2.

Ray Waddell. "Mounting Concert Ticket Surcharge Provoke Dissent." Billboard Magazine. May 26, 2001. Pg. 1.

CHAPTER TEN

Merchandising, Endorsements, & Sponsorships

*"The Woodstock generation has gone away. In the end, this business is
really not so different from Xerox or General Motors."*
Larry Stersel, Director Merchandising, Epic, Portrait & Assoc. labels, NY Times, October 2, 1983.

By the end of this chapter you should be able to:

1. Discuss the differences between merchandising, endorsements, and sponsorship.
2. Discuss the five basic ingredients in a merchandising deal.
3. Discuss how the revenues are shared.
4. Compute the average revenue splits in a merchandising deal.
5. List the factors that contribute to the size of the artist's advance money.
6. Discuss the procedures for prosecuting offenders.
7. Discus four important issues concerning product endorsements.
8. Discuss the important areas of an endorsement deal.
9. Discuss the two types of sponsorships that exist in the business.

The areas of merchandising, endorsements, and sponsorship are very lucrative for many of today's artists. Merchandising and sponsorship are relatively new to the entertainment business. Nevertheless, to some stars, the exploitation of their name and/or likeness as a property right now represents not only an important promotional vehicle, but substantial income as well. Endorsements, on the other hand, have been a revenue producing aspect of the entertainment business for many years.

THE DIFFERENCE

Merchandising

In general terms, merchandising is the buying and selling of goods for profit. In the entertainment industry, these goods feature the name or likeness of the artist (and the artist's recordings) on every good produced. The owner of the artist's name or likeness has the legal right (property or "personality" right) to exploit it for either promotional reasons or as a means of generating income.

Endorsements

When an artist endorses a product he or she gives support or approval to the product for a set fee for a limited time. Usually, this represents a relationship between the artist and the product. Extreme caution must be used when choosing a product to endorse. No endorsement deal is worth the possibility of deteriorating the artist's image.

Sponsorship

A business (or corporation) that pays an artist a fee for the right to associate its name or logo with the artist's appearance is a sponsor. The name may blatantly appear on a banner hung behind the stage in a concert hall or on merchandise sold, or it may be tastefully incorporated into posters advertising the event. Today, non-record company sponsorship support many tours.

MERCHANDISING

Its History

Artist merchandising seriously began in the rock business in the early 1970's. Winterland Productions, which is one of the biggest merchandising companies in the business, began in the early 1970s by selling Grateful Dead T-shirts at one of their concerts at the Winterland Ballroom in San Francisco.[1] However, not many people recall any substantial exploitation of an act's name prior to the Peter Frampton "Live" tour in the mid-1970's. In any case, merchandising was more or less a dirty word to the Woodstock generation, and was not a factor in the exploitation of the counterculture of the 1960's. A former employee of the Filmores East and West could not recall any act selling T-shirts or other paraphernalia in either hall.

Now it's big business. According to Debra J. Graff, Esq., revenue from merchandising in the music industry exceeded 1/2 billion dollars in 1980, and it had doubled by 1985.[2] According to Felix Sebacious, President of Blue Grape Merchandising, "In the '90s, T-shirt sales got to be about as big as box office [receipts].[3] Worldwide revenues are now in the billions of dollars, and on some tours, an average of $10+ a ticket is generated from the sale of tour merchandise.

How Does It Work?

Tour merchandising is the primary source of merchandising revenue. Fan club, e commerce, and direct mail merchandising are growing, but revenue depends on the loyalty of the group's fan base. Thanks to the internet, the industry has finally discovered direct to consumer marketing and a few independent companies have convinced record companies to use their services.

The merchandising procedure is as follows:

1. Three months prior to the start of a tour, the manager will contact the three major rock music merchandising companies and ask them to bid for on merchandising the tour. If the artist does not have any product value in the marketplace (even though he or she may have a recording contract), the merchandiser may pass on the tour, or may offer to merchandise the tour without offering any advance money. If the artist has a proven merchandising track record, the merchandiser will examine the tour dates and determine a projected "per-head gross."

2. The manager and merchandiser agree on the terms of the contract.

3. The merchandiser designs the graphics for the products and brings the designs to the manager for approval. If the tour coincides with the release of a recording (and it usually does), then the recording jacket's graphic should be incorporated into the merchandising graphics.

4. The merchandiser and the manager decide which products are to be manufactured. This decision is fairly simple. T-shirts are mandatory. Some groups estimate that they sell shirts to a quarter of their fans. The other products should be priced to cover the spending power of the audience. In other words, there should be something for every pocketbook. Common items include: T-shirts, baseball shirts, sweatshirts, visors, caps, posters, and buttons. However, towels, undergarments, sheets & pillowcases, and soccer balls have also been offered!

5. The manager approves all of the items to be merchandised accepting only high quality pieces.

The Deal

There isn't a standard merchandising deal in the music business. The power of the artist in the marketplace plays a major role in determining who receives the biggest piece of the pie. Some merchandisers will take a smaller share of the revenue to have the prestige of merchandising a superstar's tour. The number of dates on the tour and the number of countries covered are also factors.

Usually, a manager will give the merchandiser the right to exploit the name and likeness of the artist for the purpose of selling merchandise for a negotiated royalty . . . with a minimum guarantee or an advance against the royalty. The royalty for the license is negotiated and computed on either the wholesale or retail prices of the products, based on the number sold.

For an established act, the length of the deal usually coincides with the length of the tour. If the deal is with a new artist, the merchandiser will specify that the length of the deal run until the monies are recouped, for fear of not making any profit.

Lately, venues have been demanding as much as 40% of the sales which has been passed on to the consumer.

The revenue splits are roughly as follows:

Cost of the goods (including freight, security, etc.) 25-35%.

Venue (arena) receives 20-40% commission. This arrangement may vary depending on whether the merchandiser works the concessions or the venue's concessionaires are used and the venue's notoriety.

Merchandiser receives 5-10%.

Artist royalty is 15-30% or higher, depending upon his or her status.3

For example:

$30.00 shirt
  10.50 cost (35%)
$19.50
-$9.00 venue (30%)
$10.50
-$2.70 merc (9%)
$ 7.80 artist (26%)

Advance money: A number of factors come into play when negotiating the artist's advance. Obviously, the size of the advance is based on the volume of business expected. This may be calculated by the number of dates on the tour and the volume of business transacted on previous tours. Advances may range from $10,000 to $1,000,000+. The manager may negotiate a higher royalty rate in lieu of an advance if he or she is sure the artist's products will sell well and cash is not needed.

Normally, the agreement will contain a personal guarantee by the performer that minimum tour obligations will be met. If they are not met, unrecouped advances (unlike record company advances) will be repayable, with interest, by the performer.

Because the concert business has been so risky recently, advances have been given in increments throughout the tours.[4]

Selloff. The merchandiser will want to selloff unsold goods. The manager should negotiate a time limit that extends beyond the tour for the selloff to occur. The merchandiser should not be permitted to **manufacture** any additional merchandise. This prevents merchandise to be sold for an unlimited time under the old contract.

Ownership. Since the mid-1980's, record companies have not allowed new artists ownership of the recording jacket's artwork or graphics. They have made it clear that they intend to take part in all merchandising that bears the name or likeness of the artist. It may be stated in the contract as follows: **"If Records receives any payments for any use of your name or picture in connection with merchandise other than Phonograph Records, your royalty account will be credited 50% of the net amount of those receipts, after deduction of the following expenses."** The manager may negotiate the ownership (or a bigger share) from the record company to the artist for a price.

Record/Entertainment companies now own merchandising companies and offer new artists the opportunity to do business with them. (Since 1987, MCA Music has owned Winterland, Labatt Brewing of Canada is a shareholder in The Brouckum Group, Giant Merchandise is a joint venture with Warner Bros. Records and Time Warner Inc., and Polygram Diversified Entertainment acquired Great Southern Co.)5

Bootlegs And Counterfeits. During a major artist's tour, products featuring the tour logo are in such demand and sell so well that bootleg and counterfeit products are big business. Since official tour merchandise is marketed outside the arena as well as inside, a concert-goer has no way of knowing if the product he or she buys in the parking lot is "official" or not. Nor does he or she really care! Therefore, the bootlegger doesn't care if the products he or she sells are exact replicas of official products. If a bootlegger incorporates the artist's name, the latest recording's graphics, and the tour specifics, the product will sell as well as the "official" product. In fact, some claim that at times the bootleg products are designed better!

Stopping Them. Obviously, it's disturbing to the artist and manager to see bootleg and counterfeit products sold at a concert. However, it's usually the merchandiser's responsibility to police the tour.

There are several ways to curtail the sale of bootleg and counterfeit products. According to Graff, suits may be filed based on trademark infringement under the Federal Lanham Act; copyright infringement under the Federal Copyright Act; and unfair competition and misappropriation of the right of publicity under common law.6 An enforcement procedure is important, although many merchandisers do not always find it cost effective.

Until the 1980's, the best procedure is to obtain a court order prohibiting the sale of unauthorized merchandise. However, the merchandiser had to bring the bootlegger into court *before* a judge would grant the injunction. However, with the result of the **Matter of Vuitton et Fils, S.A.606F.2d.1 (2d Cir. 1979)** case, an ex parte temporary restraining order (TRO) can be obtained from a court without notice to the defendant. This allows the plaintiff to obtain an injunction, without first notifying a bootlegger, and restrains the unauthorized activities for a limited time period, usually ten days, after which the court will consider granting a preliminary injunction which will remain in effect during the pendency of the case.7 Because some bootleggers don't really have legal addresses, the courts have allowed "John Doe" TROs to be served by marshals. These TROs are enforceable during specified times and areas, usually within a three-mile radius of the concert hall, during several hours before and after the concert. This has been very helpful in curtailing the business of bootlegging.

Following is a merchandising agreement with comments in italics.

RE: Retail Merchandising Agreement

Ladies and Gentlemen:

This will confirm our agreement by which we shall have the exclusive retail merchandising rights regarding you, the artist and collectively professionally known as the artist.

1. **Territory:** **World.**

Rights:

Exclusive right throughout the term to use your name(s), group name(s), approve likenesses and other approved identification ("Licensed Property") in connection with the manufacture, distribution, advertising, and sale of merchandise to the public, to be offered for sale and sold through retail distribution channels and on the site of your live concerts. The rights granted to us hereunder with respect to retail sales include the execution of licenses for the implementation of our retail rights, and specifically exclude fan club sales, mail order sales and phone order sales. All rights not expressly granted hereunder are expressly reserved by you.

2. We agree that we shall not, without your prior written consent, (i) utilize the Licensed Property in connection with so-called commercial "tie-up" arrangements or (ii) enter into any endorsement arrangement pursuant to which you agree to endorse goods or services of any kind.

3. **Term:**

The term of this agreement shall be for a period of one (1) year commencing on January 1, it being understood that should you be on tour on January 1, the tour rights only hereunder will continue until that particular tour leg is completed. Upon the expiration of earlier termination of the term as provided hereunder all rights granted to us shall cease and revert to you automatically subject to the provisions of paragraph 7, below, and as may be otherwise specified hereunder.

4. **Royalties.**

(a) Tour; Ninety percent (90%) of our "tour net profits". The term "tour net profits" shall be defined as our "tour net sales" less hall and vendor commissions (not to exceed thirty percent [30%] of gross receipts), cost of goods sold (including artwork), road expenses (which shall be deemed to be no greater than five percent [5%] of net sales), freight and mutually agreed upon miscellaneous expenses. The term "tour net sales" shall be defined as gross proceeds actually received by us from the sale of tour merchandise less sales taxes actually included in the sales price, value added taxes, import and customs dues and reasonable and customary costs of on-site bootleg security pertaining solely to the rights granted hereunder.

Included in this clause are important definitions as well as the basics of the entire deal. Ninety percent appears to be a big piece of the pie, however, upon closer reading, the ninety percent is ninety percent of 65%, and not including freight and miscellaneous expenses. A limit of thirty percent has been placed on hall and vendor commissions......in reality many halls are receiving forty percent! This is addressed in "d" below.

(b) Retail: Fifteen percent (15%) of our Wholesale Receipts up to Two Hundred Fifty Thousand Dollars ($250,000.00) of gross receipts; sixteen percent (16%) of our Wholesale Receipts between Two Hundred Fifty Thousand One Dollars ($250,001.00) through Five Hundred Thousand Dollars ($500,000.00) of gross receipts` and seventeen percent (17%) of our Wholesale Receipts in excess of Five Hundred Thousand Dollars ($500,000.00) of gross receipts. "Wholesale Receipts" are all monies actually received by us or our agents or credited to our or their account from the retail sale of products less sales taxes, returns or credits on returns.

The retail deal is worded so that as sales increase the artist's percentage increases. Again these percentages do not include taxes, returns, etc.

(c) Licensing: Seventy five percent (75%) of our License Receipts. "License Receipts" are the total of all monies or other compensation payable or credited to our account by the licensees under licenses entered into under this agreement.

(d) We agree that upon your request we will sell T-shirts hereunder for Fifteen Dollars ($15.00), Notwithstanding the foregoing, in the event that hall fees exceed thirty five percent (35%) of the gross receipts, the parties agree that the selling price of T-shirts will be adjusted accordingly, upon the mutual agreement of the parties.

5. Products.

(a) You will provide us with a reasonable number of color transparencies or equivalent full color artwork sufficient to enable us to produce T-shirts, sweatshirts, and other specialty wearable items. All costs of creating or originating photographs, color transparencies or equivalent artwork shall be advances, which are recoupable from monies payable to you hereunder,

(b) We shall not manufacture products hereunder (except for samples) without your prior approval of the design and quality of such product, which approval may be withheld in your sole discretion. Your failure to reject any product within ten (10) days after submission of same to you shall constitute your disapproval of same.

(c) You shall have the right to approve In writing each license agreement, which we propose to enter hereunder.

6. Warranties.

(a) You warrant, represent and agree that (i) you exclusively own and control all rights in and to the names, group names and other identification of every kind, and all rights covered herein, (ii) you have not taken and shall not, during the term, take any action which would limit in any manner our full enjoyment of such rights in the Territory, (iii) you have the right to grant and do hereby grant the right to use on products hereunder the album artwork and all photographs, artwork or other materials furnished by you to us, and (iv) our use of such materials will not infringe the rights of any person and the rights granted to us hereunder shall not conflict with the rights of any person. You agree to indemnify and hold us harmless from any loss, cost, damage, liability or expense arising out of any claim, demand or action by a third party which, If proven, would constitute a breach of this agreement and which claim, demand or action is reduced to final, non-appealable judgement.

(b) We warrant, represent and agree that (1) we have the right to enter into this agreement and perform all of our obligations hereunder, (ii) all wearable products shall be made of one hundred percent (100%) cotton unless otherwise requested by you, and (iii) all Products hereunder shall be of the same style, fabric and quality as the samples which are approved by you pursuant to paragraph 5, above. We agree to indemnify and hold you harmless from any loss, cost, damage, or expense arising out of any claim, demand or action by a third party which, it proven, would constitute a breach of this agreement and which claim, demand or action is reduced to final, non-appealable judgement.

7. Unsold Merchandise.

We will have the non-exclusive right, for a period of ninety (90) days after the expiration of the term (the 'Sell-Off Period"), to dispose of any unsold merchandise remaining after the term (provided that we shall not have the right to manufacture merchandise during the Sell-Off Period or to sell those unsold products which are in excess of a reasonable inventory of same in light of anticipated demand as of the expiration of the term and provided, further, that we shall not manufacture products prior to the expiration of the term in excess of anticipated demand during the term) through retail distribution channels only and will pay to you a royalty equal to fifty percent (50%) of our Wholesale Receipts. In connection with the foregoing, we shall not sell any merchandise during the Sell-Off Period at a discount price without your prior written consent. During the Sell-Off Period, you shall have the right to purchase any unsold products from us at our cost in respect of same less only the royalty which would otherwise be payable to you pursuant to paragraph 4, above. At the expiration of the Sell-Off Period, we shall destroy all unsold products and furnish you with an affidavit certifying same.

This is a very important clause in the agreement because it defines the sell-off period (which is ninety days after the expiration of the one year term) and what rights are granted to deplete the inventory, should any remain. This clause blocks excess manufacturing of goods and bargain pricing.

8. **Force Majeure.**

(a) If, by reason of any cause or causes beyond our control or that of any affiliate or subsidiary, (i) the enjoyment by us, or our subsidiaries or affiliates of any rights or benefits hereunder is interfered with or otherwise becomes impossible or impracticable, or (ii) the performance of our obligations hereunder Is interfered with or otherwise becomes impossible or impracticable, then we shall be relieved of such obligations (other than the obligation to account and make payments to you hereunder), and the periods of time in which we shall be obligated to take any actions shall be suspended, for the period during which we are so affected. If any suspension imposed under this paragraph by reason of an event affecting no merchandise manufacturer or distributor except us continues for a period in excess of sixty (60) days after the commencement of the applicable event, you may request us, by notice, to terminate the suspension within fifteen (15) days after our receipt of your notice. If we do not do so, the term hereof will terminate at the end of that fifteen (15) day period or at such earlier time, which we may designate by notice to you, and all parties will be deemed to have fulfilled all of their obligations under this agreement except those obligations which survive the end of the term.

(b) If, by reason of any cause or causes beyond your control the performance of any of your obligations hereunder or our ability to tour is interfered with or otherwise becomes impossible or impractical, then you shall not be responsible for any loss, cost or damage to us occasioned as result thereof.

The force majeure clause appears in all contracts relating to live performance. The clause protects against any "acts of God" such as tornados, hurricanes, civil violence, or causes "beyond your control".

9. **Accounting.** Accountings and payments will be on a monthly basis within thirty (30) days following the end of each month during the term. Not later than forty five (45) days following the expiration of the term, we will render a final accounting and will pay to you the balance of royalties, if any, shown to be due pursuant to such statement.

10. **Books and Records**

(a) We shall keep, maintain and preserve for three (3) years following expiration or earlier termination of the term, complete and accurate records and accounts of all transactions relating to this agreement. Such records and accounts shall be available for inspection, copying and audit at any time or times during or within three (3) years after the term (but not more frequently than once a year) during reasonable business hours, upon reasonable notice by you, specifying the statements with respect to which you seek examination, at your sole cost and expense.

(b) (i) Such examination shall be limited to those books and records which relate to you and which are necessary to verify the accuracy of the statement or statements specified in your notice to us. All information furnished by us to auditors or sent to us by auditors including; without limitation, any reports prepared by auditors, shall be held confidential by all parties and used solely for the purpose of identifying and settling claims and disputes that arise under this agreement. Unless documents or information to any person or entity not a party hereto other than attorneys and business representatives.

(ii) In the event that any audit conducted by a certified public accountant reveals an under-reporting of royalties to you of more than ten percent (10%) less than the royalties to which you were entitled under this agreement, we shall reimburse you for the reasonable and customary coat of such audit.

(c) Each royalty statement rendered to you shall be final, conclusive, and binding on you and shall constitute an account stated unless objected to within three (3) years after the same is delivered to you. You shall be foreclosed from maintaining any action, claim or proceeding against us in any forum or tribunal with respect to any statement or accounting due hereunder unless such action, claim or proceeding is commenced against us in a court of competent jurisdiction within four (4) years from rendition of such statement or accounting.

11. **Gratis Products.** We shall provide you with fifty (50) gratis units of each product produced by us hereunder.

12. **Ownership of Logo(s) and Designs: Uses By Third Parties.**

(a) It is acknowledged that the copyrights in and to any and all artwork and designs created by you and/or furnished to us by you hereunder shelf be owned exclusively by you or your designee and we shall have no rights therein except the right to use the some on products In accordance with the terms of this agreement. We agree to place an appropriate legend, in the form supplied by you, on all products in order to provide public notice of your copyright and trademark rights, No inadvertent failure by us to place such legend on any product hereunder shall be a breach of this agreement, but we shall use best efforts to cure such failure prospectively, on the next manufacturing run after our receipt of notice of such failure.

You acknowledge and agree that, with respect to any artwork created or originated by us, we shall own such artwork; provided, however, that you may repurchase such artwork at our cost after the term.

13.   Cure of Default.

As a condition precedent to any assertion by either party that the other is in default in performing any obligation contained herein, the party alleging the default must advise the other In writing of the specific facts upon which it is claimed that the other is in default and of the specific obligation which it is claimed has been breached, and the other party shall be allowed a period of thirty (30) days (or, solely with respect to payments by us to you, ten [10] days) after receipt of such note within which to cure such default.

14.   Resolution of Disputes.

All disputes arising out of or in any way associated with this agreement, including its execution, performance or breach, shall be governed exclusively by the laws of California, whose courts shall have exclusive jurisdiction.

15.   General.

This agreement cannot be assigned by you without our specific written consent We shall have the right to assign this agreement or any rights hereunder to any third party owning or acquiring a substantial interest in our company or our assets or to any-affiliated company.

This agreement sets forth the entire understanding between the parties with respect to the subject matter and suspends all prior agreements and understandings.

Any notices required or desired to be sent hereunder shall be in writing and shall be sent by registered or certified mail, return receipt requested, to the other party at the address herein above provided, unless either party notifies the other in writing of a change of address. This shall be deemed effective when received. In the event you notify us of a change in your address, we shall thereafter furnish a courtesy copy of notices sent hereunder to our attorney.

(a) If either party hereto brings any action, suit or proceeding arising from or based upon this agreement against the other party hereto, then the prevailing party shall be entitled to recover from the other its reasonable attorneys' fees in connection therewith in addition to the costs of such action suit or proceeding.

Please sign below to indicate your agreement with the terms of this letter.

Very truly yours,

By_____
An Authorized Signature

Accepted and Agreed to:

By: _____
An Authorized Signature

ENDORSEMENTS

Product endorsement has long been a part of the entertainment industry. Celebrities have endorsed products through TV and radio advertisements and print ads for years. In 1998, the Wall Street Journal reported that Elton John received $5 million from Citibank to appear in its global ad campaign.

Others have allowed (licensed) their names or likenesses to be used in conjunction with product promotion. The royalties may be high, but caution should be taken before consenting to an endorsement deal.

An endorsement represents a relationship between the product and the artist. Potentially, it can damage the artist's image, and no endorsement is worth that risk. The manager should exercise caution and investigate the following *before* signing an agreement.

1. Is the product valid? How effective is it?

2. Is it harmful? Will certain interest groups be against its use?

3. Will the artist's fans believe the artist uses the product?

4. How accurate are the products claims? Does it do what it claims to do?

5. Has it been tested by an independent laboratory and given its seal of approval?

6. Does the artist use the product? If not, he or she should live with it to see if he or she feels comfortable with it.

The endorsement must be evaluated in terms of its effect on the long-range career goals.

The Deal

An ad agency will usually approach a manager inquiring about the possibility of an endorsement. As a manager, if you are seeking an endorsement deal, a big fan in an account services department can be helpful in working a deal.

The important areas of the contract are:

1. The length of time a commercial will appear or a print ad will run.

2. The region or number of regions of the country where the commercial or print ad will appear.

3. The media for which it is intended.

4. Advances against a royalty deal.

5. Residuals from the airing of a commercial

6. Creative control…. Does the artist have any input?

7. Rights. Who will own what?

The cola war has been going on for over a decade. Whitney Houston, Paula Abdul, Ray Charles, and others at one time have been spokespersons for either Coke or Pepsi. Presently, the ammunition is Christina and Britney. Market researchers believe that the consumer associates (and hopefully remembers) who is endorsing what. This author finds the whole commercial venture, just that, and believes that it cheapens the artist's image and degrades that very definition of the word "artist."

SPONSORSHIP

There are three methods of non-record company sponsorship active in the industry. The first involves a non-record company that pays the artist outright for the right to associate its name or logo with an artist's appearance. This usually involves some sort of bidding opportunity for the right, and in many instances in connected to an endorsement deal. The artist may be required to guarantee that s/he will complete a certain number of appearances.

The second is paying for advertising in exchange for the right to associate its name or logo with an artist's appearance; cash may also be included. It's reported that the Rolling Stones received over $3 million in advertising from Jovan (a subsidiary of Beecham Group LTD.) in the early days of sponsorship, during the 1981 tour. Also in the 1980s Rod Stewart received $4 million from Canada Dry, the Jacksons received over $5 million from Pepsi, Julio Iglesias received over $30 million from CocaCola in a multitier deal, and the list goes on.

More recently, Shania Twain received an estimated $2 million for her first national concert tour, including local tour ads. Celine is hooked up with Ericsson mobile phones, and Blink 182 dresses in Billablong clothing[8]. Forbes Magazine reported that Britney Spears' deal with Pepsi accounted for at least 25% of the $38 million she earned in 2001.[9] According to Jay Coleman of *Entertainment Marketing Communications International*, "sponsorship in rock & roll is commonplace."[10]

The third form of sponsorship involves media companies and non-record companies teaming up. For example, MTV or another broadcaster contributes a certain amount of tour support for the right to an exclusive broadcast performance of an artist. The broadcaster, with the non-record company support, sells the show to radio station affiliates who sell air time to local advertisers. The media company as well as the non-record company support the artist. This arrangement is only offered to major stars.

Sponsorship can mean millions to an artist. If appearances in commercials are included in the deal, several million dollars can be guaranteed. Jive Records believes that commercial/sponsorship exposure for the artist, can and does give the artist additional exposure to a different audience that translates into record sales. Obviously, sponsorship deals can represent a great deal of money and be very lucrative for an artist. Therefore, companies, such as Entertainment Marketing, usually take about a 15% commission from the party seeking a deal.[11]

Because the sponsor may want high visibility on the tour, a manager must be certain that any advertisements during or after the concerts are not offensive to the artist (Pearl Jam has banned sponsors from their tours). A banner hung over the stage, or an ad with an artist guzzling a bottle of beer may not have a positive effect on long range career goals. As Herbie Herbert, the manager of Journey said back in 1983: "We are going to gross $30 million in ticket sales and $10 million more on record sales, so why go out there and sell our souls for a lousy million bucks?"[12]

SUMMARY

1. Merchandising is the buying and selling of goods with the artist's name or likeness on them for profit. An artist endorses a product by giving support or approval of it for a set fee. A business that pays an artist a fee for the right to associate with him or her is called a sponsor.

2. Merchandiser's largest expansion in the rock music field occurred in the mid 1970's.

3. Revenue from tour merchandising averages billions of dollars a year.

4. The procedure for acquiring a merchandising deal is as follows: The manager calls merchandisers and asks them to bid on merchandising the tour. The terms of the contract are agreed upon and the merchandiser designs the products. The manager approves all of the items to be merchandised.

5. The revenue from the merchandising is split between the maker of the goods, the venue, the merchandiser, and the artist.

6. Advance money is based on the volume of business expected.

7. The record company shares in the merchandising revenue unless the artist buys the ownership of the graphics and artwork from the record company.

8. Bootleggers and counterfeits are difficult and time consuming to prosecute.

9. Several issues should be investigated before endorsing a product. Namely, is the product effective? How accurate are its claims? Does the artist use the product?

10. Poor endorsement choices can have a negative effect on the artist's image.

11. Several areas of importance in an endorsement contract include: The length of the advertising run, audience reach, media, advances, residuals, creative control, and rights.

12. Tour sponsorship is reserved only for major acts.

13. The types of sponsorships are non-record company sponsorship and non-record company sponsorship in conjunction with a media company.

PROJECTS

1. Design a logo for a group that incorporates the group's image.

2. Locate a local silkscreen company that will create a silkscreen for the artist's merchandise.

3. Locate a local company that would like your artist to endorse a product and negotiate a deal.

4. Do the same for a sponsorship deal

NOTES

Larry Rohter. "Pop-Music Fashion Becomes a Sales Hit." <u>New York Times</u>. 8 January 1991. pg. D9.

Debra J. Graff Esq. "Merchandising in the Music Industry," <u>The Musicians Manual: A Practical Guide</u>. Beverly Hills Bar Assn., Beverly Hills, CA. 1986, pg. 379.

Ray Waddell. "Venue Merchandising Fees At Issue." Billboard Magazine. 2 December 2000. pg. 67.

Paul B. Ungar, ESQ. "Negotiating Concert Agreements During a Recessionary Period," <u>Agent & Manager</u>. March 1992. pg. 51.

Op. Cit., <u>New York Times</u>.

Op. Cit., <u>The Musicians Manual</u>, pg. 381.

Barry I. Sloctnick, Esq. "Are Bootleggers Walking Away With The Performance Profit Center?" <u>Agent & Manager</u>. April 1992. pg. 53.

Op. Cit., Billboard Magazine. Pg. 67.

Carla Hay. "Madison Ave. Woos Musicians." Billboard Magazine. 20 April 2002. Pg. 82

Michael J. Specter. "Rock Puts On a Three-Piece Suit," <u>New York Times</u>. 2 October 1983. Section Three.

Adam Heider. "The company They Keep," <u>Rolling Stone</u>. 6 August 1998. Pg. .30.

Op. Cit., <u>New York Times</u>. 2 October 1983.

CHAPTER ELEVEN
Business Manangement

"The business manager's primary function is to maximize client's earnings while safeguarding their capital."

Marshall M. Gelfand and Wayne C. Coleman in The Musician's Business & Legal Guide. Mark Halloran (ed.) Prentice Hall, 1991. Pg. 153.

By the end of this chapter you should be able to:

1. Describe the role of the business manager.
2. Describe the various functions s/he performs.
3. Discuss the various fee structures.
4. Discuss how to choose a business manager.
5. Using your knowledge of project management, discuss in detail how to prepare a funding proposal.

There are a million stories in the rock business about artists and their money. And there are two million stories in the business about artists without their money! When money comes quickly it sometimes gets "lost in the shuffle." Take Kiss for example, as reported in the New York Times: a former employee said that "she was told by an accounting firm that about $700,000 in cash had somehow fallen through the cracks."[1] The financial woes of Mick Fleetwood from Fleetwood Mac are also well documented (see "There's No Stopping Tomorrow" by Geraldine Fabrikant, New York Times, November 30, 1997 Bus. Sec. Pg. 1), as are Marvin Gaye's, Jerry Lee Lewis', and Wayne Newton's.

One of the saddest tales is that of Stanley Kirk Burrell, a.k.a. "Hammer." Hammer's "Please Don't Hurt Me" sold 18 million copies. He won three Grammys, had a private jet, movie offers, his own record production company, and a cartoon show. According to *Forbes*, he earned $33 million in 1990 and 91. By 1996 his income totaled over $50 million. It has been estimated that if Hammer had invested conservatively, he could have enjoyed an annual income of $3 to $5 million for the rest of his life.

Instead, he spent over $11 million to build a house and bought 17 cars. While on tour, he stayed at the best hotels, traveled by private jet. Consequently, his debts total $13.7 million and he has only $9.6 million in assets. One business associate who is owed money by Hammer summed it up by saying, "In this business you have overnight-success stories, but they tend to go down very quickly. They think it will always be as good as it is now."[2]

BUSINESS MANAGER

The Role:

Business managers play an important role in the artist's career. Their relationship, as with the personal manager, is a fiduciary one, and the artist must have total confidence in their judgment. Many business management firms also act as accountants, and play a greater role in the daily fiscal activities. Therefore, the breath and depth of their role may vary depending on their function(s).

Functions

Accounting: One should expect reports (balance sheet, etc.) completed on time (on an agreed upon schedule), and accurate to the penny.

Collecting of funds: Receipts from appearances, merchandising deals, and royalty agreements, should be designated with the artist's appropriate account number, and deposited **IN FULL**, in the artist's account. Funds should be drawn against, if needed. Audits should be conducted in a timely manner, especially record company royalty account audits, which are very tedious, but unfortunately, necessary.

Budgeting: If needed, budgets for projects, as well as living expenses, should be generated by the artist and the personal manager, in consultation with the business manager. The responsibility of the business manager is to notify the personal manager when a budget is not being adhered to.

Tax Advising: If the business manager is also the artist's accountant, s/he should be a Certified Public Accountant (CPA) and knowledgeable about the current state, federal, and international tax codes. Should any project be as complicated as to require special attention, the business manager should recommend a tax specialist.

Investment Advising: Many business managers (not simply accountants) are also investment advisors. Since anyone has the ability to give advise (and one usually does), as a form of protection, the artist should look to any one of the various types of licensed financial investment advisors. However, there aren't any guarantees that anyone with or without a license has the ability to give sound financial advice AND make money. Therefore, the general advise from the investment community is to be aware of investments that can't be explained properly ("I think it's a form of plastic . . ."), are hard to understand ("It's a device that allows your computer to . . ."), and are so new that no one really knows what earnings will be ("You can get in on the ground floor!").

Fees

Fees will vary depending on location, reputation of, licenses and academic degrees held by the business manager. Fees are computed based on any one (or more) of the following factors:

1. **time:** A rate per hour charged while s/he is conducting business (spending his/her time) on your behalf.

2. **a percentage of income:** Especially when the business manager is investing the artist's income, s/he is likely to charge a percentage (usually around 5%). The artist should make certain to understand whether income from investments (passive income) is included in determining the fee due, or only on funds received from career endeavors.

3. **retainer:** A retainer is a fee charged per week, month, or quarter for the normal accounting activities. An additional fee, along with the retainer, may be charged when additional functions are being carried out. If the additional fee is an hourly rate for performing a huge task, such as auditing a royalty account, because s/he is on a retainer, the hourly rate should be lower than if the business manager was not.

CHOOSING A BUSINESS MANAGER

Reputations are usually built on word of mouth recommendations. As stated in Chapter One, a good personal manager will suggest to his/her client the names of several reputable business managers, and then allow the artist to make the choice. A good personal manager will also emphasize to his/her client, that this is an important decision, and will affect many short and long term goals of the career.

FINANCING A PROJECT

It would be a wonderful world if everyone had enough capital to fund any creative idea. But it isn't. Some say, it would be a wonderful world if we still worked on the barter system of trading. But we don't. Although people outside the entertainment industry think performers make "money for doing nothing," at the beginning of a career, there just doesn't seem to be enough available. Since robbery is against the law, attempts at raising capital for a project must be completed in an organized, convincing, businesslike manner.

Assuming that the artist is signed with a record label, the most often vehicle for borrowing money is a draw against the artist's royalty account. Assuming the artist is successful, another source of funds is a bank. However, assuming that both these resources are not available to the artist, a capital funding proposal needs to be developed.

The Deal

There are many ways to structure a capital investment deal. Below are four such possibilities. Before any deal is structured a business manager should be consulted.

1. **A loan:** The simplest and easiest way to get money is for someone to loan it you and you pay s/he back. You can compose a loan agreement describing the amount of money that is being borrowed and how and when it is will be paid back (a promissory note).

2. **A limited partnership:** As described in Chapter Two, a limited partnership is sometimes setup so that the person loaning money becomes a partner that will share in income resulting from the project. S/he risks only the sum being borrowed, and takes on no additional liability.

3. **A corporation:** Someone may loan money in return for a number of shares in a corporation. The amount of shares received in exchange is based on the amount of money loaned in relation to the number of shares outstanding. Similar to a limited partner, the only risk is the amount invested (loaned), and no additional liability is assumed.

4. **A securitization:** A music-royalty securitization is a method where an artist or songwriter issues bonds that give the artist immediate access to cash and the bond-holder/s receive/s an attractive, stable investment. David Bowie's bankers floated the first $55 million worth of bonds in 1997, issuing them against future royalties. Publishing assets clearly have the best value for application to the securitization transaction, basing the deal on future earnings.[3]

The Plan

Adapting the tools of project management discussed in Chapter One to a capital seeking proposal is one method of organizing the plan. Figure 11.1 lists the categories that should be included. A discussion follows.

FUNDING PROPOSAL
[Based on Project Management]

    I.   Problem Statement

    II.   Background Statement

    III.   Goals & Objectives

    IV.   Procedures

    V.   Plan

    VI.   Schedule

    VII. Budget

    VIII. Financing Structure

    IX.   Success Indicator

    X.   Executive Summary

Figure 11.1

I.   Problem Statement An explanation of what is perceived to be needed, what this project entails, and why it has been determined to be a solution.

II.   Background Statement This section usually begins with a description of the artist and his/her organization, his/her financial condition, the current status of his/her career, successes and any special attributes or awards that may persuade someone to believe that the artist is someone special. A description of similar situations and how the successful completion of the project solved a similar problem, must be included. This section should also include a thorough description (including statistical information) of the music business.

III. Goals and Objectives The goals and objectives, (both long an short term) of the project must be clearly stated.

IV. Procedures It is sometimes helpful to list what has to be completed before the actual plan is presented. This is especially true when the plan is very complicated and contains steps that are unique to the music business. For example, if one is seeking funds to support a tour, production, security, and catering requirements might seem elaborate to someone outside the industry.

V.   The Plan It is here that how the steps of the plan are to completed is clearly described. Who is responsible for doing what is clearly listed. If a marketing plan is needed, it should be included here. All aspects of the plan must be able to be explained easily, and no aspect of the project should be left to chance.

VI. The Schedule Describing when the steps are to be completed is the main function of this section. Critical path analysis, a method to determine what aspect of the project will take the longest, should be performed first, so that unrealistic deadlines are not proposed. The schedule should remain flexible.

VII. The Budget The budget should also include the financial statement showing the present financial condition of the artist's company requesting funding. If the artist has been in business for three years or more, the financial condition of the past three years should also be included.

VIII. Financing Structure The financing requirements are included in this section. The structure and responsibilities of the company loaning the funds, such as the formation of a limited partnership are described here. How and when the funds will be paid back are included. The projected time it will take to payback the loan is also described. The business manager must known the current "going rate" for such a project so that the artist does not pay too much for the deal.

IX. Success Indicators Projected sales should be described in intervals to act as progress report. Inherent risks and possible problems should be indicated.

X. Executive Summary This should be a one page description of the deal including all the basic requirements and financial conditions. It is intended for executives that do not have time to read the proposal. It should be concise and businesslike with an eye-catching appeal.

The old saying "you can't make money without spending money" is true than ever. What seems also to be true today, is the saying "to make a lot you need to risk a lot."

SUMMARY

1. The role of the business manager varies from artist to artist.
2. The basic functions are: accounting, collecting funds, budgeting, tax advising, and investment advising.
3. Any funds collected should be deposited in the artist's account in full and then drawn against when needed.
4. One should make certain how the fee for services is to be collected and what it is based on.
5. Business managers work on hourly fees, percentage of income, and retainers.
6. The artist's business manager has a fiduciary relationship with the artist, and should be chosen by the artist and not the manager.
7. The financing of a project will come forth easier if the funding proposal is organized, convincing, and businesslike.
8. The procedures used in project management can be adapted to be used in a proposal seeking capital.

PROJECTS

1. Develop a funding proposal for a project using actual cost estimates and a realistic time-line.
2. Ask the class to develop a funding proposal and have individuals role play as investors by examining each other's proposals.

NOTES

Geraldine Fabrikant. "The Bad Boys Start Watching Their Pockets." New York Times. February 23, 1997. Sec. Pg. 7.

John Cassidy. "Under The Hammer." New Yorker Magazine. August 26, 1996. Pg. 62.

Matthew Benz. "Securitization: Who it's right for, and when." Billboard Magazine. 27 April 2002. Pg. 21

CHAPTER TWELVE
Legal Battles

"The first thing we do, let's kill all the lawyers."
Shakespeare, Henry VI, Part 2 Act IV, Scene II

[The author thanks students from his personal management classes for their research in updating information concerning the cases listed in this chapter. Further updates may be required.]

The following are selected cases of artist manager disagreements that resulted in very publicized lawsuits. In the entertainment industry, when a substantial amount of income is achieved over a relatively short period of time, it is not unusual for allegations of the misappropriating of funds to arise. Although the law suits may result in large attorney fees, this is an "ego driven" business based on relationships, where emotions play an major role, and when someone is suspected of a misappropriation, the usual response is "I don't care what it costs, I'm going to get that sucker!" The truth of many settlements is that the attorneys are the real winners.

In reality, many artists, young or old, fail to read or fully comprehend the artist-manager agreement, and consequently set themselves up for misunderstandings. Secondly, most contracts use terms like "reasonable effort" or "best effort" to describe the behavior expected by the parties, which are obviously open to a broad range of interpretation. What follows are lawsuits that were filed for a variety of reasons. They were chosen as a representation of the various misunderstanding that occurs. They are meant to be used as learning tools for students, and not intended to be partial to the artist or manager involved.

TABLE OF CHAPTER CONTENT

Bee Gees vs. Robert Stigwood..

Billy Joel vs. Frank Weber ....

Lisa Marie Presley vs. Tom Parker & RCA Records ....

Laura Branigan vs. Susan Joseph ....

Michael Lang vs. Joe Cocker ....

Prince vs. Cavallo, Ruffalo, & Fargnoli..

Anita Baker vs. Sherwin Bash, David Braun, & Randy Bash.........................

Stephen Hutton vs. Kid Rock and Top Dog Records ....

David Lee Roth vs. Edmund Anderson..

Henry Newman vs. Hootie & the Blowfish ....

Inga Vainshtein vs. Jewel (Kilcher) and her mother, Lenedra Carroll ....

Lou Pearlman vs. 'N Sync...

Leann Rimes vs. Wilbur Rimes and Lyle Walker ....

Christina Aguilera vs. Steven Kurtz...

BeeGees vs. Robert Stigwood

The Background

The Bee Gees, Barry, Robin, and Maurice Gibb are pop singers from Australia who became one of the most successful recording groups in the world in the late 1970's. As a result of the overwhelmingly successful movie "Saturday Nite Fever," their soundtrack album, recorded for RSO Records, sold over twenty million records worldwide, and is considered by most as one of the crowning achievements of the disco era. Barry's falsetto vocals became a familiar sound on radio, television, and in elevators, supermarkets, and health clubs All accounts support that the BeeGees were on top of the industry.

Robert Stigwood, an entertainment mogul also from Australia is the principal owner the Robert Stigwood Group. Under the umbrella of the RSO Group are a number of companies that encompass many aspects of the business. In addition to RSO Records, there is a personal management firm, and a number of music publishing companies. Stigwood is considered a giant in the worldwide entertainment industry.

The Dilemma

In October 1980, the Bee Gees filed suit in a New York State Supreme Court that Stigwood had cheated the act out of more that $16 million through a pattern of fraud, breach of trust, and conflict of interest. Filed on behalf of the three, the suit asked for upwards of $75 million in damages and other costs from a host of Stigwood related companies.[1] They sued for release from all their ties with Stigwood, and charged that he deliberately mismanaged them to his own advantage and withheld millions of dollars in royalties

Details of the claim asked for $75 million from Stigwood; $75 million from Polygram, which owned half of the Stigwood Group companies; $50 million in punitive damages; and additional millions in interest and back royalties. They also asked for the return of all the Bee Gees' master recording and copyrights, and a release from all their many contracts with Stigwood.[2] The suit alleged that Stigwood diverted millions of dollars from them by creating self-servicing corporate entities that hid money and delayed royalty payments.[3] The three brothers hired Paul McCartney's father-in-law, John Eastman, to represent them, who negotiated Paul's release from the Beatles and from Allen Klein.

On the emotional level, the Bee Gees became insecure about the monopoly Stigwood had in every aspect of their career. He was their personal manager since 1968, and head of their record company. They were also signed to his publishing firm. In 1980 they questioned, as their manager, why Stigwood didn't solicit them deals from any other record companies or publishing firms. After all, as a manager, he took twenty-five percent of their gross earnings for twelve years. Weren't they entitled to negotiate deals through competitive bidding?

The suit continued to allege that Stigwood fraudulently failed and refused to account properly for royalties and other income and hid the fact that he owed them large sums of money[4]. In fact they conducted their own audit and found that they were owed millions in unpaid royalties dating back to 1968.[5]

The Stigwood group called the suit "revolting" and countered by claiming the whole suit was just a way for the three to renegotiate a better contract. Stigwood appealed in London England for an injunction against anyone who tried to usurp his interests in the group. Stigwood denied all charges and executives at RSO Records claimed that the group was being paid "excessively high royalties" and owed their careers to Stigwood.[6]

The Resolution

Although it was widely speculated that the case would be very difficult and last for quite a number of years, the suit was settled out of court and all charges dropped. Details of the settlement were not revealed, however, an industry representative claims that Stigwood gave up his rights to the group and released them from their RSO Records deal but retained their catalogue.

Billy Joel vs. Frank Weber

Index No. 20702/89
Supreme Court of New York, New York County

The Background

Billy Joel is one of the biggest record-selling artists in the world. Starting out as a songwriter/piano player, his first shot at the big time, came as the singer/songwriter/keyboards player in a keyboard and drum duo called "Attila". Recording solo albums for Columbia since the 1970's, Joel has gained the attention of the college age. In fact, at one time he was tied with the Beatles as having the largest number of platinum albums. Several worldwide tours have grossed him hundreds of millions of dollars as well.

Joel's rise to stardom did not come overnight nor without setbacks. His history as a singer in piano lounges in Los Angeles is public knowledge. His lose of ownership to many of his songs to various "parasites" in the industry is also a common hazard of this industry.

His career is bigger than ever. His marriage and subsequent divorce to supermodel Christie Brinkley has added to the aura of his public persona. He gained superstar status in the 1980's and continues to enjoy the status in the 1990's.

Frank Weber is Joel's ex-brother-in-law who began managing him in 1979. Also named in the suit were his wife Lucille, his brother-in-law Richard London, and two other in-laws. Weber's prior experience in the industry is not known.

The Dilemma

On September 25, 1989, Billy Joel filed a $90 million lawsuit against Frank Weber, accusing him of misappropriating recording royalties and tour funds over a period of ten years.[7] According to the papers filed in New York State Supreme Court, Weber "maliciously defrauded" Joel while being paid millions of dollars annually in management commissions, and funds from Joel's tours and record royalties.

Details of the allegations include:

1. misappropriation of $2.5 million in unauthorized, interest-free loans,

2. $10 million loss from risky investments,

3. double-billed Joel for production costs for music videos shot by a Weber controlled company,

4. and obtained loans from CBS Records for Joel, using his copyrights as collateral.[8]

Joel also asked to void his 1980 agreement with Weber and block him from any further compensation. Weber moved to have the claims dismissed at the start of the hearings. He claimed he was innocent. Rumors in the industry suggested that Joel's new wife at that time, Christie Brinkley, convinced Joel that his former wife's family was unfaithful to his career, and the suit was filed with a great deal of ill feeling and mixed emotions.

The Resolution

The court ruled against Weber on counts of fraud and embezzlement, and awarded Joel $2 million as compensation for funds that were allegedly drawn from Joel's bank account.[9]

Although Joel was awarded $2 million in the spring of 1990, as of May 1991, Joel collected only $250,000 from Weber. Weber has filed for bankruptcy. Consequently, Joel pursued Weber's accountants and attorney claiming they had a role in the improper transfer of $1.5 million of Joel's assets![10]

On February 25, 1993, Judge Lehner of the New York Supreme Court awarded Joel $675,670.68 in a summary judgement concerning two real estate partnership distributions.[11] The remaining claims have yet to have hearings scheduled.

Weber filed an $11 million suit against Brinkley alleging that she induced Joel to terminate the management agreement. A New York judge has moved a dismissal of the complaint as a spouse is unnamed against a claim of interference and cannot be forced to testify against his or her spouse or reveal details about private conversations.[12]

In April 1995, Joel's attorney, Leonard Marks, filed a motion in the Supreme Court of the State of New York to discontinue action without prejudice from the case so that the plaintiff is free to file a new suit on the same claim. However, at this time further action would be a waste of time and money.

Lisa Marie Presley vs. Tom Parker & RCA Records

Probate Court, Memphis TN.

The Background

(This suit was filed on behalf of Elvis' daughter, Lisa Marie in 1980.)

Elvis was (and might still be) THE KING. He was one of the biggest stars in the entire entertainment business, attracting audiences whose ages ranged from "eight to eighty." For years, his records represented one-half of RCA Records' sales. He has over 700 hundred charted songs recorded on dozens of hit albums to his credit.

Colonel Tom Parker had been Elvis' personal manager since 1956. Legend has it that the colonel and Elvis didn't have a written agreement. A handshake and trust held their relationship together on a 50%-50% basis for those many years. Many consider Parker the brains behind Elvis' enormous success. After all, it was Parker's idea to convince RCA Records to buy his contract from Sam Phillips at Sun Records in Memphis for the total sum of $40,000.

Parker was once a carnival barker. He was known to have no problem with saying anything to anyone. In fact, he was known as one of the industry's biggest practical jokers.

RCA Records is one of the oldest continuously operating record labels in the USA. RCA is a subsidiary of BMG a major international entertainment company with facilities throughout the world. Historically, their emphasis has been in the recording and releasing of country and classical music.

The Dilemma

A court-appointed guardian of Lisa Marie Presley, then twelve years old, filed a report on July 31, 1981 accusing Col. Tom Parker and RCA Records of "collusion, conspiracy, fraud, misrepresentation, bad faith, and overreaching" in their business dealings with Elvis.[13] Central to the charges was the 1973 sale of royalty rights to Presley's entire catalog to RCA for $5 million, to be split equally between Elvis and the colonel. With Elvis in the 50% tax bracket, his net would only be $1.35 million, and he would forfeiture of all future rights![14] This was certainly not a sound business decision on Parker's part for Elvis, however, it did provide a nice income for the 63 year old Parker.

The report also cited a number of side deals that the Colonel made with RCA, the Hilton International Hotel in Las Vegas, and Management III. Blanchard E. Tual, the court appointed attorney filing the suit, also claimed that Elvis lost considerable revenue by never playing outside the U.S.

Tual claimed that he never performed outside the country because Parker was never naturalized as an American citizen, and was really Andreas Cornelus van Kuijk, born in Holland on June 26, 1909.[15]

Elvis tended to ignore any attorney's advice and put his entire fate in Parker's hands. Elvis went along with the buyout by RCA that was suggested by Parker, even though the contract was not due to expire until 1975. Furthermore, RCA Records had not purchased any of its other artists' master catalogs.[16] The new 1973 seven year contract called for a royalty rate of 10c per single and 50c per album for U.S. sales, half of which was to paid to "All Star Shows," the Colonel's company. At the time, other stars such as the Rolling Stones and Elton John were getting twice the royalty and paying half the commission rates to their management.[17]

Some of the side deals cited were the agreement that RCA Records would pay All Star Shows $675,000 over seven years, and RCA Records Tours would additionally pay the same for "planning, promotion, and merchandising." Parker would also receive 10% of RCA Tours profit. RCA agreed to pay Parker a $50,000 consulting fee and another $350,000 of All Star Tours for planning, promotion, and merchandising. Tual reported that with these deals, Elvis would gross $4.65 million, while Parker would make $6.2 million, plus 10% of all tour profits.[18]

The contract contained a "no audit clause" which did not allow an Elvis representative to examine the books! By 1972, Elvis physical and emotional condition did not allow him to evaluate any agreements, and it seems obvious that Parker was interested in cashing in before the King's inevitable early expiration.

Another side deal was with the Hilton. Parker was provided with a year-round suite of offices and hotel rooms, all the food and beverages for his home in Palm Springs, and free transportation to Las Vegas anytime that he requested it. Parker was also a notorious gambler, good for $1,000,000 per year at the hotel tables. Included in this deal were the services of Elvis at $100,000 to $130,000 per week. A fee that was surpassed by acts of far less value.[19]

The Resolution

A settlement was made on behalf of Lisa Marie. However, the Colonel never was convicted of enough crimes to spend any time in jail. He died a free man.

Laura Branigan vs. Susan Joseph

The Background

Laura Branigan is a pop singer that enjoyed a number of hit records on the Atlantic label in the 1980s. Her personal manager at the time was Susan Joseph, a partner of Henry Marx in Grand Trine Management. Marx is also a partner in Ram Promotions, an independent record promotion company. Branigan is married to Laurence Kruteck who is also her business manager.

The Dilemma

In 1985, Branigan sued Joseph for failing to fulfill her obligations of the personal management agreement. Branigan then terminated her agreement with Joseph. Specifically mentioned in the suit was the use of $125,000 of Branigan's money for independent promotion of her records. Also at issue was the claim that Joseph misrepresented the role offered to Branigan in an Australian film.[20]

Branigan claimed that the $125,000 spent on independent promotion was improperly spent by Ram Promotions, the company hired by Joseph to do the job. Branigan also claimed that Joseph was a partner in the company. Over $1 million was spent on independent promotion of Branigan's records over a two year period.

The testimony revealed that Branigan had reservations about the role in the Australian film. However, she already committed herself to the project when she filed suit in 1985.[21]

According to Joseph's attorney, Branigan's husband, Kruteck, induced her to breach the contract with Joseph.

The Resolution

Branigan lost her suit against Joseph. A jury granted Joseph's counterclaim filed in federal court on November 30, 1987. They found that Joseph had not breached the contract or her fiduciary duty to the singer. Also she was not a partner in Ram Promotions. They awarded $509,238.74 to Joseph, and levied $100,000 punitive damages against Kruteck, as they believed he induced Branigan to breach the agreement. This settlement was very unusual because juries do not normally award punitive damages against a third party.[22]

Michael Lang vs. Joe Cocker

The Background

Joe Cocker is a blues oriented singer with an usual stage presence. When he performs in his raspy voice, he contorts his body and releases spasms with his hands and arms that make him appear to be suffering from a crippling disease. Cocker hit the international scene in the early 1970's with a cover version of the Beatles' "A Little Help From My Friends." His career has had its ups and downs, however, he does sell records and makes concert hall appearances.

Michael Lang and Better Music Inc. began managing Cocker in 1977. The agreement expired in 1980 but the parties agreed to continue under its terms and conditions. In 1984 they entered into a new agreement.

The Dilemma

On March 26, 1992 Michael Lang and Better Music Inc. filed suit in federal court in New York City against Joe Cocker and Adaven Productions, which sometimes acts as Cocker's agent, claiming that Cocker agreed to pay Better Music 15% of his gross earnings from recordings, concerts, merchandising rights, song royalties, and TV appearances during the term of the 1977 agreement. The suit names several albums made under the original agreement as well as singles from the soundtracks of "An Officer And A Gentleman" and "An Innocent Man."[23]

The suit claims damages of $1 million for breach of contract and $1 million for the plaintiffs' services, 15% of the net from Cocker's recordings and concert appearances, as well as court costs.[24]

Better Music continued to manage Cocker until August 19, 1991 when they were notified by the singer that he no longer required Lang's services and would no longer pay him.[25]

The Resolution

Cocker attorney denies Lang's claims and said Cocker will counter sue.

Prince vs. Cavallo, Ruffalo, & Fargnoli

Los Angeles Superior Court

The Background

Prince is considered one of the most innovative performers in the business. His creative endeavors in addition to performing include producer, songwriter, screenwriter, movie star, and multi-instrumentalist. His mixture of raw sexual appeal with rhythm and blues has made him a huge success with crossover appeal.

The Dilemma

His former managers Robert Cavallo, Joseph Ruffalo, and Steve Fargnoli reportedly filed suit against him in Los Angeles Superior Court February 1, 1991 claiming that he owes them $600,000 that he agreed to pay when he released them from their responsibilities. The three assert that they were able to collect potential earnings when he ignored their career advice. They further claim that the disagreement occurred when Prince decided to release his records "in competition with one another."

In October 1991, Prince released the Diamonds and Pearls Cd, which contained a track entitled, "Jughead," which was Prince's artistic expression of the stereotypical music manager. Fargnoli was convinced that the song was specifically written to mock him. He filed a $5 million suit against Prince's Paisley Park Studios claiming "defamation of character." The suit was eventually thrown out of court.[26]

The Resolution

A settlement has not been reached.

Anita Baker vs. Sherwin Bash, David Braun, Randy Bash

Los Angeles Superior Court

The Background

Grammy-winning artist Anita Baker is one of the greatest r & b singers of the 1990's. As an Elektra artist, her records have sold consistently well and she is recognized as one of today's most enduring female stars. Ms. Baker possesses great crossover appeal, as she is popular with the pop and jazz audiences as well.

The Dilemma

Ms. Baker has filed a breach-of-contract cross-complaint against former manager Sherwin Bash, former attorney David Braun, and Randy Bash, who administered her catalog through Big Heart Music. The filing occurred on May 14, 1996, claiming "fraud and deceit, breach of fiduciary duty, breach of contract, defamation and slander, intentional infliction of emotional distress, civil conspiracy, and attorney malpractice."[27]

Her action stems from a default judgment filed by Sherwin Bash in February, 1996, for "damages, back royalties, unpaid commissions, other revenue sources and court costs."[28] Baker stated: "Management firms and large labels don't pay you. [Bash] thinks that he should live off me the rest of my life."[29]

The suit follows another action against Bash that was filed before the labor commission of California that alleges that Bash's BNB Associates acted as a talent agent without being licensed in that state. Baker entered into a 5 year personal management contract with BNB at a commission rate of 15% in 1983 and again in 1988, with an option to terminate in 1991. Baker terminated the agreement but retained BNB on a as needed basis for 10%. On December 13, 1994, Baker advised Bash that the management contract was terminated. Therefore, her agreements with BNB are unenforceable because BNB was unlicensed and that claims on existing and future commissions, royalties, or other sums arising from previous contracts be voided. Baker's suit claims that the defendants "knowingly and willfully conspired and agreed among themselves to further their own self-interest at Baker's expense."[30]

The Resolution

A settlement has not been reached.

Stephen Hutton vs. Kid Rock and Top Dog Records

U.S. District Court, New York

The Background

Kid Rock has enjoyed a successful career mixing metal with rap. He has sold millions of records reciting nasty lyrics, and has performed his stage antics to sold out audiences throughout the world.

The Dilemma

Hutton sued Rock and his company, Top Dog Records for at least $4 million in July of 2000 alleging breach of contract and unjust enrichment.

The Resolution

The terms of the settlement were not disclosed, however, in a joint statement, Hutton and Rock said that there were glad the case has been settled fairly and that the litigation has been brought to an end.[31]

David Lee Roth vs. Edmund Anderson

Los Angeles Superior Court

The Background

Just a gigolo…………

The Dilemma

Roth filed a lawsuit against his former manager for selling unauthorized Roth T-shirts and other memorabilia on his Web site. Roth authorized Anderson to sell "certain limited surplus merchandise" in exchange for previous management and consulting services. Anderson was not authorized to make copies of the merchandise or create new Roth products. Roth authorized him to set up a website to sell the stuff on condition that Roth approve its design and that Anderson would terminate the site when Roth asked. Roth told him to take down the site. Anderson did but then allegedly put it back up at another location and is continuing to sell merchandise without permission.[32]

The Resolution

?

Henry Newman vs. Hootie & the Blowfish

The Background

Hootie & the Blowfish enjoyed one of the biggest debut albums in industry history by selling over fourteen million copies of Cracked Rear View. In 1996, the Atlantic Records recording artists also won a Grammy for the Best New Artist.

The Dilemma

Henry Neuman, the group's former manager slapped the group with a $150 million lawsuit claiming that he was wrongfully excluded from the band's recording contract. The group called the suit "meritless."

Neuman says that he discovered the band while he was hosting a talent showcase in Rock Hill, North Carolina, and signed a managerial contract with a term of three years.

He claims that the group blew him off when the record went big by pressuring him into signing a release from his contract.

The Resolution

Terms of the settlement were not disclosed, but lawyers for the band happily reported that it was cheaper to settle than to go to court![33]

Inga Vainshtein vs.
Jewel (Kilcher) and her mother, Lenedra Carroll

California Superior Court, Los Angeles

The Background

Jewel is one of today's most successful artists. With several platinum albums charted, she is one of the industry's top performers. Born in Utah, she spent her early years living in Alaska performing in Eskimo villages with her singer/songwriter father. After graduation from the Interlochen Fine Arts Academy she moved to San Diego to live with her mother. Performing her own material, she played coffeehouses in the area and met Vainshtein who signed on as her manager in 1993. Later that year, she was picked up by Atlantic Records.

The Dilemma

In November of 1998, Vainshtein filed a $10 million lawsuit charging Jewel and her mother with wrongful termination of her 'three album cycle' managerial contract. Vainshtein is seeking compensatory and punitive damages claiming that she is owed millions in commissions. She maintains that Carroll shadowed her as a co-manager to learn how to handle her daughter's business, and then fired her. The suit goes on to claim that Carroll convinced the singer that advice from Vainshtein had to be approved by a "channeler" (named Jack Snyder) who evaluated the advice by communicating with some entity referred to as "Z!" Furthermore, Carroll pressured her into sharing a portion of her commissions and directed that commission payment be calculated based on net, rather than gross earnings.

The Resolution[34]

The California Labor Commission ruled that the management contract between Jewel and Inga is void because Inga used illegal tactics in booking Jewel's appearances while she was manager, voiding the contract (supposedly without a booking license).

Vainshtein has filed an appeal to the ruling and is requesting that she be paid $1,843,450 in commissions.

Lou Pearlman vs. 'N Sync

Federal Court, Orlando, FLA

The Background

'N Sync, the boy band that followed in the footsteps of another Pearlman group, The Backstreet Boys, sold more than 7 million copies of their debut album in 1998. Presently, they are in the mist of a worldwide tour which, when completed, should be one of the largest grossing tours in history.

The Dilemma

On October 12, 1999, Pearlman, the group's creator and manager filed a $150 million law suit against them and Zomba Recording. The suit cited breach of contract and an injunction was also filed barring them from using the name 'N Sync, claiming that Pearlman had exclusive ownership.

Pearlman created, developed, and financed the boys and was instrumental in landing their exclusive distribution deal with BMG. The deal was for five albums, and they were signed to a subsidiary of BMG and then licensed to RCA.

The dispute began in July of 1999 "when the group claimed that Pearlman and his firm, Trans Continental, failed to fulfill its contractual obligations." The group then left RCA for Jive (of which Zomba is the parent company).

Pearlman's attorney, Michael Friedman, said that it is absurd to think that now that the group has been made rich and famous, they can just turn their backs on Pearlman and go someplace else. Pearlman is seeking $100 million in compensatory damages and $50 million in punitive damages.

On November 2, 1999, "N Sync filed a $25 million counter suit. The group claimed that Pearlman's financial arrangements made them virtually "indentured servants" of Trans Continental. They claimed that Pearlman et. al received 55% of all gross touring revenue plus 37.5% of the net; 75% of all record royalties and 100% of any advances; 80% of the merchandising; 100% of the music publishing; and 55% of gross celebrity endorsement monies, plus 37.5% of the net from such deals. (Pearlman filed an affidavit stating that $13 million was given to the band over the past two years.)

The court documents said that the band members "have been victims of a con man who has become wealthy at their expense. They have been cheated at every turn by Pearlman's fraud, manipulation and breach of fiduciary duty. As a final affront, Pearlman now seeks the aid of a federal court to ratify his theft and leave 'N Sync unable to pursue its career."

Group member J.C. stated that Pearlman was an "unscrupulous businessman who while hugging us and calling us family was picking our pockets, robbing us of our future and endangering our health." He also said that "Pearlman dissuaded the group from consulting lawyers, never showed them contracts for the label deals, and pressured them to hire Johnny Wright as manager and pay him more than the Backstreet Boys did in order to shift Wright's focus to "N Sync."

The Resolution

On November 24, 1999 Judge Ann Conway denied Pearlman's request for an injunction. On December 27, 1999 an agreement was reached that was not disclosed to the public. Some sources say that 'N Sync will pay royalties to BMG as part of the settlement. [35]

Leann Rimes vs. Wilbur Rimes and Lyle Walker

U.S. District Court Dallas Texas

The Background

As a teenage novice, Leann Rimes shot straight to the top of the country and pop charts with a voice reminiscent of Patsy Cline's. Today, as a holder of several Grammy awards, she is considered one of country music's top stars as she transforms her image from the teenage sensation to a sex symbol.

The Dilemma

In a suit filed May 2, 2000, Leann is suing her father, Wilbur, and former manager, attorney Walker claiming they took $7 million from her over a five year period. She claims that they paid themselves excessively as co-managers, keeping 30% of her income. The suit says that an artist of her stature "should pay 10% or less for competent management services."

She alleges breaches of fiduciary duty, constructive fraud, conspiracy, and breach of contract. Leann seeks an accounting of all transactions involving the defendants and actual damages to be determined but including at least $7 million in "excessive and unreasonable management fees."

The Resolution[36]

?

Christina Aguilera vs. Steven Kurtz

California Superior Court Los Angeles

The Background

The former Mousecateer won a Grammy as best new artist in 2000, and has sold more than 7 million copies of her debut album for RCA. As a current player in the "cola wars" she has rocketed to the top of the music business in about two years.

The Dilemma

Aguilera, who filed suit on Oct. 13, 2000, is seeking to break the management agreement and alleges that Kurtz, Marquee Management and co-manager Katrina Sirdofsky committed fraud and breached their fiduciary duties. "Kurtz exercised improper, undue, and inappropriate influence over her professional activities, as well as her personal affairs." The action also claims that the contract allowed Kurtz to collect 20% of any and all Aguilera's "Commissionable income" earned for an indefinite period of time. "The true facts are that Kurtz did not place Aguilera's interests above his own; did not act fairly and honestly in protecting her rights and interests; did not advise her independently of his own interests; took actions which inured to his own benefit; and took actions adverse to her interests."

The Resolution[37]

?

PROJECTS

1. Lawsuits involving some of the biggest stars in the music business were purposely omitted from this chapter so that students would have the opportunity to investigate the cases as a project. Two of those cases involved the following people and should be researched: Bruce Springsteen vs. Mike Apel, and Bob Dylan vs. Albert Grossman.

2. Pick any suit from the chapter and role-play the two sides of the argument. Draw logical solutions.

3. Further investigate any of the above cases.

4. Examine the trade papers for current artist-manager suits and investigate.

NOTES

1. Irv Lichtman, Peter Jones, and Mike Hennessy. "Stigwood Responds," Billboard Magazine. 18 October 1980. pg. 1.

2. Marc Kirkeby. "Bee Gees sue Stigwood, charge mismanagement," Rolling Stone Magazine. 13 November 1980. pg. 22.

3. Op. Cit., Billboard Magazine.

4. Op. Cit., Rolling Stone Magazine.

5. Ibid.

6. Op. Cit., Billboard Magazine

7. Larry Flick. "Billy Joel Sues Former Manager For $90 Mil," Billboard Magazine. 7 October 1989. pg. 96.

8. Ibid.

9. Larry Flick. "Billy Joel Gets $2 Mil In Suit," Billboard Magazine. 7 April 1990. pg. 94.

10. Irv Lichtman. "Inside Track," Billboard Magazine. 25 May 1991. pg. 80.

11. Melinda Newman. Billboard Magazine. 20 March 1993. pg. 12.

12. Billboard Magazine. 14 March 1992. pg. 92.

13. Roman Kozak. "Parker, RCA Accused Of Fraud In Elvis Dealings," Billboard Magazine. 15 August 1981. pg. 1.

14. Ibid.

15. Ibid.

16. Ibid. pg. 15.

17. Ibid.

18. Ibid.

19. Ibid. pg. 90.

20. Ken Terry. "Branigan Loses Lawsuit," Billboard Magazine. 12 December 1987. pg. 69.

21. Ibid.

22. Ibid.

23. Trudi Miller. "Ex-Manager Sues Joe Cocker," Billboard Magazine. 18 April 1992. pg. 34.

24. Ibid.

25. Ibid.

26. Irv Lichtman. "Inside Track," Billboard Magazine. 2 March 1991. pg. 79.

27. J.R. Reynolds. "Anita Baker Suing Her Former Manager, Lawyer, And Publisher." Billboard Magazine, 8 June 1996. Pg. 6

28. Ibid.

29. Ibid. pg. 15

30. Ibid.

31. Melinda Newman. "Kid Rock settles Suit With Ex-Mgr." Billboard Bulletin. 114 March 2001. pg. 3

32. Richard Skanse. "In the News." Rolling Stone Magazine. 9 December 1999. pg. 27

33. "Hootie Lawsuit Settled." Wallofsound.go.com. 14 November 1997.

34. Chris Morris. "Former Manager Sues Jewel and her Mother." Billboard Magazine. 12 December 1998.pg. 6

35. Melinda Newman. "'N Sync Responds to Tran Con/BMG Suits." Billboard Magazine 13November 1999. pg. 5 Additional material: MTV.com; Wallofsound.com; E! Online News.

36. Carolyn Horwitz. "Leann Rimes." Billboard Magazine. 20 May 2000. pg. 36.

37. Chris Morris. "Aguilera Sues Her Manager." Billboard Magazine. 28 Oct. 2000. pg. 12.